SURVIVAL
OF THE RICHEST

SURVIVAL
OF RICHEST
THE

HOW THE CORRUPTION OF THE MARKETPLACE
AND THE DISPARITY OF WEALTH CREATED
THE GREATEST CONSPIRACY OF ALL

DONALD JEFFRIES

FOREWORD BY RICHARD SYRETT

Skyhorse Publishing

Skyhorse Publishing books may be purchased in bulk at special discounts for sales promotion, corporate gifts, fund-raising, or educational purposes. Special editions can also be created to specifications. For details, contact the Special Sales Department, Skyhorse Publishing, 307 West 36th Street, 11th Floor, New York, NY 10018 or info@skyhorsepublishing.com.

Skyhorse® and Skyhorse Publishing® are registered trademarks of Skyhorse Publishing, Inc.®, a Delaware corporation.

Visit our website at www.skyhorsepublishing.com.

10 9 8 7 6 5 4 3 2 1

Library of Congress Cataloging-in-Publication Data is available on file.

Cover design by Rain Saukas
Cover photo credit: iStock

Print ISBN: 978-1-5107-2065-7
Ebook ISBN: 978-1-5107-2066-4

Printed in the United States of America

This book is dedicated to the millions of anonymous souls such as my parents, grandparents, and great-grandparents, who have been forced to live with constant financial uncertainty, because of a system that is stacked against them.

CONTENTS

FOREWORD

THE RECENT US PRESIDENTIAL CAMPAIGN pitted a rude, crude, alpha-male, reality TV star and real estate tycoon against a political insider, opportunist, and fair-weather progressive feminist.

And for the first time in living memory, the battle lines were cleanly drawn between two diametrically opposed camps. On one side was a cabal of globalists who view western liberal democracies as an annoying obstacle to the free flow of capital. Once content to pull strings from the shadows, a perceived change in the wind—namely, a nationalist fever sweeping Europe—forced them out of their lairs and into the glare. For their latest standard-bearer, they awkwardly shoehorned onto the ballot, by hook and by crook (but mostly by crook) the tired and insipid Hillary Rodham Clinton.

Across the irreconcilable breach, the brash, trash-talking disruptor Donald J. Trump defied all odds and won the White House and the hearts and minds of the disaffected with a barrage of plain-spokenness and rough-hewn truths. His ball cap–ready battle cry in defense of the sanctity and sovereignty of the nation-state was a middle finger in the face of political, corporate, and media elites. Like JFK's pledge "to smash the CIA into a thousand pieces and scatter it into the wind," Trump's anti-globalist screed may yet still prove to be his coffin's final nail.

Against this revolutionary and historic backdrop, Don Jeffries has once again proven himself to be a true and righteous chronicler of our times and for our times. In *Survival of the Richest*, he shines a disinfecting light on the dark insidious players that have, over the course of only two generations, conspired in a process that has led to the hollowing out of the flyover states and the virtual collapse of America's middle class.

Jeffries tackles his subject—the root causes of economic inequality—with all the finesse of a back-alley brawler. Understanding the urgency of America's perilous decline, he spends little time on nuance and subtlety.

Like Rowdy Piper's immortal drifter, John Nada in the John Carpenter film *They Live*, Jeffries has come to chew bubble gum and kick ass. Don Jeffries is all out of bubble gum.

—Richard Syrett is a veteran radio and television broadcaster based in Toronto, and a frequent guest-host on *Coast to Coast AM*.

INTRODUCTION

Poor—Persons who are unable to pay their taxes. For example, Vanderbilt.
—Ambrose Bierce, *The Devil's Dictionary*

THERE HAVE BEEN WEALTHY PEOPLE and poor people throughout the course of history. One cannot exist without the other, much as no one would understand what "beautiful" meant, if there wasn't a contrasting "ugly" to compare it with, and teenagers would have no idea who the "popular" kids were, if there weren't corresponding "unpopular" kids. How many organizations—from Country Clubs to Freemasons—would exist without exclusionary rules? What good is a group, after all, if *anyone* can be a member? Rich and poor, success and failure, are man-made constructs. However, when the medium of exchange in our society, which largely determines the quality of everyone's lives, is being distributed in an obscenely unfair way, then the vast majority of the people, who aren't benefiting from the present arrangement, have a right and an obligation to demand change.

This book is not meant to be an attack upon the rich. Without wealthy statesmen, which nearly all the Founding Fathers were, the United States would still be a colony of England. Historically, many rich individuals heeded the call to public service and felt an obligation to look out for the interests of their fellow human beings. They had a sense of history and were principled enough to care about liberty and justice. Joseph P. Kennedy urged all his children to enter public service, reminding them regularly of the old adage, "To whom much is given, much is expected." Can anyone picture the Koch brothers, Warren Buffet, and their ilk—the closest approximations we have today to George Washington, Thomas Jefferson, Benjamin Franklin, or Patrick Henry, sacrificing *their* lives, fortunes, and sacred honor for independence, or freedom, or any cause? When was the last time we had a leading statesman—now mere politicians—who led the troops, who was even seen near any battlefield, such as George Washington and many other signers of the Constitution?

One doesn't have to be a socialist to be concerned about the ever-widening gap between the "haves" and the "have-nots" in our society. Certainly there should be incentives for every citizen to work harder and improve their lot in life. Just like human skills and qualities are not distributed equally, the collective wealth cannot ever be distributed equally. Individuals should be allowed to become rich. But when things have reached the point where the richest four hundred people in the country have more wealth than the bottom 50 percent of the population combined, then we simply must recognize the extent of the problem and address it rationally. Even more incredibly, on an international scale, the richest *eighty-five individuals* in the world now have as much wealth as the poorest half of their fellow human beings around the globe.[1]

As F. Scott Fitzgerald once notably said, "The rich are different from you and me." The wealthiest 20 percent of Americans, especially the ones in the rarified air of the top 1 percent, have no concept of the problems their fellow citizens in the bottom 80 percent face every day. It used to be that those in the middle class were nearly as removed from the struggles of the lower class. That is no longer the case; the middle 40 percent of Americans—what is left of the steadily shrinking middle class—are in most cases a few paychecks away from joining their unfortunate brethren in the lowest 40 percent, whom collectively have less than 1 percent of the total wealth in this country. Put another way, the six heirs to Sam Walton's fortune have as much wealth as these hapless 40 percent at the bottom of the economic scale.[2] In fact, a 2013 survey from Bankrate determined that 76 percent of Americans are now officially living paycheck-to-paycheck. It was found that less than one-quarter of Americans possess enough money in savings to cover at least six months of expenses, cushion the blow from the loss of a job or unexpected illness, or deal with any other unforeseen emergency. Fifty percent had less than a three-month supply of savings, and 27 percent had *no savings at all.*[3] An updated 2015 survey from GoBankingRates found that 62 percent of Americans had less than $1,000 in savings.[4]

According to an eye-opening article on the March 1, 2013, Minimum Wage Union Workers of America blog, after adjusting for inflation, 90 percent of Americans were earning less than what minimum wage earners made in 1950. When factoring in the productivity rate, they conclude that the minimum wage in America should really be about $28.56 per hour in 2010 dollars. They cited movie projectionists as just one example of a formerly high-paying, union job that gradually atrophied into minimum wage work, with the accompanying lack of benefits. I had a great-uncle who made a wonderful living doing this for decades. *Business Insider,* on December 2, 2013, published a graph showing the federal minimum wage since 1960, adjusted for inflation. Based upon this, the minimum wage peaked in 1968. Inspired by the 2016 Bernie Sanders presidential campaign, the Democrats' platform included a provision to raise the federal minimum wage to $15 an hour.

Those with great power invariably have lots of money. The system is run by the rich, for the rich. As the great Ferdinand Lundberg, author of *The Rich and the Super-Rich* and other books put it:

It is true that all persons have their compensation for work determined by a market. The elite, however, do not have their revenues impersonally determined by a market, to the dictates of which they submit. They make market rules pretty much suit their inclinations. Members of the labor force, high and low, come up against a decree that says: So far and not further. They have not acquiesced in this decree, they have not been consulted about it, they are often opposed to it but they are powerless to push it aside. It looks very much as if this decree has been handed down from some esoteric group.

Conservatives love to blather on about the "marketplace deciding" what someone's work is worth, which always happens to be "what the market will bear," and is seldom enough to provide a decent standard of living for the vast majority of Americans. The fact is the wealthy control the marketplace, so they decide that CEOs and other high-ranking executives must be constantly rewarded, while determining that the value of the average worker is minimal at best. Why is it that "anyone" can do low-paid, menial jobs, according to the wealthy, but evidently only a special breed is qualified to be what talk-show host "The Black Eagle" Joe Madison, a longtime fixture in Washington, DC, talk radio, once cogently referred to as "vice presidents in charge of looking out of the window?"

The mainstream media continues to parrot wildly inaccurate figures regarding unemployment in an overt attempt to paint a misleading, less pessimistic portrait of our economic situation. The official numbers only include Americans who are presently filing for unemployment benefits, thus all the long-term unemployed and those who didn't qualify for unemployment or opted not to take it are left out of the statistics. Obviously, the real unemployment rate is much higher than what is being reported. A more accurate measure of our economic woes was revealed in 2014, in the incredible statistic that 20 percent of American households have *nobody* working, according to the Bureau of Labor. Even this shameful figure is a low estimate, as the Bureau of Labor counts persons who worked fifteen or more hours weekly, in an unpaid capacity, in "an enterprise operated by a member of the family" as being employed. There are, in fact, more Americans now living off of inadequate government benefits than are gainfully employed. "The number of Americans getting money or benefits from the federal government each month exceeds the number of full-time workers in the private sector by more than 60 million," according to Michael Snyder, of the excellent End of the American Dream website. Add to this the fact that an increasing number of companies now have an official policy of not hiring the unemployed.[5]

The great disparity in American wealth is likely to continue unabated, simply because anyone in a position of influence, in any sphere of our society, is among the 20 percent of wealthiest Americans. The politicians passing legislation, the lobbyists who control most of these officials, the executives in charge of hiring and firing most workers, the judges who reign in every courtroom, the reporters who cover the issues, and their bosses who determine what is and isn't important news, are all paid more than average Americans can ever dream of making. They don't have to worry about unemployment or low credit scores. It isn't in their vested interest to solve any of the problems that beset the poor and working classes. From their perspective, there is nothing to complain about. The system is working great for them. But this shortsightedness on the part of the financially secure, this tendency to declare, "*I'm* doing okay, why aren't you?" ignores the simple reality that, without all the unwashed masses to prop their system up, and sustain their wealth, everything will eventually crumble.

The US Census Bureau tells us that more than 146 million Americans are either poor or low income. The wealthiest 1 percent of Americans presently has more wealth than the bottom 90 percent combined. US families with a head of household under the age of thirty have a 37 percent poverty rate. Half of all children in cities such as Miami, Cleveland, and Detroit are now living in poverty. The poorest residents of Miami live on $11 per day, in the midst of high-rise buildings being financed by money from Hong Kong, Venezuela, and Argentina. Assessing the situation, Dr. Pedro "Joe" Greer, who had spent the last twenty-five years treating the homeless and uninsured in the city, declared, "Miami isn't the gateway to Latin America; Miami has the same economic demographics as Latin America. Seventy percent of the families we work with bring in less than twenty-five thousand dollars a year."

In fact, US cities such as Miami, Atlanta, and New Orleans have a higher income inequality rate now than Buenos Aires and Rio de Janeiro and are on a par with Mexico City.[6] A study by the Brookings Institution added San Francisco and Boston to this list, and detailed Atlanta's inequity further; while the richest 5 percent of households in the city earned more than $280,000 in 2012, the poorest 20 percent earned less than $15,000.[7] More than a million students in our public schools are now homeless.[8] During the course of the Obama administration alone, the number of Americans on food stamps has gone from 32 to 47 million. Nationally, the Census Bureau would report the shameful news that, as of 2015, 13.5 percent of Americans were living in a state of poverty. The statistics vary slightly, depending upon the source, but all tell the same tragic story. Ross Perot's prediction that if our wrongheaded policies didn't change, then this generation of Americans was going to become the first in a long time to have a lower standard of living than their parents is unfortunately coming true.

As recently as 1988, the *Economist* would grade the United States as the best place for a person to be born. Today, the United States is tied for *sixteenth* place in this category. There were more Americans working in manufacturing in 1950 than there are today, even though the population has more than doubled, according to the Department of Labor. One of Donald Trump's most convincing talking points in his 2016 presidential campaign was his oft-repeated references to the seventy thousand factories that have closed in America since 2001.[9] A study released in 2007, by the University of California at Berkeley, exposed the stark reality that income inequality in the United States had reached an all-time high, including even the darkest years of the Great Depression. As Naomi Klein recently described it in the *Shock Doctrine* documentary, "We are witnessing a transfer of wealth of unfathomable size." Near the end of 2016, news reports indicated that the wealthiest 10 percent of Americans control 76 percent of the wealth, and the top 50 percent control 99 percent. These new alarming statistics reveal the horrific reality that half of the country has 1 percent of the collective wealth.[10]

My favorite Bible verse comes from Matthew 19:24, where Jesus himself advises us that, "It is easier for a camel to go through the eye of a needle, than for a rich man to enter the kingdom of God." You aren't likely to hear your local preacher quote *that* particular verse on any given Sunday. Every Christian I have ever recited this verse to reacts in the exact same way; they deny a literal interpretation of Christ's words, which is strange considering how they literally interpret their own favorite verses. To take the words of Jesus here literally, and still remain a Christian, is to forego any chance of ever attaining great wealth, which is a goal that most of us aspire to. In the same vein, no man of the cloth ever mentions all the references in the Bible to the Year of Jubilee, which was a tradition in those times of absolving citizens of all their debts. Just imagine what a Year of Jubilee would do for the 80 percent of Americans who are feeling the full impact of this dreadful economy.

The promising Occupy Wall Street movement, which began in September 2011, kindled hopes in many that proper attention would finally be focused upon the disparity of wealth between the One Percent at the top and everyone else. Left largely unreported by the mainstream media was the unsettling fact that some eight thousand Occupy activists were arrested in less than three years. Included among these was Cecily McMillan, who was mindlessly convicted of assault by a useless jury in May 2014 and sentenced to three months in prison and five years of probation. McMillan was accused of elbowing a New York City police officer in the face, which she claimed was an instinctive response to having her breast grabbed. The officer went on to severely beat McMillan, who suffered a seizure and was hospitalized after the incident.[11] Considering the multitude of videos featuring law enforcement officers manhandling and beating young Occupy protesters, none of whom were ever charged with anything, it is a special indictment of our society that McMillan received a prison sentence for trying to defend herself against one of these overly aggressive officers.

We see an 80-20 percent split of resources in all the research. These numbers go back to Italian economist Vilfredo Pareto, who observed that 20 percent of the population had 80 percent of the wealth. Like casinos, our economy seems built on the precept that the vast majority of citizens must lose in order for the lucky ones at the top to keep winning. Following the great recession of 2007, the fairly consistent figure of the wealthiest 20 percent of Americans owning 80 percent of the wealth actually went up to an astounding 87.7 percent.[12] While the much-talked about One Percent has wealth of an unfathomable scale, the 19 percent below them, who are the ones primarily running the system, are doing just fine. An increasing number of young people, who must contend with the college debt explosion and a horrific job market, are becoming politically astute on this subject. The popularity of the 2016 Bernie Sanders presidential campaign certainly reflected the economic anxiety of the young. That economic anxiety, coupled with anger at the status quo in Washington, was the driving force of the 2016 presidential election. Donald Trump's campaign, meanwhile, resonated with mostly older Americans, who had lost good jobs to outsourcing, foreign visa workers, and the general globalism Trump frequently decried.

There is a class war going on all right, and it's been going on for a long, long time. It's been a one-sided war, with those being relentlessly attacked apparently unaware that there *is* a war. Sure, they might wonder why annual raises are no longer part of what we are told is the "new normal." Neither are pensions, vacation and sick leave, or any other traditional perks for an increasing number of workers. They also may grumble, among themselves, about the huge bonuses their bosses are getting, and perhaps even notice how seldom they seem to be doing anything at all to justify their outrageous salaries. But while they scratch their heads in confusion, they appear reluctant to identify the enemy who is waging war on them as surely as any military force ever has. This class war is being waged by the wealthy, against the rest of us.

1 ARE THEY WORTH IT?

The few own the many because they possess the means of livelihood of all. . . . The country is governed for the richest, for the corporations, the bankers, the land speculators, and for the exploiters of labor.
—Helen Keller

MOST PEOPLE SHY AWAY FROM the simple question; do those who are paid the most in our society deserve to be compensated like that? If a particular individual was the driving force behind a cure for all cancer, or instrumental in significantly increasing the human life span, I think most everyone would agree that their value to society would be such that they'd be entitled to millions, even billions of dollars. But the world's wealthiest individuals do not, in fact, seem to have contributed in such a way that they have earned a distinction placing them above the masses, garnering more money in less than a year than what virtually everyone else earns in a lifetime. According to the Bloomberg Billionaires Index, which ranks the world's richest three hundred people, these incredibly wealthy elite saw their net worth jump by $52.4 billion in 2013. On July 21, 2016, *Bloomberg* would recount how Amazon founder Jeff Bezos had surpassed Warren Buffet as the third richest person in the world, thanks to a tidy increase of $5.4 billion in his personal fortune in 2016. Meanwhile, the vast majority of workers, who desperately need a significant pay raise, are simply not getting one.

The wealthiest people in our society don't appear to be improving any lives but their own, and they don't seem to have special qualities or skills that explain why they're being compensated so much more extravagantly than the rest of us. Warren Buffet, like so many very wealthy people, made his fortune with investments. Multi-billionaire Mexican Carlos Slim Helú is another whose occupation is investor. When we examine any list of the richest Americans, we find names such as notorious corporate raider Carl Icahn, whose more polite title is investor, George Soros, who is yet another investor, hedge fund managers John Paulson and James Simons, and plenty of financiers, bond mavens, chairmen, and others with predictable titles that assure us, whatever they do, they aren't positively impacting the lives of the bulk of humanity, The very wealthy, in all reality, can generally be defined as those who are abnormally good at making money.

Bill Gates's Microsoft was primarily known for creating an operating system with numerous flaws, charging excessive prices for all the unnecessary upgrades and new versions, and engaging in monopolistic practices. Apple founder Steve Jobs would declare that Gates had "shamelessly ripped off other people's ideas." Jobs had a right to feel that way; most people think that Microsoft stole many essential features from Apple. Of course, many believe that Jobs himself stole from Xerox. Gates acknowledges that advances in technology, including robotics, "will reduce demand for jobs particularly at the lower end of the skill set."[13] Senator Jeff Sessions, now President Trump's attorney general, was a fierce critic of Gates's call for increased foreign visa workers at the same time Microsoft announced plans to lay off eighteen thousand workers in 2015.[14] The Heritage Foundation has estimated that the disastrous June 2013 immigration "reform" bill, which Gates and every other pillar of the establishment supported, would cost taxpayers some $6.3 trillion over the next few decades.[15]

Like almost all modern corporate leaders, Jobs used cheap, if not slave, labor in foreign countries to build his beloved iPhones. Both

Herbert Hovenkamp, a law professor at the University of Iowa, and Bill Black, author of *The Best Way to Rob a Bank is to Own One,* referred succinctly to Jobs as "a walking antitrust violation." Walter Isaacson, author of a biography on Jobs, declared that the founder of Apple "always believed that the rules that applied to ordinary people didn't apply to him."[16] Bill Gates is about as pedestrian a personality as one can imagine; in an interview with Christine Amanpour, he declared that "Clearly, you can't raise the taxes we need just by going after that 1 percent."[17] In his 2014 annual Bill and Melinda Gates Foundation letter, Gates expounded upon his delusional misinformation, writing, "By almost any measure, the world is better than it has ever been." Well, it's certainly become a better place for *him.* If it could be demonstrated that either Gates or Jobs had single-handedly invented the personal computer, they might indeed be worth their fortunes. By any definition, that clearly isn't the case.

We hear regular, nonsensical references in the mainstream media about the difficulty of finding suitable executive talent and thus the need to compensate them extravagantly in order to beat the competition. It is never explained just what talent one requires to be an executive in a large corporation. One can't quantify this kind of talent in any measurable way, the way one can assess the skills of an athlete, a musician, or an artist. Many powerful corporate leaders attain their positions in the most traditional manner, through simple nepotism. Sam Walton's children, for example, exhibited no talent whatsoever in inheriting their father's fortune. The Koch brothers inherited an oil refinery firm from their father. Fidelity's Abigail Johnson is merely continuing the family tradition of running the company her grandfather established. Donald Trump began life as the son of a multimillionaire, which made the arduous climb to billionaire a bit easier. Bill Gates did not come from a "middle-class" family; his parents were quite wealthy, and his father was was on the board of Planned Parenthood. Warren Buffet's climb up the corporate ladder was undoubtedly aided by the fact he was the son of a United States congressman. Nike founder and chairman Philip Knight's father was a newspaper publisher. Hedge fund magnate James H. Simons grew up the son of a factory owner. Any present-day Rockefeller, Rothschild, Carnegie, Mellon, Morgan, etc. invariably succeeded because of their names and their inherited wealth, while Facebook cofounders Mark Zuckerberg, Dustin Moskovitz, Eduaro Salverin, Chris Hughes, and Justin Rosenstein all came from wealthy families and met at the ultimate breeding ground for the elite, Harvard University. Horatio Alger stories, if they ever existed to any great degree, are clearly a thing of the past.

Amazon founder Jeff Bezos spent much of his childhood on a 25,000-acre Texas ranch with his maternal grandfather, who was a regional director of the US Atomic Energy Commission. Liliane Bettencourt, presently estimated to be worth more than $33 billion, earned her riches by inheriting L'Oreal, one of the world's biggest companies, from her father. Google founder Larry Page's father Carl was a pioneer in computer science and artificial intelligence. Forest Mars Jr., worth some $21 billion, achieved his success through inheriting the giant candy company from his father, who had inherited it from his grandfather. His siblings, John and Jacqueline, are also worth $21 billion each. They mirror the work ethic of Sam Walton's children, yet undoubtedly many Americans, from all income levels, would argue that they earned this incredible wealth. When he uttered the statement, "You didn't build that," Barack Obama inadvertently tapped into the strong personal belief most Americans possess, that they have attained whatever success they've achieved solely through hard work or their own brilliance. Those who make it almost always have been fortunate in different ways. They might have been born into a supportive, financially stable family. They might have known someone who opened the right doors for them. They might have been blessed with a set of genes that made them physically attractive enough that others want to help them. They might simply have been in the right place at the right time. For whatever reason, human beings seem to blanch at the notion that they've been lucky. Senator

Elizabeth Warren echoed Obama's comments, saying, "There is nobody in this country who got rich on his own."

Author Chrystia Freeland, in her 2012 book *Plutocrats: The Rise of the New Global Super Rich and the Fall of Everyone Else,* explored the attitudes of these unfathomably wealthy people. She found that each of them felt strongly that they'd earned their great wealth. Just as unanimously, though, they all thought that at least some of their billionaire brethren hadn't earned theirs. Oddly, this attitude seems just as prevalent among the upper middle class, the middle class, and even many in the lower middle class. I can't tell you how many times I've heard working-class people moan that "I worked hard for what I got," or "nobody helped *me.*" When talking about redistributing the wealth, I've often been met with fierce opposition from those who have no wealth to share, and thus would benefit in some way from such a proposition. They love to counter with statements such as, "How do you define rich?" or "I guess rich means anyone who has more than you." Another perennial favorite, from those who've made it as well as those who haven't, is, "If you divided up all the money in the world evenly, in a few years, the same people would have it all again." This is, of course, a very convenient defense for those who have hoarded all the wealth. Why should society even bother to distribute the wealth more fairly, when everyone knows the money would just magically gravitate back to them?

Slightly below this lofty top level of multibillionaire investors and the like are entertainers and athletes. By 2016, the *average* salary for a Major League Baseball player had risen to $4.4 million a year. In the NBA, it was an even more incomprehensible $5.2 million annually. NHL players average $2.5 million, and NFL players "only" $2.1 million each year. The biggest movie stars are in the "$20 million club," indicating they command that kind of salary per picture. Tom Hanks hauled in as much as $49 million from *The Da Vinci Code.* Often these figures don't factor in the considerable residuals that can result from a huge box office hit. Tom Cruise made $290 million from his four *Mission: Impossible* films alone.

Keanu Reeves, meanwhile, piled up $262 million from the three *Matrix* movies. Reeves is an unusually generous sort and gave up some profits from his back-end points in order to help finance the special-effects team and costume designers for the sequels.[18] By the end of the long-running *Friends* television show, each of the six cast members was garnering a million dollars per episode. Even if one accepts categorically that these athletes and entertainers are that exceptional and wildly talented, can anyone maintain they deserve to be so lavishly compensated?

By the end of 2013, the distribution of wealth in America had become so unequal that we no longer could be classed among the First World, developed nations in this category. According to the Credit Suisse Global Wealth Databook, 75.4 percent of all wealth in the United States belongs to the richest 10 percent of the people. Comparable nations (none of them as bad as the United States) in terms of wealth disparity include Chile, Indonesia, and South Africa. The bottom 90 percent of American citizens own only 24.6 percent of the aggregate wealth, while the norm for developed countries is around 40 percent. Meanwhile, under Obama, who was often accused of being a socialist, the wealthiest 1 percent of Americans received 95 percent of the income gains during the alleged economic "recovery."[19] During his 2016 presidential run, Bernie Sanders would embrace this issue with statements such as "something is profoundly wrong when the twenty richest people in our country own more wealth than the bottom half of the American population—150 million people." FactCheck.org claimed that the situation for the 40 percent at the bottom of the ladder has grown even more dismal, declaring that by early 2016, they actually had a combined negative financial worth. Every statistic on income and wealth disparity supports the notions of Ferdinand Lundberg, who postulated in his 1937 book *America's Sixty Families* that, "The United States is owned and dominated today by a hierarchy of the richest families, buttressed by no more than 90 families of lesser wealth."[20]

While millions of Americans have lost their homes and were financially devastated by this undeclared Depression, the wealthy continue to be rescued from their own mistakes, time and time again. The 2008 Banker Bailout was one of America's most disgraceful acts. With foreclosures and bankruptcies at all-time highs, the criminal banks who orchestrated it all were given the kind of security net denied to those suffering individuals across America. When individual Americans experience a terrible financial setback, they are told it's their own fault and to try harder and pull up their bootstraps. Helping them somehow is a handout most Americans resent giving. But when the wealthiest groups in our society—the big banks, General Motors, etc.—make bad decisions and should ostensibly suffer the consequences, they aren't penalized at all. They don't feel the wrath of the vaunted marketplace, as powerless individual citizens do.

The liberal political advocacy group Common Cause would report that the banks bailed out by the taxpayers certainly didn't stop lavishing excessive benefits on their top executives. Lloyd C. Blankfein, CEO of Goldman Sachs, was given over $70 million in total compensation in 2008, despite his company having been gifted $10 billion in the bailout. J. P. Morgan Chase's James S. Dimon earned nearly $28 million, while his company had taken $25 billion from the taxpayers. The list goes on, as huge conglomerates such as American Express, Bank of America, and Capital One bestowed millions on their CEOs, only months after begging for handouts from the unwashed masses who were struggling to make ends meet, and to whom were still being told to sacrifice for the good of the country. All told, nine banks that begged the struggling taxpayers to bail them out awarded cumulative bonuses of nearly $33 billion in that same year of 2008, including $1 million each to some five thousand employees. Exposing the lie that these economic excesses are connected to the ironclad manifestations of an all-knowing marketplace, six of the nine banks *paid out more in bonuses than they earned in profit*. The Obama administration reacted to these shameful figures with a statement by Robert Gibbs, "The president continues to believe that the American people don't begrudge people making money for what they do." Citigroup, which received about 25 percent of the bailout money going to the nine banks, bestowed an incredible $98.9 million in compensation on Andrew Hall, head of their energy-trading unit Phibro LLC, which dwarfed the $38 million they paid CEO Vikram Pandit in 2008.[21]

As has been widely reported, only a few relatively small fry—loan officers and the like—were ever prosecuted for crimes related to the 2008 financial crash. By comparison, the much smaller Savings and Loan crisis of the 1980s resulted in over thirty thousand criminal referrals and one thousand felony convictions by the Department of Justice.[22] In contrast, only one banker—the Egyptian-born Kareem Serageldin—was ever sent to jail for the 2008 financial crisis. Despite that even the judge admitted that others at Credit Suisse were guiltier and that Serageldin was merely "a small piece of an overall evil climate within the bank and with many other banks," he nevertheless sentenced him to thirty months behind bars. The overall lack of prosecutions related to the worst banking crisis in American history reflected a disturbing trend. From 1995–1997, the percentage of federal white-collar prosecutions was 17.6 percent. In the period from 2010–2012 however, this figure dipped to only 9.4 percent. As multiple sources within the banking industry told the *New York Times,* federal authorities appeared to lack the courage to go after powerful corporate figures, part of an overall change within the Justice Department of seeking settlements in lieu of prison sentences.[23]

CEOs are not only given wildly excessive salaries and "performance" bonuses; they are often given parting "gifts" that boggle the mind. ConocoPhillips CEO James Mulva, for example, was gifted an unbelievable $260 million from the company when he left them in June 2012. Evidently the $141 million total compensation package he'd accrued in 2011 wasn't enough. Mulva's package paled in comparison to the more than $417 million doled out to John Welch, in honor of his twenty-year tenure at General Electric.[24] But perhaps Welch was deserving of such an honor, considering General Electric *paid no taxes* at all in 2010, according to the *New York Times* and numerous other mainstream media outlets. In 2015, Citizens for Tax Justice claimed that GE had again paid no taxes, along with fourteen other Fortune 500 companies.[25] These lucrative deals, often called golden parachutes, are extended to overpaid executives even when they fail miserably at their jobs. The magazine *Mother Jones* calculated that the average golden parachute for these CEOs was an amount equal to forty-nine lifetimes' worth of work for a median income employee. In the case of Welch, this would rise to 203 lifetimes' worth of work.[26]

Some executive pay rates are so astronomical that they defy belief. John Hammergren, CEO of drug giant McKesson, made $54.4 million in 2010. This works out to $210,000 *a day*, and that daily salary would be more than nearly 99 percent of Americans make *annually* ($250,000 a year is generally considered the basement level for the top One Percent). Health Care pays its executives extremely well, too, which goes a long way toward explaining the spiraling, out of control medical costs in this country. Anthem Blue Cross and Blue Shield paid CEO Larry Glasscock a $42.5 million bonus in 2004, which nicely dwarfed his $3.6 million compensation for the year.[27] As an anonymous wit on a conspiracy forum noted in outrage over this, "At my former salary, I would have to work 1,214 years to make $42.5 million. That's over twelve centuries." To show just how rapidly, and drastically, the gap between upper management and workers is growing, during the 1980s, executives made about forty times what average workers did. By 2015, the ratio of CEO to worker pay was 204 to 1.[28] During the Clinton years, the average pay for CEOs increased more than 400 percent.

While paying no tax at all in 2010, GE, citing merely one example of corporate tax "fairness," paid an average of just one-eighth of a percent in taxes between 2002 and 2011. In response to these astonishing statistics, GE CEO Jeff Immelt termed the US tax system, "old, complex, and uncompetitive."[29] Uncompetitive with what, one wonders. Immelt exemplifies everything wrong about present-day America; since he took over as GE's CEO, the company's stock lost 50 percent of its value, and GE had closed thirty-one factories and laid off nineteen thousand workers. For this dazzling performance, Immelt earned over $12 million a year.[30] *Forbes* magazine ranked Immelt as the fourth worst CEO in America in its May 2012 issue. Perhaps Immelt possesses that indistinguishable executive talent we've heard so much about.

One could fill a good-sized book with the excesses of CEO compensation alone. The figures are mind-boggling. Angelo Mozilo was the cofounder and longtime CEO of Countrywide Financial. During one eight-year period alone, Mozilo earned $521.5 million from his company, according to compensation research firm Equilar. Mozilo became the first executive to be penalized for the losses incurred by millions of investors during the mortgage collapse when he agreed to settle with the Securities and Exchange Commission in a civil fraud case. Of the $67.5 million Mozilo was assessed, Countrywide agreed to pay $20 million as part of the indemnification agreement he had with the company. Mozilo, like many of the highest-paid corporate leaders, received innumerable, valuable perks along with his millions. For instance, his compensation package covered annual country club and golf course dues. Mozilo knew how to take care of his influential friends, too; Senator Christopher Dodd, for example, was given a $75,000 reduction in mortgage payments at below-market interest rates, that in real terms worked out to be a sweetheart deal worth over a million dollars. Other luminaries who benefited financially from being "friends of Angelo" included members of Congress Kent Conrad and Barbara Boxer, as well as Nancy Pelosi's son, Fannie Mae CEO Jim Johnson, and Democratic Party figures Richard Holbrooke and Donna Shalala.[31]

The unfathomable salaries CEOs regularly give themselves are, for all intents and purposes, tax subsidies from the government. Congress, in 1993, capped the tax deductibility for executive pay at $1 million but still allowed US corporations to profit from deducting so-called performance-based pay, including stock options. Thanks to this provision, corporations regularly use these stock options to lower their taxes, making large executive bonuses in effect tax free. The total yearly cost to taxpayers from all these shenanigans is some $7 billion, according to the Economic Policy Institute. The fast-food industry has been especially noteworthy in this regard; the Institute for Policy Studies found that fast-food CEOs had deducted about $183 million of this performance pay, which decreased their tax liability by $64 million over two years. These are the same folks who are claiming no one will be able to afford their putrid food if they were forced to pay their employees a living wage. McDonald's CEO James Skinner, for example, received a performance bonus of $23 million in 2012, while David Novak, CEO of Yum! Brands (which includes Taco Bell and KFC), was given more than twice that amount, with a $48 million "performance" bonus.[32]

While these CEOs are earning unconscionable amounts of money, their workers are often forced to make ends meet on $20,000 annually or less, with decreasing benefits every year. Walmart has become notorious in this regard; their employees are even given instructions on how to apply for welfare and food stamps during their orientation. The fact that some of these companies are paying their workers so little that they qualify for government subsidies seems to have largely escaped the attention of the public, who have been trained to focus their anger on the poorest individuals, benefiting from some nominal form of government assistance. In the minds of many Americans, it's fraud for a decidedly poor person to be on government assistance and still have what appears to be too good of an automobile or television for someone of their lowly lot in life, but it's okay for huge corporations to be given unlimited handouts from taxpayers to subsidize the shameful pittances they pay their employees.

During the 2013 holiday season, Walmart launched a canned-food drive for its own employees. Somehow, I don't expect Sam Walton's children to reexamine their priorities, despite all the attention and criticism this campaign received. No less ironic was the incredible boast from Walmart's CEO Bill Simon, the month before, during a presentation about the opportunities at his corporation, that 475,000 Walmart associates earned salaries of at least $25,000. There are about a million Walmart employees, so this means that less than half of them are paid even this kind of paltry salary. The Committee for Better Banks surveyed bank tellers in New York and found that 39 percent of them were on some form of public assistance, because their salaries were so low. By the end of 2012, the top ten CEOs each were making over $100 million a year. Facebook CEO Mark Zuckerberg led the way, with $2.28 billion. Almost all of Zuckerberg's earnings came through stock options, which meant a very low tax bill.[33]

The results of a study published in the *New York Times* on July 22, 2013, confirmed that whether you're born poor or born rich you tend overwhelmingly to stay that way. Nationally, a Pew poll found that 43 percent of Americans born in the bottom fifth of the economic ladder never move up at all, while 70 percent never reach the middle rung. Even students from wealthy families with lower test scores are more likely to graduate from college than poor students with higher test scores.[34] So few people control the marketplace that, according to the Institute for Policy Studies, the top One Percent own half of all the stocks in this country, while the bottom 50 percent own only .5 percent of them. Sociologist and author G. William Domhoff revealed, in an illuminating report on his *Who Rules America?* website, that the One Percent has only 5 percent of the collective personal debt, while the bottom 90 percent has 73 percent. When we contrast the distribution of income and debt, it becomes obvious just how difficult economic upper mobility is in present-day America. Joseph Stiglitz went over much of this material in an excellent article in the May 2011 *Vanity Fair,* titled "Of the 1%, by the 1%, for the 1%." There is probably no truer saying than the chestnut, "The rich get richer and the poor get poorer."

As Ambrose Bierce once defined it, a corporation is an ingenious device whereby individual profit is obtained without individual responsibility. Those who suggest that top executives are indispensible and crucial to the success of the company should try a simple experiment; allow a week to go by without any executives reporting to work (or even telecommuting, one of their countless perks). Then go a week without the janitorial staff. It will be crystal clear to everyone just who is doing the important work.

2 Deindustrialization and Free Trade

Riches—the savings of many in the hands of a few
                                    —Eugene Debs

As far back as the 1896 presidential campaign, populist William Jennings Bryan criticized what would later be called the trickle-down theory of economics. "There are those who believe that if you just legislate to make the well-to-do prosperous," Jennings said, "that their prosperity will leak through on those down below." Jennings was the Democratic Party's unsuccessful candidate for president three times. There is little question that this would have been a better country with him in the oval office. In 2013, Pope Francis would blast trickle-down economics as "opinion, which has never been confirmed by the facts, [that] expresses a crude and naïve trust in the goodness of those wielding economic power."[35]

The post-World War II economy, which provided baby boomers of all income levels with a wonderful sense of security, is now just a fond, distant memory. A variety of factors have contributed to the lowering of wages for some 80 percent of workers over the past thirty-plus years. Our disastrous free-trade policies, combined with a lack of punitive tax measures for corporations that move offshore, have decimated America's once vibrant industrial base. The loss of viable unions, and national labor as a force to be reckoned with, has resulted in depressed wages and benefits across the board for blue-collar workers. Immigration, especially illegal immigration, was probably the biggest culprit, as both Democrats and Republicans alike clamored to court a new voting bloc and tap into an unending source of cheap labor, respectively. As far back as 1999, a joint report from the Department of Labor and the Department of Justice concluded, "unions have been weakened directly by the use of recent immigrants."

As Patrick Buchanan noted in a World Net Daily column on June 18, 2012, when NAFTA was enacted in 1993, the United States had a trade surplus with Mexico of $1.6 billion. By 2010, we had a trade deficit with Mexico of $61.6 billion. Few statistics tell a clearer story than that. Bureau of Census figures show that our trade deficit with China went from $6 million in 1985 to more than $365 billion by 2015, which is the largest trade deficit one nation has ever had with another. Overall, according to the Department of Labor, the United States has piled up an astounding $8 trillion trade deficit with the rest of the world since 1975. The United States, with its affinity for disastrous trade deals that Ross Perot was so adroit at criticizing, stands in stark contrast to countries such as Japan, Germany, and China, which all take great pride in protecting their industries from foreign competition. Much as the establishment has learned to demonize critics of our immigration policy as racists or xenophobes, they instinctively blanch at any opposition to free trade, labeling it as protectionism.

NAFTA demonstrated how bogus the "left" and "right" paradigm is. NAFTA was conceived during Reagan's administration, negotiated by Bush the Elder, and pushed through Congress by Bill Clinton in an alliance with numerous Republicans and corporate lobbyists. NAFTA not only produced the "giant sucking sound" Ross Perot forecast, it dramatically increased the number of Mexicans illegally crossing our border. NPR acknowledged this in a December 26, 2013, story titled "Wave of Immigrants Gained Speed After NAFTA." George W. Bush copied the NAFTA template with the World Trade Organization and more than a dozen additional awful trade treaties, including one that opened American markets up to China by admitting them into the WTO. That deal alone, according to the Economic Policy Institute, cost this country some 2.7 million jobs. A recent study conducted by Federal Reserve Board economist Justin Pierce and Yale's Peter Schott found that granting permanent normal trade relations to China in 2000 had caused the loss of almost a third of American manufacturing jobs.[36] To quote Economic Policy Institute blogger Jeff Faux, "By any measure, NAFTA and its sequels have been major contributors to the rising inequality of incomes and wealth."

Nike exemplifies the disastrous impact globalization has had upon average blue-collar workers. Depending upon the study one uses, it appears that the total cost to make an Air Jordan tennis shoe is somewhere between $15–20. The newest Air Jordans sell for over $200 a pair. These wildly overhyped sneakers, advertised during Michael Jordan's playing days under the slogans, "Just do it," and "Be like Mike," are manufactured in foreign plants that pay their employees slave wages. In one of Nike's Indonesian plants, the military was utilized to force factory workers into accepting $3.75 per day, which was below the already absurd Indonesian minimum wage of $4 a day. Labor activists claimed this was not an isolated incident. Another Nike factory in Indonesia was accused of failing to pay its workers for 600,000 hours of overtime over a two-year period, according to the *Guardian.* Workers in a Converse factory in Indonesia (Converse is owned by Nike, in yet another example of the countless phony competitors our predatory system provides consumers) alleged they were physically assaulted by their supervisors.[37] Philip Knight, Nike's cofounder and former CEO, has an estimated worth of $18.4 billion. Michael Jordan has a $650 million fortune. Since the early 1990s, inner-city youths all across America have been killed over these glorified tennis shoes. *Sports Illustrated,* in a twenty-five-year anniversary update to its May 14, 1990, cover story on the subject, acknowledged that "robbing people for sneakers was, and still is, not a media fabrication."

Using Department of Labor figures, in 1980, more than 80 percent of American adult men had jobs. By 2013, less than 65 percent were employed. The Civilian Labor Participation Rate in late 2016, of close to 63 percent, was the lowest since the 1970s. Some 53 percent of American workers now make less than $30,000 annually. The persistent mantra from politicians, touting the importance of small business, and American entrepreneurs, stands in stark contrast to the economic reality; only 7 percent of all non-farm workers in the United States are self-employed. And since over 90 percent of small businesses invariably have yearly revenues of less than $250,000, the conservative talking point about how raising taxes on the wealthy will hurt small business is plainly ludicrous. Although the failure rates for small businesses vary according to the source, *Small Business Trends* reported recently, "The typical new business started in the United States is no longer in operation five years after being founded."[38] Despite the handful of examples trotted out to support the myth, in reality America is actually falling behind the rest of the world in terms of creating entrepreneurial wealth. A 2014 study by Barclays found that while 40 percent of millionaires from around the world cited a business sale or profit as their source of wealth, only 21 percent of those in the United States did. The number of businesses less than a year old dropped from 4.1 million in 1994 to 3 million in 2015, according to Bureau of Labor statistics. All the numbers show that start-up businesses have been declining for three decades, and have dropped significantly within the last ten years.[39]

Large corporations saw their offshore profits rise by 14 percent in 2012. General Electric alone admitted to withholding some $108 billion in profits overseas. Just as companies have found it much easier to move their factories to other countries, where they can pay slave-labor wages while providing no benefits and avoiding health and environmental regulations, they use their profits garnered offshore to avoid paying taxes. The *Wall Street Journal* researched sixty big US corporations and found that they were keeping over 40 percent of their annual profits out of the country. An April 14, 2016, article in the *Atlantic* reported that the fifty largest American corporations were storing more than a trillion dollars offshore in order to avoid taxes. Apple, Cisco, Oracle, and other corporate giants chant the familiar mantra about such tax breaks creating jobs. It was reported in late 2013 that the Walt Disney Company had saved an estimated $315 million in taxes through offshore profits.[40] A May 2013 Senate hearing exposed the fact that Apple had paid only 2 percent tax on its estimated $74 billion in profits. Apple CEO Tim Cook told the committee that his company had paid "all the taxes we owe." If offshore tax shelters were outlawed, these large corporations would be paying somewhere between 30–35 percent in taxes.[41]

According to the Bureau of Labor, only 31 percent of American workers were offered a traditional pension plan by their employer in 2010. Eighty-two percent of the dwindling number of unionized employees, however, were still being offered such a pension. By 2013, BLS figures showed that only 8 percent of private-sector companies were offering pensions. The difference between public and private industry was even greater; some 84 percent of state and local government workers had a top-notch pension plan, while only 20 percent of private-industry employees did. Of those working less than full-time hours, as an increasing number of Americans are, only 14 percent have a pension.[42] The corporate world has gradually, over the past thirty years or so, basically outsourced the pension. Popular 401(k) plans shift the responsibility from employer to employee. While 401(k)s give individuals more control over their retirement, they also eliminate the benefit loyal workers used to enjoy, a guaranteed, regular income upon retirement. As the Social Security Administration put it in its 2009 bulletin *The Disappearing Benefit Pension,* "DB [or defined benefit] pensions are tied to employers who, consequently, bear the responsibility for ensuring that employees receive pension benefits. In contrast, DC [or defined contribution] retirement assets are owned by employees who, therefore, bear the responsibility for their own financial security."

The *Wall Street Journal* reported in 2011 that the nation's largest corporations, such as General Electric, Microsoft, Walmart, Intel, Oracle, Cisco, Stanley Works, etc., had cut their workforces by 2.9 million over the past decade, replacing them with 2.4 million overseas workers. Cisco alone went from 26 percent of its workforce abroad at the beginning of the decade to 46 percent by the close of it. In 2009, representatives from many of the nation's most powerful corporations attended the "2009 Strategic Outsourcing Conference." The majority of executives attending responded to a conference poll by indicating they had increased outsourcing. The primary reason for the outsourcing, according to another question in the poll, was "increased operating costs." Of course, this absurd rationale was belied by all the monstrous severance packages, golden parachutes, and regular compensation doled out to their top executives.[43]

Much of the left is hypocritical on the labor issue. In the revealing book *Do As I Say, Not As I Do,* by Peter Schweizer, it was revealed that film director Michael Moore owns shares in companies such as Haliburton, Honeywell, and Boeing and does his postproduction film work in Canada to avoid paying union wages in the United States. On top of that, he owns *nine* homes, including a 10,000-square-foot mansion in Michigan.[44] Democratic Party leader Nancy Pelosi owns a Napa Valley vineyard that uses nonunion labor, but this didn't stop her from getting the 2002 Cesar Chavez Award from the United Farm Workers. Some have alleged that Pelosi uses not only nonunion labor, but illegal immigrants.[45] Senator Elizabeth Warren made dubious claims about having Native American heritage, which helped her to land a coveted job at Harvard University where she was paid $350,000 to teach a single class. She lives in a $5.4 million mansion and certainly ought to know the truth behind her sound bite that "the system is rigged to benefit the rich."[46]

Unions have become so ineffectual that in recent years some of them have instituted a policy of outsourcing their own picket lines! They utilize unemployed, sometimes homeless people to walk picket lines in protest of layoffs and, yes, company outsourcing.

The pay is minimum wage with no benefits, and, in the new normal American tradition, is in cash with no taxes recorded.[47] The few remaining unions still make the kinds of mind-boggling decisions and allocations of funds that led them into unethical collusion with organized crime and resulted in the McClellan Senate investigation in the 1950s, which first brought both Senator John F. Kennedy and his ambitious younger brother Bobby to national prominence. For example, according to the Department of Labor, then MSNBC talking head Ed Schultz purportedly received at least $177,000 from unions in 2012. Why would any organization devoted to representing the interests of blue-collar workers waste this kind of money on a wealthy, nonunion talking head? While accepting this kind of extra income, Schultz refused to publicly support unionization of employees at NBC, the company that paid his own excessive salary (according to Celebrity Net Worth, Schultz has a fortune of $11.5 million). In the best establishment liberal tradition, Schultz had been a vocal critic of private aircraft, but he actually owns at least *four* private jets himself, according to the *Daily Caller*.

With the passage of the Taft-Hartley Act in 1947, so-called unfair labor practices, such as wildcat strikes—spontaneous acts of defiance on the floors of factories and shops—were forbidden. Most of the union power went to leaders at the top, who were tasked to police their dissident members, who often ended up, in the words of many old union members I heard when I was young, in bed with management. This period also saw the beginning of misnamed "right-to-work" laws, which don't guarantee someone a job, as the name implies, but instead give employees the right to resist joining a union. In reality, these laws, which still exist in several states, have had a lethal impact on the formation and effectiveness of unions. The merger of the AFL and the CIO in 1956, along with several big union strike successes in steel, auto, rubber, and other major industries and the activism of the United Auto Workers, kept Big Labor afloat as a political force to be reckoned with for a few more decades, but by the Reagan era, the antiunion, anti–big government trend was clear.

The expression "new normal" comes from venture capitalist Roger McNamee's 2004 book *The New Normal: Great Opportunities in a Time of Great Risk.* The book advises Americans to look for niche areas to exploit, usually on a temporary basis, because secure full-time jobs, guaranteed pensions, and real chances for advancement are rapidly vanishing for blue-collar workers.

The average American worker today faces a lethal combination of dwindling benefits, stagnant pay, increased expectations, and uncertain futures, all born out of corporate greed. This greed has been nurtured by the massive influx of immigrants into the workforce, the destruction of private sector unions, and a pacified public.

3   PART-TIME JOBS

Board of Directors have to make certain kinds of decisions, and those decisions are pretty narrowly constrained. They have to be committed to increasing profit share and market share. That means they're going to be forced to try to limit wages . . .

—Noam Chomsky

MANY WORKING AMERICANS HAVE BEEN forced to supplement their income with a second job over the past few decades. The wealthy elite also often have part-time jobs. Their part-time jobs are certainly not taken out of financial necessity, however, and the compensation they receive in this regard is often as unfathomable as their full-time salaries are.

Both for-profit and nonprofit corporations are required by law to have a governing board of directors. These directors are supposed to oversee the company's activities and represent its shareholders. While nonprofit board members are theoretically not supposed to be paid, for-profit directors usually are. The average compensation for a board of directors member at S&P 500 companies rose to a record $251,000 in 2012, for an average of 250 hours of "work."[48] A 2015 director compensation study revealed the average compensation had risen to $276,667.

Bill Gates serves on the board of directors for Warren Buffet's Berkshire Hathaway, He is upholding a family tradition, as his "middle-class" mother served on the board of directors for First Interstate BancSystem and United Way. Further making a mockery of the legend that Gates grew up middle class, one of his grand-fathers was also a bank president. Buffet pays Gates a ridiculous $1,800 annual salary to sit on his company's board, and he reaps the benefits of glowing mainstream media praise for that, reports a story in the March 15, 2013, *Wall Street Journal* for example. What even the *Journal* concedes in its puff piece is that Gates also gets *billions* of Berkshire shares in compensation, which are funneled through his Bill and Melinda Gates Foundation.

Al Gore is on the board of directors for Apple. *Reuters* reported that in 2008 alone, as the recession was first hitting America, Gore was paid an incredible $633,000 to attend the five obligatory board meetings that year. Imagine that—being considered worth well over $100,000 a meeting. He also received some real sweetheart deal in Apple stock options to add to his lucrative compensation package. Gore's full-time gig is Chairman of Generation Investment Management, for which we can safely assume he is very well compensated.

There are a great many celebrities who, despite the lack of any seeming qualifications, sit on the boards of large corporations. Deepak Chopra, high-profile doctor and author, is a member of the Men's Wearhouse board of directors. Former NBA player Julius "Dr. J" Erving sits on the Fusion Telecommunications board, and Michael Jordan is a director for Oakley Inc. Opera star Beverly Sills sat on Time-Warner's board, while actor Sidney Poitier was with Disney. And ex-Pittsburgh Steelers wide receiver Lynn Swann trumps them all; he sits on the board for H.J. Heinz, Hershey Entertainment and Resorts, Transdel Pharmaceuticals, and Harrah's Entertainment.[49]

Naturally, politicians also get in on the action. Al Haig and Colin Powell served on the board of directors for America Online. Henry Kissinger, as might be expected considering his exalted posi-tion within the establishment, has been associated with the boards of numerous companies, including Revlon, American Express,

Union Pacific, and Macy's. Even Chelsea Clinton, at the tender age of thirty-one, was named to the board of IAC/Interactive Corp., largely controlled by powerful entertainment mogul Barry Diller. Longtime United States Senator Sam Nunn at one time sat on *seven* different boards, including the Coca-Cola Company, Dell Computer, and General Electric.

The online community Democratic Underground charted many examples of these multiple-board positions. Leonard S. Coleman, for instance, whose last known full-time job was as unofficial president of Major League Baseball's National League, sits on a slew of powerful boards: H.J. Heinz Company, New Jersey Resources, Omnicom, Cendant Corporation, Aramark, Churchill Downs, and EA (Electronic Arts). As Democratic Underground put it, "With so many commitments pulling him in so many directions, how does Coleman develop a true understanding of what makes any of these companies tick?" Perhaps Coleman is a special breed, a professional board member, possessing that innate, unquantifiable executive "talent." Professor G. William Domhoff has long been researching what he calls the "interlocking directorates in the corporate community."

The June 28, 2010, *Milwaukee-Wisconsin Journal Sentinel* exposed the outrageous part-time salaries already wealthy individuals were garnering from multiple Wisconsin companies. As their article stated, "An accountant, a lawyer, and two retired executives each collected more than $475,000 last year—and one topped $600,000—doing part-time work for multiple Wisconsin companies. The men are members of corporate America's most elite club: the board of directors." Thomas Fischer, who ran the Milwaukee office of Arthur Andersen for a decade, made $575,864 for sitting on four boards in one year. "It's a hell of a lot of money," Fischer admitted but made sure to note, "The responsibilities are huge." Again, how could anyone hope to perform even mundanely at *four* different jobs if each of them required any substantial amount of time, let alone carried "huge" responsibilities? Fischer went on, "You have to pay them a competitive wage or you're not going to get the highest caliber board members or officers." There it is again; the allusion to that elusive executive talent. It's hard to believe that this situation isn't being mirrored all across the United States.

A puff piece, attempting to explain all these often high-paying positions being bestowed upon those who most decidedly don't need them appeared in the May 10, 2011, *UK Financial Times.* Headlined, "One Woman, Multiple Boards: Rise of the Super-Connected Director," the story chronicled the career of Charlene Barshefsky. The article informed us that Barshefsky, a former US Trade Representative, "began getting offers to sit on corporate boards" during her tenure as a globe-trotting bureaucrat. Barshefsky is associated with some real heavyweight boards: Estee Lauder, American Express, and Intel. The article routinely informed us that fifty-nine men sit on the boards of four or more large US companies, with at least one being a Fortune 500 business. The thrust of the article was that females are under-represented on these boards; we learn, for instance, that only twenty-one women sit on such multiple boards. The article quoted the 2002 bestseller *Linked,* which described how "a sparse network of a few powerful directors controls all major appointments in Fortune 1000 companies."

Countless ex-politicians supplement their incomparable pensions by sitting on the boards of powerful corporations. Former Senator Spencer Abraham is director for Occidental Petroleum, for example. NBC aired a rare, hard-hitting report on this subject on June 13, 2012. They covered a scandal involving Chesapeake Energy, wherein CEO Aubrey McClendon had invested in drilling projects his company was associated with, and noted how two of Chesapeake's board members were Oklahoma's ex-Senator Don Nickles and former Governor Frank Keating. The board members were charged with using the company's private planes for travel. NBC cogently noted, "It is equally reasonable to ask why politicians, with their backgrounds unrelated to running big companies, were even appointed to the board." NBC further noted, regarding the question of politicians in general serving on boards of directors:

"The common thread among the directors on this list is that they have been paid very well in their roles. Most make more than a quarter of a million dollars a year. Most also have stock ownerships or grants that add substantially to those payments and usually amounts to millions of dollars."

One might wonder how much work is required to earn all that money. As you might guess, not much. McDonald's board members attended all of eight meetings in 2012. The lowest-paid members of McDonald's board of directors are paid $250,000 annually, while Chairman Andrew J. McKenna was paid *over a million dollars.* Eight meetings. Over a million dollars. McDonald's proxy statement reveals other interesting gems; a glaring example of a typical incestuous corporate relationship is revealed in the fact McDonald's board member Enrique Hernandez Jr. is the CEO of Inter-Con Security Systems, Inc., which happens to be the provider of physical security services for McDonald's home campus. We also learn that McDonald's former president Jeffrey Stratton has both a son and a son-in-law whose businesses "have been significant suppliers of products and services to the McDonald's system."

Nabors Industries, a global oil and drilling company, sent the members of its board to Bermuda—four times in 2009 alone—for three days of "round-the-clock meetings." In addition to this incredible perk, Nabors was paying its board of directors an average of $420,000 each as of 2009. And all this came a year after the value of the company stock dropped 60 percent. Shareholders have attempted to vote out some of these highly paid board members but have been unsuccessful in doing go.[50] Intuitive Surgical, a robotics health-care equipment provider, paid its seven non-employee directors an average of $697,000 in 2009. They held five meetings that year. Apple paid its board of directors a standard $633,000 (as noted earlier, including Al Gore), which adds up to $127,000 per meeting. Intuitive Surgical's spokesman Ben Gong said, regarding their board's compensation, "We are certainly comfortable with that." Corporate watch-dog website Footnoted.org editor Michelle Leder stated the obvious here, "If you had a part-time job that was paying you $300,000, $400,000, $500,000 a year, and you didn't have a lot of work to do, would you rock that boat?" In 2008, members of the Goldman Sachs board of directors were each paid $298,000, although they did have to attend sixteen meetings, more than most companies have. Morgan Stanley's board was even "busier," with twenty-eight meetings, but their average pay of $312,000 was still impressive for any full-time, let alone part-time work.[51] The highest-paid board members in 2016 included those at Vertex Pharmaceuticals, where they were paid a median of over $1.2 million; Goldman Sachs, which paid an average of more than $595,000; and Regeneron Pharmaceuticals, Inc., which received an incredible average of over $2 million each.[52]

The revolving door at the highest levels of finance should come as no surprise. President Trump's Secretary of the Treasury, Steve Mnuchin, worked for Goldman Sachs and several hedge companies. When Barack Obama appointed ex-Federal Reserve Bank of New York president Timothy Geithner as Secretary of the Treasury, he was not only following a long political tradition of asking foxes to guard the henhouse, he was getting a real blue blood. Geithner's father had been a high-ranking Ford Foundation official, and his mother was a Mayflower descendent. His grandfather was an advisor to President Eisenhower and a Ford Motor Company, vice president. Bill Clinton's Treasury Secretary, Robert Rubin, came from Goldman Sachs, where he'd been a vice chairman and co-chief operating officer. After the Clinton years, he went on to serve on the boards for the Harvard Corporation, Mount Sinai/NYU Health and Citigroup, the New York Stock Exchange, the Ford Motor Company, and others. He was on the board of trustees for several powerful organizations, including the US Securities and Exchange Commission and the Carnegie Corporation of New York. Clinton's second Treasury Secretary, Lawrence Summers, came from the World Bank. After Clinton left office, Summers kept busy, serving on the boards of numerous companies, including Center for American

Progress, Teach for America, Center for Global Development, and the Partnership for Public Service, as well as rock star Bono's foundation ONE. He also manages to fit in writing regular columns for the *Washington Post,* the *Financial Times* and *Reuters.*

Incidentally, in addition to Lawrence Summers, Bono's phony ONE foundation features luminaries like Warren Buffet's son Howard, Condoleeza Rice, and Maria Shriver's brother Bobby as board members. Since it has been widely reported that ONE has overhead expenses of more than 98 percent, spending barely 1 percent of donations on helping anyone, it can be safely assumed that they are all generously compensated.

Once federal rules requiring disclosure of such compensation began, the public became privy to the startling fact that not only was the median board salary $251,000 for an average of 250 hours of work per year, companies such as Fidelity National Information Services (which handed out a $9.5 million retention bonus), News Corp., and Costco Wholesale Group (which awarded some directors $1 million consulting fees), were creating a situation where the part-time directors on these boards were receiving nearly six times the average salary of a full-time American worker.[53] As has been the case with CEOs and other high-ranking officials of large corporations and their salaries and benefit packages, the success or failure of the company often is in direct contradiction to the compensation bestowed upon those who serve on the board of directors. Hewlett-Packard, for example, while losing more than 50 percent of its stock value over the previous few years, led the nation in director compensation in 2012. According to the feisty Internet website, 247wallst.com, the average compensation for individual HP board members was $941,802. (By 2016, average board salaries at HP had apparently dropped significantly, as they failed to make the top twenty list of the highest compensated.)

The rich and famous can also supplement their fortunes with astronomical speaking fees. In 2006, Donald Trump was paid $1.5 million *an hour* to speak at Learning Annex seminars.[54] Hillary Clinton charged over $200,000 to speak to everyone from apartment developers to equity managers. In a revealing example of the "oppos-ing" nature of our two major political parties, Hillary was discovered to have been paid $225,000 by an education group associated with Jeb Bush.[55] Her husband Bill really built his fortune up in this area; he was paid $750,000 for an address to a telecom company in Hong Kong and after leaving the presidency, he had accumulated some $106 million from paid speeches by 2013, according to CNN. In February 2016, CNN reported that the Clintons had accumulated $153 million in speaking fees. Bernie Sanders was highly critical of Hillary's willingness to address big corporate groups for lucrative fees. During one debate, he declared, "I don't take money from big banks. I don't get personal speaking fees from Goldman Sachs."[56] Sanders is in a distinct minority on the issue. On his 2008 pres-idential candidate financial disclosure form, Rudy Giuliani listed $9.2 million in income from speaking engagements over a thirteen-month period. Al Gore's speaking demands are "$100,000, plus travel, hotel, security, and per diem expenses." George W. Bush made at least $15 million from speeches from the time he left office in 2009 until the summer of 2013.[57]

Celebrities can even earn pocket change merely by attending parties or nightclubs. Sisters Paris and Nicky Hilton (who each earned their successes as heiresses to the old hotel fortune) hauled in $500,000 for attending a 2008 New Year's Eve party at a Las Vegas nightclub. Brittney Spears was paid $350,000 the year before to host a New Year's Eve bash at another Las Vegas club. Pamela Anderson was paid $110,000 for partying at a Las Vegas nightspot.[58] In addi-tion to being paid, these professional partiers are flown by private jet, and receive free luxurious suites, free food, and free booze. Kim Kardashian gets $50,000 for a nightclub appearance. How many human beings could not do an adequate job of partying or appearing somewhere? As if these ridiculous appearance fees weren't enough, celebrities can actually get paid for tweeting on Twitter. Kim Kardashian, for instance, gets $10,000 *per tweet* to hawk a particular product.[59] Her lesser-known sister Khloe gets $8,000 per tweet as well. Celebrities even frequently employ a hungry young ghost tweeter for this purpose. Celebrities such as Rhianna and Fergie have been paid as much as $100,000 to sit in the front row at fashion shows. Even those categorized as C-list celebrities can still make $15,000 at these fashion shows.

When celebrities merely want to gratify their egos, they can always rely on some prestigious academic institution to award them an honorary degree. Robert DeNiro has been given two doctorate degrees. Meryl Streep has been given five honorary doctorates from the top colleges in America: Harvard, Yale, Dartmouth, Princeton, and Indiana. Yoko Ono has two honorary doctorates. Singer Aretha Franklin has four honorary doctorate degrees. Author J. K. Rowling has six honorary doctorates, including one from Harvard. Boxer George Foreman has two doctorates. Celine Dion, William Shatner, Stephen Colbert, Oprah Winfrey—the list is endless in terms of celebrities being handed the most valuable pieces of paper any student can obtain.[60]

More than seventy years ago, the great populist Huey Long recognized the danger of such a concentration of power in the hands of so few. In a US Senate speech on April 4, 1932, Long declared, "I find that the Morgan and Rockefeller groups alone held, together, 341 directorships in 112 banks, railroad, insurance, and other corporations." Clearly, things have not changed in this regard over the last seven decades.

Obviously, something is wrong with a system that bestows such unlimited financial compensation, and endless opportunities for more wealth, for doing virtually nothing productive, on those who least need it. How can anyone say that those who sit on a board of directors and are paid six figures for attending a handful of meetings that year are worth the compensation? Or that anyone on earth deserves to be paid extravagantly to attend a party? There is no way to defend the notion that this kind of inexplicable extra income is being earned.

4 SPECIAL PERKS OF THE WEALTHY

Competition is a sin.

—John D. Rockefeller

THE NATIONAL FOOTBALL LEAGUE GENERATES $9 billion a year in revenues, but it enjoys a special tax-exempt status, because it portrays itself laughingly as a nonprofit organization. The league garners an estimated $30 billion from its television contracts alone.[61] Former NFL Commissioner Paul Tagliabue garnered $12.5 million in fiscal year 2010 even though he retired from his position in 2006.[62] By 2014, it became public news that Commissioner Roger Goodell was making more than $34 million yearly.[63]

United States Senators Angus Young and Tom Coburn are attempting to strip the NFL of its tax-exempt status. "For every dollar that goes out in a case like this," Young said, "that's a dollar my constituents have to pay in income taxes." The two lawmakers estimate that their PRO Sports Act, which would bar professional sports organizations with annual revenues of $10 million or more from their charitable status, would add some $10 million annually to federal coffers. The National Hockey League and the Professional Golf Association also claim tax-exempt status, while Major League Baseball voluntarily abandoned it in 2007. The NFL manages its money much like many wealthy individuals do; out of the $254 million it collected from its teams in 2011, it gave only $2.3 million to charity, and almost all of that was funneled to the Pro Football Hall of Fame.[64] The owners, naturally, don't have to fork over taxes on the dues they pay to the league, because of their nonprofit status." Meanwhile, the NHL paid its Commissioner Gary Bettman some $8.3 million in 2011.[65] Bettman has been a terrible executive by any definition of the word, allowing his sport's contract with ESPN to lapse, leaving it largely unpublicized to millions of Americans, and losing an entire season of play because of a labor strike. He is another corporate executive being extravagantly rewarded for failing miserably at his job.

The most powerful perk the wealthy enjoy is a veritable above-the-law status. If Michael Jackson had been a working stiff, and been saddled with that many allegations of improper conduct with children, he would undoubtedly have been imprisoned for a long time, and local groups would have led the way with pitchforks and flaming torches. There are countless examples every year of NFL players alone being caught for their second, third, or fourth DWI, or their second or third allegation of sexual assault, and getting the kind and gentle treatment from the law that average citizens never do. If the case isn't dropped altogether (which is what usually happens), then their "punishment" is invariably what I call the "celebrity special"; community service and/or a suspended sentence. Community service usually entails hosting a golf tournament or signing a bunch of autographs for adoring fans.

Fringe NFL wide receiver Donte Stallworth was caught not only driving drunk, but hitting and killing a pedestrian while doing so, in March of 2009. Normally, a member of the public caught drunk behind the wheel after killing a pedestrian would have faced a long prison sentence. In fact, Stallworth could have received fifteen years in prison. Instead, he was sentenced to *twenty days* in jail. Miami-Dade County State Attorney Katherine Fernandez Rundle cited the lack of a previous criminal record, cooperation with police, and Stallworth's willingness to accept responsibility as factors in the incredibly light punishment. "For all of these reasons, a just resolution of this case has been reached," she rationalized.[66] Stallworth resumed his playing career afterwards; in all these cases, the NFL won't even do the minimum and simply ban even marginally talented offenders from playing in their league again. A local representative of Mothers Against Drunk Driving (MADD) didn't criticize the sentence but publicly applauded it. "I think there are a lot of kids as well as adults who will listen to his message," stated Janet Mondshein, MADD's Miami-Dade Director. "I think he'll do more good being out of jail and being active in prevention than he would be in jail."[67] This is a common theme where wealthy or famous defendants are involved—the notion that it would serve no purpose in sending them to prison. Couldn't this argument be made on the behalf of any defendant?

It's sobering to consider that since many police officers are just as starstruck as the rest of us, the majority of athletes and other celebrities caught in the midst of various misdeeds are probably let off with a warning, perhaps even a request for an autograph or a picture. In April 2016, *TMZ* reported that police had covered up country singer Zac Brown's involvement in a Palm Beach, Florida, hotel drug bust. A May 25, 2011, story in the *New York Daily News* detailed how NYPD police had fixed a summons for New York Yankees star Alex Rodriguez. Singer Kid Rock was stopped in Nashville in 2005 on suspicion of drunk driving, but the officer opted not to perform the standard sobriety test and indeed asked for an autograph. The officer's police captain, defending his underling as they always do in these cases, stated, "We don't have any way of knowing, had the field-sobriety test been done, how that would have come out."

Even when they are caught, celebrities fare far better than the unwashed masses when they enter a courtroom. Actress Michelle Rodriguez, for instance, was caught driving under the influence while serving a three-year probation for a previous DUI that was also a hit-and-run (and for good measure, she was driving with a suspended license). Although she was sentenced to sixty days in jail,

Rodriguez was released after a little more than four hours. As *Prison Legal News* editor Paul Wright put it, "you have one system of justice for the poor and politically unconnected and another system of justice for the wealthy and politically connected."[68]

On the rare occasions when someone of means actually has to serve time behind bars, they are often treated like royalty. For well over a decade, Southern California jails have been renting out upscale cells to affluent citizens convicted in Los Angeles County. These private cells are known as self-pay jails and include amenities such as iPods, cell phones, computers, and work-release programs. These special prisoners are referred to as clients and are often permitted to bring in their own food. At the same time, conditions in the Los Angeles County jail are so deplorable that, according to federal judge Dean D. Pregerson, inmates must constantly remain in their bunks, because there is no room for them to stand in their cells.[69] Like most penal institutions, the population of the self-pay jails consists overwhelmingly of pretrial detainees; in the case of Los Angeles County this figure is a staggering 85 percent. "If you're going to be in jail, it's the best $75 per day you'll ever spend in your life," declared proud Fullerton County Police Lt. John Petropulos, "You don't have to worry about getting beat up by a guy with a shaved head and tattoos." As *Prison Legal News* astutely observed, "The implication, of course, is that poor prisoners who can't afford pay-to-stay jails should be worried about such violence." While the poor and unconnected are instantly incarcerated and frequently have a lengthy wait until their trial, wealthy persons charged with crimes often are given "bail monitoring" arrangements, that permit them to stay in their homes.[70]

Radio personality Rush Limbaugh received a sweetheart deal when he was caught with illegally obtained prescription drugs in 2006. Limbaugh was released on $3,000 bail, and prosecutors agreed to dismiss the charge if he submitted to some hardly taxing terms for eighteen months (not owning a gun, submitting to drug tests, participating in substance abuse treatment, and paying

$30,000 to cover the costs of the doctor-shopping investigation). An even-more-outrageous example was the slap on the wrist billionaire investment banker Jeffrey Epstein received. On June 30, 2008, Epstein pleaded guilty to felony charges of soliciting prostitutes and procuring minors for prostitution. Epstein admitted to having sex with girls as young as fourteen at his Palm Beach, Florida, mansion. After agreeing to an eighteen-month sentence, the federal investigation against him was dropped. He served a year in prison and then spent an additional year on house arrest. Epstein's dream legal team included former Special Prosecutor Kenneth Starr and renowned attorney Alan Dershowitz. There were few protests from women's groups, who certainly would have been more vocal had Epstein been a garden-variety pedophile.

On May 18, 1978, John Daniel Christian, the thirteen-year-old son of Lyndon Johnson's one-time press secretary George Christian, shot and killed his English teacher in front of the entire class. He was arrested and charged but never prosecuted. Two psychiatrists testified that putting the youngster in a juvenile detention center would only increase the severity of his mental illness. The fact his father was friends with District Attorney Ronnie Earle was purely coincidental. After spending two years in a mental hospital, he went on to become an attorney and is presently practicing in Austin, Texas. Online references to this case are scant; I had to rely on an article written by Michael Corcoran on his website for information. Author and beat generation poet William S. Burroughs shot and killed his wife Joan Vollmer on September 6, 1951, during a drunken game of "William Tell" at a party in Mexico. Burroughs spent all of thirteen days in jail before his wealthy parents managed to buy his freedom (Burroughs was referred to as an heir in a *New York Daily News* September 8, 1951, headline, and it reported that his grandfather was the inventor of the adding machine). He was eventually convicted of manslaughter in absentia, and received a two-year suspended sentence. Actor Matthew Broderick killed a mother and daughter while driving drunk in Ireland on August

5, 1987. Eventually the charges against him were reduced to the extent that he was found guilty of careless driving and paid a $175 fine. The family of the victims was hardly assuaged by the note Broderick left them saying how sorry he was, and called the punishment "a travesty of justice." It wasn't until fifteen years later that Broderick finally met with the now forgiving family.[71]

Actress Rebecca Gayheart, not exactly a household name, ran over and killed a nine-year-old boy in 2001, but escaped with the typical celebrity special of suspended sentence/community service.[72] Billionaire Howard Hughes struck and killed a pedestrian in 1936, but after a witness conveniently changed her story to corroborate his account that the man had suddenly stepped out in front of his vehicle, the negligent homicide charges were dropped against him.[73] On September 25, 1933, young screenwriter and future Hollywood director John Huston killed a female pedestrian at a Los Angeles intersection. After an investigation, charges were never filed against him.[74] Keith Moon, wild and crazy drummer for The Who, ran over and killed his bodyguard outside a London pub in 1970, but it was ruled an accident and no charges were filed.[75]

NBA player J. R. Smith, who despite seven recent citations and the fact his driver's license had been suspended *five times* in just one nine-month span, was somehow said to have a driving record in good standing at the time of a fatal car crash on June 9, 2007. Smith was found to have run a stop sign, driving around another vehicle while doing so, and was struck by an oncoming vehicle that had the right of way. Smith's passenger died in the wreck, but he avoided vehicular manslaughter charges, spending twenty-four days in prison and serving five hundred hours of community service. Even the families of victims killed by celebrities seem to have an undue amount of magnanimity in their hearts; in Smith's case, Wanda Bell, mother of the dead man, hugged him after the sentencing and stated, "I told him I loved him."[76]

The saturation coverage given the tragic death of six-year-old JonBenet Ramsey in 1996 too often avoided asking the obvious questions. For instance, does anyone really think that the Ramseys were treated the same as a poor or middle-class family in such a situation would have been? John Ramsey, JonBenet's father, was worth a reported $6.4 million at the time of the murder. The Ramseys behaved about as strangely and suspiciously as a family could, yet they were treated with kid gloves by the Boulder, Colorado, police and were permitted to basically speak (or mostly refuse to speak) to the authorities at their discretion. The case led many to believe it was an inside job; although a ridiculous, rambling ransom note was found on a seldom-used back stairway, the child's body was left in the basement, to be discovered later by her father. The note, called "the War and Peace of ransom notes" by critics, strongly bore the earmarks of having been written by JonBenet's outgoing, eccentric mother Patsy. I don't think there is any doubt that if police entered the home of an inner-city family, found a ransom note like that and then the body of the "kidnapping" victim inside the residence, that family would have been taken immediately to the nearest jail.

It's astounding how routinely celebrated or wealthy accused individuals are acquitted, in the rare instances in which they are actually prosecuted—while most often the justice system arranges a deal with them or simply drops the charges altogether. Poor and working-class defendants receive quite a different deal. The conviction rate for federal prosecutions is a North Korea–like 97 percent. The swelling prison population has increased the workloads of public defenders tremendously, and as a result they spend almost no time with their clients, and that time is spent on plea bargaining. The average public defender in New Orleans spends *seven minutes* with those they are representing. It's not surprising, therefore, to learn that 90 to 95 percent of those represented by public defenders plead guilty.[77] The incarceration rate in the United States has roughly quintupled since the 1970s. Needless to say, those being imprisoned are not coming from the top 20 percent of wealthiest Americans. Considering how difficult it is to find a job in today's marketplace for those with a perfectly clean record, imagine how difficult it is for ex-convicts to be hired once they reemerge into society.[78]

Diplomats, in America and around the world, enjoy complete immunity from the law. In this country, attention has been occasionally focused on the fact that foreign diplomats can bring domestic workers into America on special visas reserved exclusively for them; the Freedom Network found that workers employed by diplomats in the United States have made allegations of rape, sexual assault, forced labor, involuntary servitude, labor law violations, and human trafficking against their employers. As the *Washington Post* reported, regarding diplomatic crime, "In each instance, the diplomat has walked" and "tolerance of abuse remains the norm."[79]

US Ambassadorships have always been a plum prize, since the time of the Revolutionary era, when Benjamin Franklin enjoyed his position in France so much and became the toast of Paris. The most sought-after ambassadorships, in places such as Italy and France, typically go to the highest bidder—wealthy donors to that particular president's campaign. Colleen Bell was just one of Barack Obama's huge donors so rewarded, when she was named ambassador to Hungary. Frequently, the typical suspects from the corporate world gravitate to ambassadorships; one such example is former HBO vice president James Costos, who is the current ambassador to Spain. As always, it helps to be related to somebody; the present ambassador to Sweden is Mark Brzezinski, son of veteran elite insider Zbigniew Brzezinski, and brother of television talking head Mika Brzezinski. Former child star Shirley Temple Black served as ambassador to two different countries, under two different presidents. Actor Sidney Poitier, whose parents came from the Bahamas, has been the Bahamian ambassador to Japan since 1997.

The ambassadorial perks are impressive; in some countries they live (for free, of course) in sprawling estates. London's Winfield House, home of the US Ambassador to the United Kingdom, boasts twelve and a half acres of private gardens, exceeded only by Buckingham Palace. The US ambassador to Italy can walk through historic catacombs to access a three-story, five-thousand-bottle wine cellar in Rome.[80] Ambassadors also get paid personal staffs, body-guards, and an automobile (with driver). The salaries are good, even without the free housing and generous expense accounts. Barack Obama was particularly shameless about his ambassadorships; when he tapped former Goldman Sachs executive Bruce Heyman as ambassador to Canada, he was the twenty-first high-rolling cam-paign contributor to receive a top diplomatic post during his second term in office. These ambassadors had raised at least $13.8 million cumulatively for Obama's political committees since 2007, accord-ing to research from the Center for the Public Integrity.

The perks the rich and powerful receive are seemingly endless. To cite just one industry alone, New York University was caught giving its former president, John Sexton, a $1 million loan to purchase a vacation home. While condemning this, Cary Nelson, former pres-ident of the American Association of University Professors, revealed that this was hardly an isolated case. "Assistance with mortgage by providing no-interest or low-interest loans is a necessity if you want people to live anywhere near the campus," Nelson stated, "But what the hell do they need a second home on Fire Island for, financed by the university?" Why it is necessary to provide special loans to a particular profession, one that pays extremely well, when average workers are never given this kind of benefit? NYU was exposed by the *New York Times* for a history of making loans to faculty and administrators, as well as paying them large bonuses. One of those who benefited from this practice was Jack Lew, a Secretary of the Treasury under Barack Obama. NYU forgave almost a third of Lew's $1.5 million mortgage when he left NYU in 2006. Although he was charged with helping to cover up the child sex scandal at Penn State University, President Graham Spanier was paid $2.9 million afterwards, more than any other college president in the country, and remains on paid leave to the tune of $600,000 annually. City University of New York paid disgraced former CIA Director General David Petraeus, who'd been caught in an adulterous scandal with his biographer, a ridiculous $200,000 to teach a single seminar. The New School gave its outgoing president, former US Senator Bob Kerrey, a $1.2 million "exit bonus" in 2010.[81]

These examples culled from the academic world should surprise no one. College has become a huge industry. Any notions that we are a meritocracy are contradicted by ugly statistics like the fact only 3 percent of students at the top 146 colleges come from families in the bottom income quartile. Even more incredibly, only 10 percent come from the bottom half.[82] The College Board reported that the average costs for tuition and fees at a private university was $33,480 for the 2016–2017 school year, while public colleges were $9,650 per year for in-state residents and $24,930 for out-of-state residents. College placement is tied closely to a student's SAT scores. The SAT is a standardized test that has become more powerful than anyone ever envisioned; a mediocre score can keep even students with topflight grade point averages from being accepted to a university. In 2009, former West Virginia Governor Gaston Caperton, the president of College Board, the "nonprofit" owner of the SAT entrance exam, received $1.3 million in compensation, more than the president of Harvard University. Nineteen executives employed by College Board were being paid in excess of $300,000 yearly. SAT's primary rival, the ACT exam, paid their CEO Richard Ferguson $1.1 million in the same year. Excessive executive compensation concerns led the Iowa State Attorney General to recommend that the IRS review its nonprofit status. Educational Testing, which develops and administers millions of tests all over the world, paid its seventeen trustees a combined $475,000 for attending four annual meetings. All told, thirty-nine college officials earned more than $1 million in 2014.[83] The average annual compensation package for the president of a private university in 2014 was $521,817.[84]

Wealthy families can sometimes literally buy their children's way into colleges they aren't legitimately qualified for. Meg Whitman, sometimes dubbed the world's stingiest billionaire, made an uncharacteristically generous donation of $30 million to

Princeton University at the same time her troubled son was applying for admission there. Her son had already been booted out of two expensive prep schools for unacceptable behavior and was subsequently accused of raping and beating a female student after being accepted into Princeton. After escaping any punitive measures whatsoever over the rape allegation, he was charged with felony battery in another incident involving a female. His case was dismissed after nine different court dates. Whitman's donation was turned into a brand-new dormitory named after her. Author Daniel Golden explored this subject in his provocative book *The Price of Admission: How America Buys Its Way Into Elite Colleges—and Who Gets Left Outside the Gates.* Former US Senator Bill Frist also managed to get his son accepted into Princeton after his family "had lavished tens of millions of dollars on a new student center." Oil magnate Robert Bass's daughter got into Stanford on the heels of a $25 million gift to the university from her father. Real estate developer Charles Kushner, who spent time in jail for illegal campaign contributions and witness tampering, spent $2.5 million at Harvard to successfully get his son Jared accepted there; Jared went on to buy the *New York Observer* and marry Donald Trump's daughter Ivanka. Golden established definitively that higher education is "not a meritocracy . . . but a marketplace." He determined that "as many as 60 percent of the places in a top school are already spoken for by higher bidders," making a mockery of a school like Harvard's advertised rate of accepting one in ten applicants. He even exposed a kind of secret society for parents, Harvard's Committee on University Resources (COUR), where donors generally give at least $1 million, and membership virtually assures your child admission into the most prestigious college in the country. Golden wrote, "By examining 'Who's Who' entries, alumni records and other sources, I found that 218 of 424 COUR members, or more than half, have had at least one child at Harvard."[85]

College scholarships are not necessarily tied to the financial circumstances of the student. Consider the case of Justin Combs, son of Sean "P Diddy" Combs, who has a net worth of at least $580 million. Justin was inexplicably awarded a $54,000 football scholarship to UCLA in 2012. When the news went public, a great deal of understandable criticism arose. Justin was defiant about the gift on Twitter, tweeting "Regardless what the circumstances are, I put that work in!!!! . . . PERIOD." Rapper Romeo Miller, better known as "Lil' Romeo," sprung to the defense of his fellow heir to wealth (Miller's father was a rich and famous rapper himself), claiming it was unfair to ". . . throw the rich baby to the side, we don't want him to be successful . . . " Young Justin was given a $360,000 Maybach automobile for his sixteenth birthday by daddy Diddy, so he is certainly accustomed to being the recipient of lavish gifts.[86]

The debate over these scholarships, primarily conducted on ESPN and other sports shows, was about as one-sided as a mainstream discussion about "conspiracy theories." Every talking head passionately defended the absurd giveaways, and many revealed that their children, too, had benefited from this regressive brand of assistance. Mike Golic, a former NFL player turned talk-show host, admitted that both his sons were given scholarships to Notre Dame, as was his daughter. Former NFL player Calvin Hill's son, Grant Hill, was awarded a scholarship to Duke, as was Austin Rivers, son of NBA coach and ex-player Doc Rivers. Joe Montana's son got a scholarship to Notre Dame. The late reggae star Bob Marley's son won a football scholarship to the University of Miami. To his credit, actor Denzel Washington asked Morehouse College to give the scholarship his son had been awarded to someone else because he could afford to pay the tuition. Michael Jordan reportedly did the same thing with his son when he was awarded a scholarship.[87] All these gifts to those who most decidedly don't need them are juxtaposed against the over $1 trillion of collective student debt.[88]

The sad fact is that so-called merit-based scholarships, which go overwhelmingly to students from middle-class and wealthy families, now comprise some 30 percent of state aid. About one in five students from families with incomes over $250,000 receives some form of merit assistance from their school, while only one in ten from families making less than $30,000 do. As reporter Catherine Rampell summarized things, "more aid is helping kids who need it less." As is the case with so many of these freebies for the rich, the rationale offered is that doing so is somehow good for business. In this case, the presence of more wealthy students boosts a school's ranking. "The U.S. News rankings are based largely on the student inputs," said Donald Heller, dean of Michigan State University's College of Education. "The public universities in general . . . are moving away from their historical mission to serve a broad swath of families across the state." The number of college graduates in America has dramatically increased over the past few decades, but almost all of that growth has been among children of wealthier families. By 2014, 77 percent of twenty-four-year olds from the top-income quartile were college graduates, while only 9 percent from the bottom quartile were.[89]

One angry graduate wrote a scathing letter to his university, which was widely disseminated on the Internet in May, 2014. "I'm sorry to hear that the university's $750 million endowment has fallen to $500 million because of the recession . . . I'm also sorry to hear that you're dealing with declining enrollment due to the fact that middle-class families are no longer willing or able to bet their homes on a $45,000-a-year higher education for their children." the unhappy graduate continued, "I know that I got a master's degree at your fine institution, but that master's degree hasn't done jack shit for me since I got it! I have been unemployed for the past TWO YEARS [emphasis original] and I am now a professional resume-submitter." This irate individual, known only as "Alumnus," also pointed out that "since 1987, higher education expenses have gone up 450 percent." The cost of a college education has effectively priced the poor and lower middle-class out of the higher education market, further cementing class and income distinctions. As the mouthpiece of the corporate world, *Forbes,* described it in a February 1, 2012, article, "Even with adjusted, or lowered, expectations, millions of

Millennial college graduates find their only opportunities are for positions where $10 an hour is aiming high, benefits are nonexistent, and a paid vacation is a laughable concept."

According to a study by Emory University sociologist Sabino Kornrich, spending on education for the top 10 percent jumped 35 percent during the recession. "People at the top just have so much income now that they're easily able to spend more on their kids," said Kornrich. This has contributed to a surge in the salaries of SAT tutors, who now average twice the US median pay rate of $24.45 per hour. As senior economist from the Brookings Institution Melissa Kearney described it, "If you're at the bottom, and the top keeps pulling away, you're just further behind." Echoing the statistics we quoted earlier, Postsecondary Education Opportunity reported that while 79 percent of students born into families in the highest income quartile obtain bachelor's degrees, only 11 percent of those born into the lowest income quartile do.

As UCLA law professor Richard Sander put it, "It's a far greater disparity than anything we'd talk about with race. The pervasive problem in admissions offices is class-ism." More incredibly, at the most prestigious law schools such as Harvard and Yale, only 5 percent of the students come from the bottom half of the socioeconomic spectrum. Sander's research found that as of 1999, there was only a 4 percent chance that a black student with SAT scores about 1200, but from the bottom 20 percent of the economic ladder, would even apply for admission to one of the elite colleges.[90]

As if celebrities needed any financial help, they also benefit from the nonsensical swag packages that provide them with lots of free stuff. Nominees at the 2012 Academy Awards were given swag bags valued at over $62,000, with the highlight being a five-day Premier Tours Elephant Back African Safari. Every college football bowl game is permitted to give up to $550 in gifts to each player. Notre Dame players, for instance, were all given the brand-new Playstation 4 game console, while Rutgers players settled for a $450 gift card to Best Buy. One of the lesser bowls, the Royal Purple Las

Vegas Bowl, featured gifts of new Samsung Galaxy tablets to all the players.[91]

Carvel, as a special promotion in honor of their seventy-fifth anniversary, gave out seventy-five "black cards" to celebrities, which permitted them to eat free ice cream for seventy-five years.[92] It is unknown just how many celebrities have been given a black card by Subway, but judging by the fact it was widely reported that NFL rookie Jarvis Jones, hardly a household name, received this nice little benefit, we can assume that a good number have. Chipotle has adopted an official marketing strategy where they send interested pro athletes a card that grants them a free burrito every day.[93] These corporate giveaways to those who least need them are universally seen by those in the media as astute business decisions. The Nando's restaurant chain, headquartered in Great Britain, gives black cards to the least needy celebrities imaginable, including soccer star David Beckham, Ricky Gervais, singer Ed Sheeran, American recording artist Jay Z, and American billionaire Oprah Winfrey.[94]

Celebrities receive on average about $100,000 annually in free stuff from companies eager to publicize their products. This can include free automobiles; while celebrities could easily afford a new car every year, they are often given free long-term leases from companies such as General Motors and Audi. Oscar nominees routinely get, in addition to their swag gift bags, things like free coupons to dine at expensive restaurants and offers to perform free laser eye surgery. When Tom Cruise threw a seventeenth birthday party for his son at LA's Staples Center, companies lavished gifts like luxury vacations and free cars on him.[95] Celebrities can often get free dresses from top designers, free haircuts, expensive watches, and vacations when they attend the Cannes Film Festival. When a celebrity has a baby, they are instantly bombarded with free offers from diaper companies and stroller manufacturers.[96] A few years back, Gibson gave $3,000 guitars to celebrities like Mariah Carey, Jamie Foxx, Carlos Santana, Kelly Clarkson, Ellen DeGeneres, and Les Moonves, then copresident of Viacom, later to become CEO of CBS.[97]

As if all this wasn't enough, the innovative crowdfunding service Kickstarter, which allows project creators to ask volunteers for contributions, is now being used by wealthy, established stars. Zach Braff, who makes a reported $350,000 for each episode of *Scrubs,* lobbied for fans to cough up $2 million so he could produce a follow-up to his 2004 indie film *Garden State.* Braff explained his rationale thusly, "I was about to sign a typical financing deal. . . . It would have involved a lot of sacrifices I think would have ultimately hurt the film." We all know that the bottom 80 percent of Americans have a monopoly on sacrificing. Rob Thomas, creator of the show *Veronica Mars,* with the assistance of former series star Kristen Bell, raised an incredible $5.7 million through Kickstarter for a movie version of the show. Whoopi Goldberg raised a relative "chump change" amount of $74,000 for her documentary on fabled comedian Moms Mabley.[98] One can easily imagine this trend growing; after all, if the public is willing to foot the bill, why should any filmmaker finance their own projects?

The multimillionaire celebrities abusing Kickstarter were only following the practice established long ago by professional sports team owners. When the Minnesota Vikings wanted a new stadium and issued the usual owner threat to move the team if they didn't get their way, the state legislature, while facing a $1.1 billion deficit, capitulated. It cost the taxpayers $506 million, a full half of the bill for the new facility. Vikings' owner Ziggy Wilf is worth 1.3 billion dollars. It's estimated that taxpayers have contributed about a billion dollars to build, and then later renovate, the New Orleans Superdome. Saints' owner Tom Benson is worth $1.2 billion. Seattle taxpayers coughed up $390 million of the $560 million construction costs for the Seahawks' Century Link Field. The Seahawks are owned by Bill Gates's former business partner, Paul Allen, one of the world's richest individuals. Taxpayers paid $260 million to build the Steelers' Heinz Field, and to take care of the debt from their old stadium. In 2012, Hamilton County, Ohio, taxpayers paid some $33 million annually in debt service for the stadiums of the NFL's Bengals and

Major League Baseball's Reds. Hamilton County cut $23.6 million in health and human services spending at the same time.[99]

Harvard University Professor Judith Grant Long estimates that 70 percent of the costs for NFL stadiums have been footed by the taxpayers, not the billionaire owners. Plenty of cities, counties, and states even pay team costs for power, sewer, and stadium improvements. MetLife stadium in New York, as a matter of fact, is the only NFL facility that wasn't built with some public financing.[100] It's even been discovered that taxpayers gave fourteen NFL teams a total of $5.4 million, courtesy of the Department of Defense, in return for all those tributes honoring the military before, during, and after games.[101]

None of this is new; the Los Angeles Coliseum was built entirely with taxpayer funds in 1923. Both Chicago's Soldier Field in 1929 and Cleveland's Municipal Stadium in 1931 were financed by the taxpayers. By the 1950s, public financing of sports facilities became commonplace.[102] The struggling taxpayer helping out the poor billionaires is really no different than the adoring fans buying millionaire athletes a drink in local bars. Or restaurants letting them eat free, golf courses letting them play for free, car dealerships giving them free cars. It's a damning indictment of our society that few find much to protest in this, but a great many become worked into a lather about the "handouts" going to welfare recipients or those on food stamps.

So how do these incredibly wealthy owners continue to get taxpayers to give them such generous amounts of welfare? Just as our representatives keep being re-elected at a rate of over 90 percent in every election, while polls show the approval rating of Congress to be under 10 percent, these publicly financed stadiums also fly in the face of popular opinion. In the case of the recent extortion from Minnesota Vikings owner Ziggy Wilf, according to the *New York Observer,* "Polls have consistently shown that Minnesotans overwhelmingly oppose using taxpayer money to finance this billionaires' playground." This is just another area where the public will is being constantly thwarted, and as always, it's being thwarted for the exclusive benefit of the very wealthy.

The wealthy have proven adept at squeezing money from the government in arenas beyond sports. Senator Tom Coburn led a study that found that taxpayers were paying vast amounts in benefits for millionaires—$74 million in unemployment checks, $316 million in farm subsidies, $89 million for preservation of ranches and estates, $9 billion in retirement checks, $75.6 million in residential energy tax credits, all totaling more than $9.5 billion. Largely due to these kinds of perks, the study found that some four thousand millionaires paid no federal income tax in 2011.[103] From 2003–2009, $9 billion was paid to millionaires in Social Security benefits. This is one of the most outrageous aspects of our backwards society; few Americans realize that only the first $119,000 of income is subject to Social Security taxes. Ross Perot gently suggested allowing *voluntary* means testing for Social Security during his first presidential run. He was shouted down by the AARP and other lobbying groups. A rational way to solve the Social Security crisis would be to make means testing mandatory. But, as Perot discovered when he proposed something far less radical, those at the top are never, ever supposed to sacrifice. That is something reserved exclusively for the common riffraff. One of President Trump's 2016 campaign populist statements was his suggestion, a la Perot, that he and his fellow One Percenters opt out from getting benefits they don't need. Social Security's Old Age and Survivors Insurance ran a $39 billion deficit in 2014, while paying benefits to forty-seven thousand millionaires. Since income is nonsensically not a factor for federal direct college loans, over $16 million has been loaned out since 2007 to millionaire college students, parents of college students, and graduate students.

The Shaw Group made a unique deal with CEO James Bernhard. They agreed to pay him (or his heirs) $15 million when he left the company, dead or alive, if he promised not to compete with them for two years. Don Tyson, of Tyson Foods (tied to several political scandals through connections with Bill and Hillary Clinton), was granted innumerable perks during his tenure with the company. Even after his 2001 retirement, Tyson Foods financed vacations and paid the credit card bills of Tyson and his friends, and spent an unconscionable $203,675 to clean five different homes owned by Tyson or his friends, as well as $84,000 in lawn maintenance costs. During the 1990s, Occidental Petroluem paid $5.8 million of CEO Ray Irani's state income taxes. Occidental, responding to criticism of this unusual deal, paid Irani a lump sum of $95 million in 1997 to rescind it. *Forbes* estimated that Irani earned $1.2 billion during his tenure as CEO.[104] One of Oracle CEO Larry Ellison's perks is company payment for his elaborate home security system, which includes security personnel, adding up to some $1.4 million annually. General Electric—which paid zero income taxes in at least three separate years, doled out a variety of embarrassing perks to CEO Jack Welch, both before and after his tenure. These included courtside seats at Knicks' games, a personal staff for his New York apartment, a skybox for Red Sox games, and VIP seating at the French Open.[105]

Golfers such as Tiger Woods make most of their money in lucrative endorsement deals. Woods, Phil Mickelson, and other multimillionaires on the PGA tour don't have to foot the bills for clubs, balls, bags, caps, shirts, pants, or shoes. And they are awarded handsome endorsement money on top of all the freebies. They are paid to wear top-of-the-line designer clothing and use the best equipment. If you've ever played the game, you know how expensive even the balls are. Golf has basically become the new polo, a sport only those with plenty of money can afford to play. Pro golfers not only can earn astronomical amounts of money without ever even winning a single tournament, they receive some outstanding perks off the links as well. *Golf Today* cited some examples from just one tournament, the Ford championship at Doral. PGA players had the opportunity to "take a few 150-mph spins in Ford-sponsored NASCAR racers" at a professional raceway, to eat free at a couple of pricey local restaurants after the first and second rounds, in addition to "the usual tournament perks—courtesy cars, free food, and day care for the kiddies." The HP Classic in New Orleans offers players fresh red-fish, cooked personally for them on the practice range by celebrity chefs such as Paul Prudhomme, and the Funai Classic at the Walt Disney World Resort offers the families of each player free tickets to all the different amusement parks. Nearly every golfer on the PGA tour came from an upper-class family; without all those expensive lessons, and plenty of playing time to gain experience, it would be extremely difficult for even the most natural golfer in the world to compete at that level. If a golfer wins just the Players Championship tournament, he would be awarded $1.7 million. That's quite a take for four rounds of golf.

Professional tennis players, who also are invariably from upper-class backgrounds (again, due to the cost and necessity of extensive private lessons), do pretty well in the perk department, too. Bob Bryen, a top-ranked doubles player on the ATP tour, refreshingly admitted to ESPN, "The money's great. You get so much free clothes. Hotels are awesome, and you get free food. In Indianapolis (at the RCA Championships), they give you a free stereo and a camcorder. It's a great lifestyle. I'd rather be doing this than working in an office."

Former world-record hurdler Renaldo Nehemiah, hardly a household name even at the height of his career, was just as candid on the subject with ESPN. "The sporting world is full of gracious-ness and people who want to do things for you," Nehemiah declared, "I still enjoy the amenities of my former status. I like to play a lot of golf, and I get to play for free on some of the finest courses in the world." If a relative nonentity like Nehemiah is still getting those kinds of incredible perks, years after he was in the public eye, just imagine what more high-profile athletes are getting. Do you really think regular golfers such as Michael Jordan or Charles Barkley, for instance, are paying for their tee times? Some active professional athletes have free golf club memberships written into their lucrative contracts. Again, the perks of the marketplace go to those who least need them.

NBA players sign sneaker deals, thus avoiding the tiresome and costly chore of paying for their own footwear, while being paid handsomely to wear that particular company's shoes. NASCAR drivers get sweetheart endorsement deals from corporate giants such as General Motors, Johnson & Johnson, Kraft, Anheuser-Busch, Wrangler Jeans, and XM Satellite Radio. Major League Baseball's Alex Rodriguez signed an incomprehensible $275 million deal with the Yankees in 2007, and had part-time millions raining in from companies like Nike and Rawlings. He also reportedly once had an arrangement with exclusive clothier Georgio Armani that permitted him to select whatever he wanted from any of his high-end stores, at no charge.[106] The myth that paying already-wealthy athletes or other celebrities to hawk a company's products, and giving them those products free as an additional lucrative perk, is a shrewd business practice was shattered by a poll taken by Word Press in 2014. The poll revealed that almost no one—96 percent of respondents—wanted to see celebrities promoting products. A study done a few months earlier by advertising agency Ace Metrix concluded that "TV ads containing celebrities underperformed those without."[107]

In a 2014 interview, comedian Chris Rock stated, "If poor people knew how rich rich people are, there would be riots in the streets. If the average person could see the Virgin Airlines first-class lounge, they'd go, 'What? What? This is food, and it's free, and they . . . what? Massage? Are you kidding me?'" The December 1, 2014, *Huffington Post* published his comments and revealed some of the other perks that the wealthy get. The article noted, "Rich people often get paid to wear jewelry. They get paid to lose weight. They're given free laptops and TVs. . . . Their kids' birthday parties have corporate sponsors." Rock should certainly know all about this subject, as his net worth is some $70 million.

Why does the system operate like this? The great masses of workers are denied even a minimum yearly raise that doesn't even keep up with the cost of living, while the richest people in our society are continually given valuable things for free, and twist and squeeze every benefit they can from the rotten mess, accumulating more wealth than they could ever hope to spend.

5 HATING THE POOR

Poverty is the worst form of violence.

—Mahatma Gandhi

NOT ONLY DO THOSE WHO'VE made it attempt to justify the unfathomable wealth that so few possess, they strive to blame the poor for their own poverty. Bashing the poor has become a popular pastime among Americans. Even those who are struggling financially seem attracted to the notion that those who have money are somehow inherently entitled to it, because they're special and/or have worked tremendously hard to attain it.

Adam Carolla expressed his feelings about rich people and poor people clearly (and seriously) in an interview with *The Daily Caller.* "[Rich people are] better than poor people. They just are," he declared. "They work harder, generally. More focused. . . . The poor people I grew up with, fairly lethargic, did a lot of complaining, smoked a little too much, drank a little too much, blamed everyone but themselves a little too much." It is difficult to picture the son of a psychologist, raised in North Hollywood, Los Angeles, having any poor people around to "grow up with."

Authors such as Tom Corley in his book, *Rich Habits—The Daily Success Habits of Wealthy Individuals,* outright suggest that the rich are simply a superior breed, much as Adam Carolla has. When he notes that the poor are far more likely to gamble, eat fast food, and not exercise regularly, while the rich are more likely to listen to audio books on the commute to work and are focused on accomplishing particular goals, he fails to mention the obvious. Poor people are struggling to survive, unlike the wealthy. They eat fast food because it's cheap, they are attracted to the lottery and other forms of gambling because they offer what appears to be their only chance of escaping poverty, and they certainly aren't in a position to afford audio books, let alone listen to them on the way to work. As Ben Cohen noted in the November 27, 2013, edition of *The Banter,* "the notion that you can change behavior patterns and become richer is simply laughable. . . . If you've been brought up with money you don't worry about things like paying off student loans because you didn't have to fork out for it in the first place. The rich can do things like go to the gym three times a week, listen to Tony Robbins tapes in the car, and eat organic food because they aren't worried about paying the electricity bill and putting food on the table." Ziad K. Abdelnour, author of the book *Economic Warfare,* defends the rich with wildly inaccurate statements such as "The overwhelming majority of people I refer to as 'the rich' are independent-minded, maverick entrepreneurs and business owners who risk their own capital, sweat, and tears to provide a good or service of value to the world around them." Abelnour also defines those who inherit their wealth as being "so small that they don't really matter."[108]

Economist Walter E. Williams, darling of right-wingers because he's a rare black Republican, once issued the following statement, "If you're a poor adult in America, for the most part, it's all your fault." Simultaneously, conservatives also like to claim that the poor aren't really poor when compared to the rest of the world. They will cite statistics like "66 percent of the 'poor' have air-conditioning," "62 percent of the 'poor' have cable or satellite TV," or "75 percent of the 'poor' own a car" to prove their case. Comedian George Carlin summed up this collective mind-set brilliantly when he said, "Conservatives say if you don't give the rich more money, they will lose their incentive to invest. As for the poor, they tell us they've lost all incentive because we've given them too much money." The feeling seems to be that if you're poor, you don't deserve to have the Internet, or watch television, or be distracted from your dismal set of circumstances for even a few moments. And you certainly must never try to drown your problems out with alcohol or drugs, like the rich and famous are wont to do.

Sarah Miller satirically responded to Adam Carolla's "the rich are better" comments with a piece in the June 2, 2014, *New Yorker.* She wrote, sarcastically, "I'm not afraid to tell it like it is: mowing lawns and picking up dog shit off of people's lawns is pretty fucking easy . . . try doing something harder, like being the voice of an animated éclair-policeman in a Disney movie, or being the spokesperson for T.G.I. Fridays." On the subject of voice-overs, the cast members for *The Simpsons* have been paid as much as $400,000 an episode to read scripts. Is anyone reading scripts worth hundreds of thousands of dollars for participating in a twenty-two-minute cartoon?

We take it for granted that we're more enlightened than our ancestors were a few centuries ago. However, it's easy to imagine Americans agreeing with economist Bernard de Mandeville's 1732 explanation that if slavery wasn't permitted, then the wealthy must have at their disposal a vast, permanent underclass to support them. Do we really wish to return to the era of the 1820s, for instance, during which researchers for the American Economic Association have found that approximately 84 percent of the world lived in extreme poverty? The nineteenth-century spirit is alive and well, however, in people like Steven Malanga, with the Manhattan Institute of Policy Research; in a February 4, 2007, piece in the *Chicago Sun-Times,* Malanga declared that, "It's not that the adults who head families in poverty don't earn enough; they don't work enough." Malanga is the author of *The Myth of the Working Poor,* a favorite book of conservatives. And, of course, 2012 Republican presidential nominee Mitt Romney made these unforgettable remarks; "There are 47 percent of the people . . . who are dependent upon government, who believe that they are victims. . . . These are people that pay no income tax . . .

and so my job is not to worry about those people. I'll never convince them that they should take personal responsibility and care for their lives." Mitt Romney was born the son of Michigan Governor George Romney, who was also a failed presidential candidate.

Journalists like Bill O'Reilly freely make denigrating comments about poor Americans. In a festive December 2010 column, he wrote that "the Baby Jesus wants us to provide, no matter what the circumstance" and quoted again the old misnomer, "the Lord helps those who help themselves," which is nowhere to be found in the Bible. Regurgitating the new normal party line, he also declared, "there are millions of Americans who are not responsible, and the cold truth is that the rest of us cannot continue to support them." Bill O'Reilly has a net worth of $85 million. It's almost as if the O'Reillys of the world are itching to start an Ebeneezer Scrooge fan club.[109] The Heritage Foundation's Christine Kim states that since we've spent some $20 trillion on means-tested welfare programs since the mid-1960s, "Clearly, the solution to alleviating poverty is not more of the same." And Kim stresses another new right-wing talking point on this issue, which is that if only single mothers would marry, poverty would be eliminated.

Fox News business reporter Stuart Varney has been over the top about bashing the poor. During one appearance on *Fox and Friends,* host Gretchen Williams gently chastised him for being mean-spirited, to which Varney replied, "I am. I am being mean to poor people. Frankly, I am." On the February 4, 2014, edition of *Fox and Friends,* right-wing reporter John Stossel interviewed several purportedly poor people and asked them each whether they had air-conditioning, cell phones, and television. This is a familiar theme we remarked on earlier, that someone who has these kinds of basic modern amenities can't really be considered poor and doesn't really deserve them. On another edition of *Fox and Friends,* Stossel masqueraded as a panhandler and was able to collect a lot of money from sympathetic pedestrians. The exposure of fake poor people, begging for money on the streets, is an issue of paramount importance to many conservatives. I thought they loved entrepreneurs. According to a February 2012 survey conducted by the Salvation Army, some 27 percent of Americans think the poor are lazy, and 43 percent said they believed "people living in poverty can always find a job if they really want to work." The research also revealed that a person's income skewered the way they viewed poverty; higher-income respondents thought there were fewer poor people, while those with lower incomes believed there were more.[110]

These attitudes flourished during the Reagan years. OMB Director David Stockman told Congress in 1983 that the official poverty number "substantially overstates the rate of poverty, because it ignores $107 billion in in-kind medical, housing, food, and other aid that tangibly raises the living standards of many low-income families."[111] Reagan himself appears to have been the originator of the welfare queen imagery. The Gipper would frequently invoke the case of a welfare queen from Chicago who drove, naturally, a Cadillac, and had stolen some $150,000 from the government by utilizing eighty aliases, thirty addresses, multiple social security cards, and four fictional dead husbands. Journalists searched in vain, hoping to interview her, but were unable to verify that such a person ever existed. In a 1984 *Good Morning America* appearance, President Reagan responded to the exploding number of homeless people by saying, "people who are sleeping on the grates . . . are homeless, you might say, by choice." Reagan elaborated on this in a 1988 interview with author Edmund Morris, explaining that homelessness had "been so exaggerated. . . . There aren't millions . . . a lot of those are the type of people that have made that choice. For example, more than forty percent of them are retarded, mentally deficient people, that is the result of the ACLU."[112]

Author and philosopher Ayn Rand, although she personally despised Ronald Reagan, had a tremendous impact upon him, as well as more recent politicians like Paul Ryan. She particularly influenced longtime Federal Reserve chairman Alan Greenspan. Rand hated the concept of democracy; she divided the world into groups of what she called makers and takers. She often referred to the takers as looters. Rand told reporter Mike Wallace in a 1959 interview that she was "the creator of a new code of morality . . . a morality not based on faith." Rand was a devout atheist, bragging rather illogically that, "I am against God." How can you be against God if you don't believe in him? It's ironic that many of those in the conservative movement in America now, including leaders of the Religious Right, support this woman who scorned faith. Talk-show host Glenn Beck exclaimed, "you've got to love Ayn Rand. She's great." United States Senator Ron Johnson called Rand's *Atlas Shrugged* his "foundational book." Rush Limbaugh calls her "brilliant" and loves her credo of selfishness. Rand's obscene quotes are plentiful; "What I am fighting is the idea that charity is a moral duty," or "You love only those who deserve it," or "Nobody has ever given a reason why man should be his brothers' keeper." Rand's philosophy rejects the very concept of empathy, rejoicing in the Darwinian mantra of survival of the fittest and the elitist predilection for eugenics. As Gore Vidal noted, "Ayn Rand's 'philosophy' is nearly perfect in its immorality, which makes the size of her audience all the more ominous. . . . To justify and extol human greed and egotism is to my mind not only immoral, but evil." Like all good hypocrites, Rand made sure to collect her own Medicare and Social Security benefits, while passionately opposing those programs.

Prominent Republican Tom DeLay once stated, "You know, there is an argument to be made that these extensions of unemployment benefits keep people from going and finding jobs." DeLay's ignorance of the system is appalling, especially considering his long career receiving a hefty salary and perks in Congress. One is required to file weekly for unemployment benefits, and to list at least two jobs applied for, with contact details, to get the next check. DeLay is another prominent beneficiary of our dual-standard justice system. He was originally convicted by a Texas jury in 2010 on money laundering and conspiracy charges. He could have served as much as ninety-nine years in prison but was sentenced to three. DeLay appealed this slap on the wrist, and in September 2013, the Texas Court of Appeals simply overturned his convictions, entering an acquittal. Reflecting the new Republican mind-set, Nevada Senator Dean Heller asked sarcastically, during a debate on jobless benefits, "Is the government now creating hobos?" Former Pennsylvania governor Tom Corbett assessed the employment situation thusly; "The jobs are there. But if we keep extending unemployment, people are just going to sit there."

Georgia Republican Rep. Jack Kingston seriously proposed that children who receive subsidized meals in schools should perform manual labor in exchange for this taxpayer largesse. Children have to be living in families who are at or below 130 percent of the poverty line in order to be eligible for free meals. Not to mention, of course, that children are not responsible for the level of income in their household. "Why don't you have the kids pay a dime, pay a nickel, to instill in them that there is, in fact, no such thing as a free lunch?" Kingston asked, "Or maybe sweep the floor of the cafeteria." Predictably, when a local TV station did a bit of digging, it discovered that Kingston had enjoyed quite a few free lunches himself while serving in Congress. According to their investigation, Kingston and his staff ran up a bill for nearly $4,300 of "meals for business purposes" with various lobbying groups. When he was asked if members of Congress work hard, Kingston had the audacity to claim he was putting in sixty-seventy hours a week on the job. When asked by a reporter if the over $145,000 in meals expense on the campaign trail weren't free lunches, Kingston ignored the question and replied, "This is what we need in America. We need workfare over welfare."[113] A few years earlier, former House Speaker Newt Gingrich had proposed something similar, commenting, "You say . . . you shouldn't go to work before you're what, fourteen, sixteen years of age. . . . Most of these schools ought to get rid of the unionized janitors, have one master janitor and pay local students to take care of the school." Gingrich didn't specify which students would be working, but I think it's easy to guess what economic level they'd inevitably be chosen from.[114] It comes as little surprise to learn Kingston's work ethic was developed while growing up the son of a widely published university professor who was a cofounder of the National Reading Conference.

Rep. Steven Fincher paraphrased a Biblical passage to defend the premise that the poor don't even have a right to food when he quoted, "The one who is unwilling to work shall not eat." Fincher certainly is not adverse to accepting handouts for his own family business; US Department of Agriculture data revealed that his seventh-generation company Fincher Farms had received $8.9 million in subsidies over the past decade. Fincher also lobbied for large cuts to the Supplemental Nutrition Assistance Program, formerly known as Food Stamps. The devout Christian Fincher was found to have violated federal election laws by accepting a $250,000 loan in 2010 from the Gates Banking and Trust Company, where his father sits on the board of directors.[115] Televangelist John Hagee, worth an estimated five million, has echoed this "Christian" theme that the poor don't really have a right to food, and bemoaned the welfare loafers that many conservatives are so obsessed with.[116] The Wisconsin State Legislature recently pushed a measure that would ban food stamp recipients from buying crab, lobster, shrimp, or any other shellfish.[117] Meanwhile, Rep. Trent Franks, admonishing the Pope over his remarks about wealth distribution, had the audacity to state that the pope doesn't understand scripture. Fierce Israeli defender Rep. Jeff Duncan was just as irate over the pontiff's call for recognition of a Palestinian state. Yet another Republican, Rep. Louie Gohmert, called the Palestinians "haters," and intimated that the Pope only spoke for Catholics.[118]

Maine Governor Paul LePage announced in July 2014 that he was requiring all able-bodied recipients of food stamps to work for their benefits.[119] A few months later, Indiana Governor Mike Pence announced that the state would begin enforcing previously waived requirements that food stamp recipients be either employed, seeking employment, or in a job-training program, eliminating an estimated sixty-five thousand people from the program. Evidently, by wasting twenty hours weekly on some kind of work or volunteer activity that brings no financial compensation, food stamp recipients will either learn a hard lesson or become magically more likely to climb out of poverty. It obviously would leave them less time to search for a paying job. In reality, by being paid nothing for twenty hours of work, their benefits from food stamps would be effectively canceled out.

These kinds of work requirements, born under Richard Nixon as workfare in 1969, became an essential part of President Clinton's welfare reform in 1996. As Kenan Malik, author of the book *The Quest for a Moral Compass: A Global History of Ethics,* points out, workfare was the brainchild of New York University professor Lawrence Mead, who argued that the problems of the unemployed weren't due to a lack of jobs, but because of their own behavior. A 2008 British governmental study concluded that "There is little evidence that workfare increases the likelihood of finding work." Just as the mainstream media and politicians refuse to acknowledge the truth that a drop in the unemployment rate is merely an indicator that claims for unemployment benefits have fallen, they boast of the successes achieved in the wake of Clinton's workfare programs. While the welfare rolls were cut basically in half because of workfare, the majority of those, according to Malik, "lived in dire poverty and few had proper jobs." Fewer people on welfare don't logically translate into fewer poor people, much as lower unemployment claims doesn't mean there are fewer people out of work.

Author Barbara Ehrenreich, in her provocative book, *Nickel and Dimed: On (Not) Getting by in America,* revealed how, "It is expensive to be poor." Ehrenreich, while researching her book, took several low-paid, dead-end jobs. As she put it, "What I discovered is that . . . these jobs . . . pay so little that you cannot accumulate even a couple of hundred dollars to help you make the transition to a better-paying job. They often give you no control over your work schedule, making it impossible to arrange for child care or take a second job." Ehrenreich deserves to be quoted further:

I was also dismayed to find that in some ways, it is actually more expensive to be poor than not poor. If you can't afford the first month's rent and security deposit you need in order to rent an apartment, you may get stuck in an overpriced residential motel. . . . If you need a loan, as most poor people eventually do, you will end up paying an interest rate many times more than what a more affluent borrower would be charged. Most private-sector employers offer no sick days, and many will fire a person who misses a day of work, even to stay home with a sick child. A nonfunctioning car can also mean lost pay and sudden expenses. A broken headlight invites a ticket, plus a fine greater than the cost of a new headlight, and possible court costs. If a creditor decides to get nasty, a court summons may be issued, often leading to an arrest warrant. No amount of training in financial literacy can prepare someone for such exigencies—or make up for an income that is impossibly low to start with.[120]

What Ehrenreich terms "the criminalization of poverty" is no exaggeration. Under lobbying by conservative groups like the Criminal Justice Legal Foundation and the Center for the Community Interest, there is even a movement to make homelessness illegal. We're not talking about the government decreeing that no one can legally be homeless, and providing shelter for those who don't have it. We mean making it against the law to exist in a state of homelessness. In many communities across America, sleeping, eating, even sitting in public spaces has been outlawed, with what the National Coalition for the Homeless charges is selective enforcement against persons known to be homeless. More than fifty US cities have adopted "anti-camping" or "anti-food sharing" laws, which are often strictly enforced by police. Police in Raleigh, North Carolina, threatened to arrest members of Love Wins Ministries because they were distributing sausage biscuits and coffee to homeless people. In Orlando, Florida, these laws have been upheld in court. New York's billionaire Mayor Michael Bloomberg banned the donation of food directly to homeless shelters, because of the salt, fat, and fiber content![121] In October 2014, Fort Lauderdale, Florida, passed a new ordinance that strictly curtailed efforts to give food to the homeless. Some of the first police citations were issued to members of the advocacy group Love Thy Neighbor, which was providing lunch to homeless people in a park.[122]

The brutal beating death of homeless man Kelly Thomas in July 2011 was made all the more tragic by the fact a jury found the officers not guilty, even though the entire incident—in which the unarmed, helpless Thomas kept pleading for them to stop and calling for his father—was caught on video. In a 2012 incident, six Michigan police officers fired forty-six shots into homeless Martin Hall, because he pulled out a small penknife when a police dog lunged at him. The US Department of Justice's investigation failed to find "sufficient evidence of willful misconduct" by the officers.[123] In yet another case, Albuquerque, New Mexico, police shot homeless man James Boyd in the back and killed him in March 2014. Boyd had taken to the foothills to camp out because the local homeless shelters were closed, but he was considered to be illegally camping. It was discovered that twenty-six people had been killed by Albuquerque police since 2010, a per-capita rate that was higher than that of New York City and Chicago.[124] A dashboard recording revealed one of the officers calling the homeless Boyd a "fucking lunatic," and threatening to shoot him in the penis, two hours before the confrontation.[125] District Attorney Kari Brandenburg predictably cleared the officers of any wrongdoing, which kept alive her perfect record. In thirteen years as district attorney, not a single officer had been charged with a crime, despite the fact that over $30 million in settlements from such cases had been paid out by the city.[126] The police are growing increasingly militarized all over the country, but even they appear to hold a special antipathy for the poorest of those citizens they're ostensibly sworn to protect.

The most hypocritical criticism of the poor came from the world's richest woman, Australian Gina Rinehart. This deluded elitist proclaimed, "If you're jealous of those with more money, don't just sit there and complain. Do something to make more money yourself—spend less time drinking or smoking and socializing, and more time working." She also urged the Australian government to lower the minimum wage—which is $15.96, a much more reasonable amount than we have in the United States. Considering the insufferable arrogance of the world's elite, it is laughingly ironic to learn that Ms. Rinehart built her $30 billion fortune entirely by inheriting it. Meanwhile, Mexican Carlos Slim, at the time the world's wealthiest individual, was a bit more tactful, suggesting only that countries who are struggling economically raise their retirement ages to seventy, which is one increasingly popular solution suggested by the rich and powerful in this country.[127]

On the February 14, 2014, edition of CNBC's *Squawk Box,* Bud Konheim, CEO of fashion company Nicole Miller, declared that "We've got a country that the poverty level is wealth in ninety-nine percent of the rest of the world. So we're talking about woe is me, woe is us, woe is this . . . the guy that's making, oh my God, he's making thirty-five thousand dollars a year, why don't we try that out in India or some other countries we can't even name. China, anyplace, the guy is wealthy." This is another theme we hear trumpeted regularly—that the poor should be grateful for what they have because things are worse in Third-World or overtly totalitarian countries. Konheim, again quite predictably, became wealthy by inheriting the family business, which dated back to the turn of the twentieth century. He went to Philips Exeter, an elite prep school that features a glittering array of past and present alumni, including Facebook founder Mark Zuckerberg, novelists Dan Brown and John Irving, Franklin Pierce, Daniel Webster, Robert Todd Lincoln, Ulysses S. Grant Jr., and assorted Rockefellers.

Echoing this "poor aren't really poor" theme was the wealthiest member of Congress, Rep. Darrell Issa. The good representative built his nearly $450 million fortune primarily through a car alarm business. Issa told *CNN Money's* Cristina Alesci that America's poor are "the envy of the world. . . . If you go to India or you go to any number of other Third-World countries, you have two problems: You have greater inequality of income and wealth. You also have less opportunity for people to rise from the have-not to the have." Issa sounded the familiar theme that poor people have air-conditioned homes, cable television, and 75 percent own their own automobile. Referring to what statistics show is largely an imaginary road toward upward mobility, Issa declared that "with hard work, anybody can become the next American success story."[128] The popular notion that poor people will simply waste any aid given to them on drugs, alcohol, or cigarettes has been contradicted by numerous studies, including one conducted in 2016 by researchers from the World Bank and Stanford University. The study found that when poor people are given actual money, the consumption of such "temptation goods" tends to instead go down.[129]

Following the mortgage meltdown in 2008, the mainstream media directed attention away from where it should have been focused: on our corrupt, unsustainable banking system. Instead, we heard innumerable commentators criticizing the hapless borrowers, effectively blaming them for being approved by the lenders. As *Businessweek* charged, in a March 2008 article, "borrowers themselves should assume primary responsibility for the current subprime crisis. Millions of borrowers, all over the country, knowingly signed mortgage contracts they cannot now afford to honor." The article, transparently titled, "Subprime Borrowers: Not Innocents," defended the humble bankers who were the ones offering the decidedly nonexpert public these loans, by declaring "there's no particular evidence" that the banking institutions had engaged in fraud. Most audaciously, the article claimed, "the mortgage lenders not only are innocent of the predatory practices borrowers complain about but also are feeling the pain right along with them." As we have clearly shown earlier, after the taxpayers bailed these shameless plutocrats out, they went on to lavish even greater rewards upon themselves. Whatever pain they might have been feeling, it certainly wasn't financial. Thomas

Sowell of the Hoover Institution chimed in on the subject, predictably maintaining that antipoverty activists "made business impossible for banks until they surrendered to demands that they make billions in loans that they wouldn't otherwise have made."[130]

In August 2013, the journal *Science* published research suggesting that while there is an undeniable average IQ gap of some thirteen points between those living in poverty and those not, the difference is not genetic but is created primarily by the impoverished conditions. Conservative groups counter this with arguments that entitlement programs take away industriousness and create dependency. The Heritage Foundation called such programs "disincentives to marriage because benefits are reduced as a family's income rises." On the contrary; ever since the implementation of the Personal Responsibility and Work Act, passed in 1996 under President Bill Clinton, welfare has been dramatically altered. The former Aid to Families with Dependent Children was abolished, and a lifetime limit of five years for receiving benefits was established, reflected in the new name Temporary Assistance for Needy Families. Many were alarmed at these draconian reforms. As the ACLU said in 2003, "The solution to getting people out of the cycle of poverty is not to prematurely kick them off welfare . . . creating a false impression that the number of people who need help has decreased." The myth that welfare queens are living high off the hog, garnering additional income with each illegitimate baby, is belied by the fact that the amount per child doesn't come close to covering reasonable expenses. Sixteen states already cap the assistance and don't give any extra money for new births. The official poverty line for a family of four is $21,954. Welfare recipients have to be in a truly dismal financial state to get any help at all from the government.

In reality, only about 12 percent of our budget is spent on safety net programs to help the needy. Conservatives, and even many liberals, love to lump Social Security, Medicaid, and Medicare into the mix, which adds an additional 43 percent to what they call entitlement programs. The difference, of course, is that every one of your paychecks has deductions for Social Security, Medicare, and unemployment insurance; if you collect unemployment insurance, you are getting *your* money back. When you get a Social Security check or Medicare benefits, you're simply being returned money that you paid into the system for your entire working life. This is something that critics inevitably ignore when chastising those on unemployment as freeloaders or inferring that Social Security and Medicare are handouts. These programs are funded by taxpayers, through paycheck deductions, for just such a purpose.

Over 60 percent of the bankruptcies in the United States are the result of insurmountable medical bills. "Unless you're a Warren Buffett or Bill Gates, you're one illness away from financial ruin in this country," said Harvard professor Steffie Woolhandler, MD.[131] South Carolina Lt. Governor Andre Bauer declared, in January 2010, that helping the poor was akin to feeding stray animals that persistently breed. Portly Rush Limbaugh had the audacity to attack the eating habits of the poor in the following statement, "the obese poor buy Twinkies, Milk Duds, potato chips, six-packs of Bud, then head home to watch the NFL on one of two color TVs and turn off their cell phones, and that's poverty in the US."[132]

Fellow right-winger Glenn Beck poked fun at those who are relegated to begging for spare change, saying, "A good response is 'Sorry, I only carry hundreds.' It gets 'em every time." Former presidential candidate Michele Bachmann reiterated Mitt Romney's concerns about nearly half the country being takers when she responded to a legitimate question about corporations paying little or no taxes by bemoaning the fact poor people don't, either. "We need to broaden the base," she told the South Carolina Christian Chamber of Commerce, "so that everybody pays something, even if it's a dollar."[133] Hopefully, Bachmann meant what she said and will urge the estimated thirty-five thousand American citizens with incomes over $200,000 who paid no taxes at all in 2009—not even "a dollar"—to contribute their fair share.[134]

No one in their right mind would want to be on one of these government programs. It's not something that anyone aspires to. Linda Blanchette, deputy secretary of the Pennsylvania Department of Public Welfare, dismisses the fantasies many have of welfare queens driving Cadillacs and living royally off of their food stamps. "You only get TANF (Temporary Assistance to Needy Families) if you're poor, poor, poor," she stated. "A mother and two kids get around $403 a month. You have to work or be in job training thirty hours a week, and there's a five-year limit. Who wants this?"[135] And none of this takes into consideration the social ostracism one faces when accepting government benefits, even from close family members. It's not only expensive to be poor, it's very, very humiliating.

In a July 2013 speech in South Africa, President Obama told his audience that, "if you think about all the youth that everybody has mentioned here in Africa, if everybody is raising living standards to the point where everybody has got a car and everybody has got air-conditioning, and everybody has got a big house, well, the planet will boil over."[136] Even more telling, during a March 2014 town hall meeting with Spanish-language media, Obama responded to a question from someone who earned $36,000 annually and could not find health insurance for his family of three for less than $315 per month under the new "affordable" health-care act, by declaring, "If you looked at their cable bill, their telephone, their cell phone bill . . . it may turn out that, it's just they haven't prioritized health care." He went on to admonish the questioner by reminding the audience, "if a family member gets sick, he will wish he had paid that $300 a month."[137] This is identical to the poor-bashing rhetoric we hear from Rush Limbaugh and all the other right-wing opponents of Obama—more reproaches about frittering away money on items that have become essential to modern living.

It is decidedly uncool to be poor. One can almost picture the Paris Hiltons of the world scrunching their noses in disgust and uttering, "ewww" in their presence. Trust fund princess Rachel

Sacks, daughter of a prominent fertility doctor, loves to blog. She has an affinity for jarring, attention-grabbing titles such as "I'm Not Going to Pretend That I'm Poor to be Accepted by You," and "I'm the 'Rich' Girl You Love to Hate and You're all Idiots for It." Sacks is obviously a typical, immature twenty-year-old, but she is symptomatic of the way younger people are being indoctrinated: to look down upon those less fortunate than themselves, to cavalierly throw around once-frowned-upon sobriquets like "retard." Donald Trump was taken to task for his absurdly juvenile mocking of a disabled reporter during the 2016 presidential campaign. Look at the despicable videos, freely available online, where mindless "bum fights" are incited, to the apparent delight of the viewing audience. There have been too many cases of young men seeking out defense-less, homeless people and beating them mercilessly with baseball bats, while their friends laughingly videotape the whole thing. On Black Friday in 2011, a man collapsed and died in a West Virginia Target store, while customers ignored him and continued shopping for their bargains. Some witnesses reported people were actually stepping over the man's body, without stopping or rendering aid.[138] Those who are dependent upon others or the state in any way, not only elicit little empathy from others, they are sometimes, literally, as in this tragic, shameful case, nonexistent to them.

Americans of all income levels have long held a curious dis-dain for the poorest among them. Until Robert Kennedy visited the poverty-stricken populace of Appalachia in the mid-1960s, for instance, no politician had ever publicized their plight. The great Kurt Vonnegut wrote in 1969:

America is the wealthiest nation on Earth, but its people are mainly poor, and poor Americans are urged to hate themselves . . . . Every other nation has folk traditions of men who were poor but extremely wise and virtuous, and therefore more estimable than anyone with power and gold. No such tales are told by the American poor. They mock themselves and glorify their betters. . . . Americans, like human beings everywhere, believe many things that are obviously untrue. . . . Their most destructive untruth is that it is very easy for an American to make money. They will not acknowledge how in fact hard money is to come by, and, therefore, those who have no money blame and blame and blame themselves. This inward blame has been a treasure for the rich and powerful, who have had to do less for their poor, publicly and privately, than any other ruling class since, say, Napoleonic times.

What kind of system operates like this? Why is giving free food and coffee to police and firefighters, or Government Purchase Cards to an unknown number of government employees, or loads of free swag to multimillionaire celebrities, perfectly appropriate, while extending minimal assistance to the poorest members of society is labeled a handout, which is the first entitlement seemingly every politician, and most citizens, want to eliminate?

Due to the rapidly diminishing sense of empathy in much of the public, and a seeming ignorance of the once widespread belief that "There but for the grace of God, go I," it's become open season on the poor. There is a thin line between the Darwinian credo of survival of the fittest and the current, prevalent attitude of "sucks for you." Like the physically and mentally handicapped, the elderly, and unattractive females, the poor have become perfect targets for disrespect, scorn, and laughter.

6 HUEY LONG

A mob is coming here in six months to hang the other ninety-five of you damned scoundrels, and I'm undecided whether to stick here with you or go out and lead them.

— Huey Long, United States Senate floor speech

INSPIRED BY WILLIAM JENNINGS BRYAN and the other leading populists of the 1890s, Huey Long invented his own special brand of progressivism and wore the mantle of champion of the little guy proudly. As a young lawyer, Long specialized in helping the disadvantaged and often boasted that he'd never taken a case against a poor man. He was especially renowned for representing those battling big business and banks. Long opposed the Ku Klux Klan, a courageous act for a southern politician of his time. At age thirty-five, Long was elected Governor of Louisiana in 1928. He ran on a platform strongly opposing Standard Oil, which had been founded by John D. Rockefeller, just one of his prominent adversaries. In response to his attempts to enact a new tax on crude oil refined in Louisiana, Standard Oil and other powerful forces led an unsuccessful impeachment effort against him in 1929. Long ran for and was elected as US Senator in 1930 and his populist ideas gained a real national platform.

Long's primary political issue as a United States Senator was redistribution of wealth, which makes his career, and his untimely death, an appropriate subject for inclusion in this book. Long unveiled his Share Our Wealth program on February 23, 1934. The plan originally proposed to cap personal fortunes at $50 million (approximately $700 million today), but would later be dropped to $5 million (around $60 million today), through a progressive federal tax. Long also proposed to cap all inheritances at $5 million and to limit annual income to $1 million (some $12 million today), while providing a yearly stipend for families earning less than one-third the average national income. At the time, this was declared to be a suitable amount to provide enough for a home, an automobile, a radio, and other necessary conveniences. Long's ideas gained resonance with the millions of Americans struggling through the Great Depression; one in four people were out of work, and long lines of hungry citizens waiting for soup or bread became a commonplace sight. According to the book *Daily Life in the United States 1920–1940*, by David E. Kyvig, animals at the Detroit Zoo were slaughtered in 1933 to feed the hungry.

To say Huey Long was ahead of his time is to severely understate things. In an era when the forty-hour workweek hadn't yet been established by law, the fiery populist leader was advocating a thirty-, possibly even twenty-hour workweek, as well as an annual four-week vacation for every worker. As he explained numerous times, this was to permit everyone to enjoy more leisure time and all "the blessings bestowed upon us." Long was basically advocating a form of universal health care, well before any other American politician, and as governor provided free health care clinics and immunizations across the state. He also expanded the Charity Hospitals in Louisiana, creating a much more extensive network of facilities available to the poor, and as a result, the death rate in the state dropped by 30 percent. He built institutions for mentally disabled children and epileptics, and his many prison reforms included providing dental and health care to inmates.

Long's speeches still radiate with modern audiences. He was full of charisma, and captivated a crowd like few other politicians of any age. His great "barbecue" speech deserves to be quoted extensively:

> How many men ever went to a barbecue and would let one man take off the table what's intended for nine-tenths of the people to eat? The only way you will be able to feed the balance of the people is to make that man come back and bring back some of that grub he ain't got no business with. How are you going to feed the balance of the people? What's Morgan and Baruch and Rockefeller and Mellon gonna do with all that grub? They can't eat it. They can't wear the clothes. They can't live in the houses. But when they've got everything on the God-slaving earth that they can eat and they can wear and they can live in—and all that their children can live in and wear and eat and all their children's children can use—then we've got to call Mr. Morgan and Mr. Mellon and Mr. Rockefeller back and say, "Come back here. Put that stuff back on this table that you took away from here that you don't need. Leave something else for the American people to consume."

Long's rural, country vernacular belied a sharp, focused mind. Former president turned chief justice of the Supreme Court William Howard Taft called him "the most brilliant lawyer who ever practiced before the United States Supreme Court."[139] His enemies despised him and feared him. They knew that, unlike other Southern politicians of the era, he never resorted to race-baiting or anti-Semitism. To this day, blacks and whites in the poorest communities of Louisiana still revere his memory. Long's achievements in Louisiana were extraordinary. When he took office as governor, there were less than three hundred miles of paved roads in the entire state. One in four adults was illiterate. He paved the highways; launched a massive program to build bridges, roads, hospitals, and schools; opened up night schools for illiterate adults; abolished the poll tax; and took mental patients out of jail cells and put them in modern institutions. He eliminated the lottery and other gambling in the state. He fought prostitution and the corrupt police commissioners of New Orleans' notorious City Ring.[140]

Using figures compiled by the Long Legacy Project, by 1936, Long's policies were saving the average Louisiana family more than $425 annually in living expenses, comparable to $5,100 today. Personal property taxes were slashed with his Homestead Exemption, which eliminated taxes on the first $2,000 of property, saving the average Louisiana home owner the equivalent of $780 a year in today's money, and in fact, 80 percent of home owners paid no personal property tax at all under his system. Automobile license fees were cut, and personal property taxes on cars were eliminated. Utility rates were reduced; the average family saved what would be $324 per year today in electricity costs alone. Long's Debt Moratorium Act stopped foreclosures and created a grace period for mortgages to be paid and debts settled.

Every move he made was calculated to benefit ordinary people, often at the expense and chagrin of the very wealthy. Huey Long still ran a tight financial ship; during his tenure, Louisiana had the third-lowest operating costs of any state government, while managing to provide unprecedented services. As he explained, "we expect to have this state ruled by the people and not by the lords and the interests of high finance." It was during this time, when Long was delivering unheard of services to the people, that he really came under attack, with allegations he was corrupt and a demagogue from rival political forces and from the establishment press. Long circumvented these relentless attacks with statewide radio broadcasts, delivered extemporaneously, which provided a direct bond with the common people of Louisiana. He would begin each broadcast by saying, "Ladies and gentlemen, it's Huey P. Long again, telling you how we're going to clean out this rotten bunch of grafters."[141] A Democrat, Long chastised both parties for being carbon copies of each other, referring to them as High Popalorum and Low Popahirum, noting that one skinned you from the ankle up, and the other from the ear down. At other times, he snickered and called them Tweedledum and Tweedledee.

Once he arrived in Washington, DC, Long showed little respect for the traditional decorum of the Senate; shortly after he entered the august body, he regularly antagonized Senate Majority Leader, Democrat Joe Robinson. Huey once read a lengthy list of the corporate clients of Robinson's law firm into the Congressional Record, and then declared, "I want now to disclaim that I have the slightest motive of saying, or that in my heart I believe, that such a man could to the slightest degree be influenced in any vote which he casts in this body by the fact that this association might mean hundreds of thousands and millions of dollars to him in the way of lucrative fees." Powerful Senator Harry Byrd asked that his desk be moved away from Long's, "even if I have to sit on the Republican side."[142]

Long accumulated an assortment of powerful enemies, on both the left and the right, who were equally frightened and threatened by his growing national influence. Long even had the audacity, and the self-confidence, to write a book titled *My First Days in the White House*, which was published posthumously. The book featured bold, imaginative conversations between President Franklin D. Roosevelt and former President Herbert Hoover, which were none too flattering to either. Long disparaged Roosevelt by demoting him to secretary of the navy in his fictional administration. In his narrative, Long also chose General Smedley Butler, author of the conspiracy classic *War is a Racket,* as his secretary of war. Butler, who had shared the stage with Long in support of legislation to pay the bonuses still owed to World War I veterans, called this "the greatest compliment ever paid me." In a private letter, he wrote that "with Huey Long's death I lost most of my interest in the present political picture."[143] In contrast, President Franklin D. Roosevelt called Huey Long "one of the two most dangerous men in the country" (the other being Douglas MacArthur).

By April 1935, Long was receiving sixty thousand letters a week in his Senate office. Foreshadowing the way future presidents would use every apparatus at their disposal to damage their political foes, FDR had the Internal Revenue Service investigate Huey Long's finances, to no avail. Crowds flocked to the Senate to hear him speak, like they had never done before or have done since. The number of Share Our Wealth clubs had grown to twenty-seven thousand, with more than seven and a half million members. Membership was free, and members were kept abreast of things by the newsletter *American Progress,* which was mailed to them at no cost. Huey was clearly building a national, grassroots movement. Long took on Standard Oil, the mainstream media, which he charged were pawns of Wall Street, and increasingly, President Roosevelt himself, who he had allegedly taken to calling Prince Franklin. He also infuriated the president with barbs like the NRA (National Recovery Administration) program really stood for Nuts Running America, and called his Secretary of Agriculture Henry Wallace "Lord Corn Wallace."[144] Long took seriously his campaign slogan of Every Man a King, which he explained was "the great plan of God and the Declaration of Independence, which said, 'All men are created equal.'" Long was a huge foe of the big bankers and an early critic of the Federal Reserve System.

Long was anathema to the leadership of both political parties. Despite being part of the Democratic majority in the Senate, the Kingfish, as Long was popularly known, was unable to get a single bill, motion, or resolution passed during his three years in the Senate. During one debate, another senator told him, "I do not believe you could get the Lord's Prayer endorsed in this body." He did, however, side with progressive Republicans in pushing through a bill extending bankruptcy privileges for farmers coping with the Great Depression, over the opposition of the Roosevelt administration. Long concentrated his attention exclusively on domestic issues; he had strongly opposed our involvement in World War I and would today undoubtedly be labeled an isolationist.

Long's proposals were very different, and much more dangerous to the establishment, than those typically raised by liberals. For instance, his progressive tax rate would have been zero on the first million dollars of *wealth*. By taxing wealth, and not merely income, the superrich couldn't have dodged it with their usual loopholes and legal shenanigans. The second million would have been taxed at 1 percent, the third at 2 percent, the fourth at 4 percent, gradually increasing until anything past the eighth million (about sixty million dollars today) would be taxed at 100 percent. Even so, Huey assured the rich elite in his colorful style that they would not lose their "fish ponds, their estates, and their horses for riding to the hounds."

Long was clearly talking about the vaunted One Percent footing the entire bill for programs that would benefit all those who desperately needed assistance. FDR was terrified of the prospect of an inter party bid for the 1936 Democratic nomination from Long, or an independent Third Party movement led by him. Not only were Long's ideas revolutionary, his magnetic appeal was unmatched, and he exceeded even Roosevelt's impressive oratorical skills.

Long was a true antitrust advocate, and ranted regularly against monopolies. Plank seven of his Share Our Wealth program decreed that every child should have an equal opportunity at all levels of education, through college, based "on the capacity of children to learn, and not on the ability of parents to pay the costs. Training for life's work to be as much universal and thorough for all walks of life as has been the training in the arts of killing." He fought entrenched plutocrats that he termed feudal lords and referred to the newspapers invariably as "the lying press." To deal with a state banking crisis, Long invited all the bankers to a big dinner at the governor's mansion, locked the bankers inside until they resolved things, then audited every one of their banks. Most other states lost hundreds, even thousands of banks, to the depressed economy. Long's Louisiana lost only seven. He increased the severance tax—the tax a company pays to remove resources (Standard Oil especially opposed it), on the large interests that were tapping the natural resources of the land and water. The Kingfish also instituted a protectionist tax on the foreign oil, mostly from Venezuela, which was being sold by Standard Oil and others, to the detriment of independent citizens and companies in Louisiana. Rockefeller's Standard Oil, in conjunction with armed anti-Long forces calling themselves the Square Dealers, briefly seized the courthouse in Baton Rouge. The National Guard had to be called out, and it was able to quell the rebellion.

Considering everything he did to help the poor and working-class people of Louisiana, and the fact that he turned much of the state from a backwards swamp into a thriving metropolis, Huey Long should be considered an icon of the left. By any measure, he accomplished a great deal and did exactly what self-proclaimed liberals are always maintaining they wont to do. It would be hard to name another politician of any age whose actions so directly benefited common people. But Long is not a hero to modern-day liberals. In fact, his memory is totally reviled by the establishment left. In my view, this is because Long walked the walk, and poor people saw direct, tangible benefits from his policies. Harry Truman said he was a liar and "nothing but a damn demagogue." There was Robert Penn Warren's ugly portrayal of a thinly veiled Long in *All the King's Men,* which was not surprisingly awarded the Pulitzer Prize and later became a major motion picture. Establishment historian William E. Leuchtenburg, who wrote extensively about every Democratic president since FDR except for the similarly dreaded John F. Kennedy, dismissively declared that "Huey clowned his way into national prominence."

Ironically, leaders of both the Socialist and Communist parties opposed Long as well. New York Communist Alex Bittelman wrote, "Long says he wants to do away with concentration of wealth without doing away with capitalism. This is humbug. This is fascist demagoguery." Socialist leader Norman Thomas called the Share Our Wealth plan a dangerous delusion, stating that it was this "sort of talk that Hitler fed the Germans." In January 1935, the *Nation* called Long a "plain dictator." FDR's Postmaster General, James Farley, admitted in his 1938 autobiography, *Behind the Ballots,* that the Roosevelt administration was wary the renegade populist might very well "have the balance of power in the 1936 election." John T. Flynn, in his book *The*

Roosevelt Myth, referred to anonymous editors that compared Long's plan to "the weird dream of a plantation darky."

After his death, the mainstream media only thinly disguised their disdain for Huey Long. While claiming it was "no longer necessary to speak except with charity" about Long in its September 11, 1935, obituary, the *New York Times* could not hide the enmity that the powerful forces who determined "all the news that's fit to print" still held for him. The obituary stated that Long had "destroyed self-government," and had been "an unquestioned dictator." Misleadingly, the establishment's flagship newspaper noted that "Many observers thought that he had already passed the peak of his national influence." Richard Wall, in a December 3, 2003, piece for the libertarian website lewrockwell.com, accurately assessed this obituary as "subtly vicious" and cited it as the beginning of Huey Long's bad press. What is most unfair is the way the establishment took one of Huey's famous expressions, "If Fascism ever comes to America, it will come wrapped in an American flag," and turned it on its head, continually calling Long himself a fascist. Historian and FDR and JFK aide Arthur Schlesinger Jr. was among those critics who cynically claimed Long never had any real affinity at all for the downtrodden, and simply used them as a means to obtain power. Richard Wall quoted one of Long's many explosive comments about the rich and powerful, when he referred to them as, "a handful of financial slave-owning overlords who make the tyrant of Great Britain seem mild," and asked quite reasonably whether "powerful interests might well have wanted to stop Long in his tracks in his incipient presidential campaign, which gave all the appearance of having the potential to succeed."

It was Long's pressure on Roosevelt that was largely responsible for much of the good that came out of the second New Deal: the forty-hour workweek, vacations, and pensions for workers, Social Security, among others. The Kingfish had initially supported FDR, who'd been aided significantly in the 1932 presidential campaign by President Herbert Hoover's heavy-handed overreaction to the Bonus

Army of World War I veterans who had assembled in Washington, DC, to demand their promised $500 bonuses. Ironically, unlike Long and Smedley Butler, Roosevelt himself would not support Rep. Wright Patman's proposal to actually pay the veterans. Long recognized, when he saw autocratic Wall Street figures—such as Bernard Baruch, an advocate of monopoly capitalism like Adolph Berle, and James Warburg, a powerful banker whose father Paul had been instrumental in founding the Federal Reserve System—sitting as members of Roosevelt's ballyhooed Brain Trust," that the Roosevelt administration was not truly interested in helping the common people.

On August 9, 1935, almost exactly one month before he was killed, Huey Long made a speech on the floor of the United States Senate in which he delineated the details of a plot to assassinate him by anti-Long leaders in Louisiana. The alleged plotters had been bugged by some courageous Long supporters, and among the remarks recorded were, "The entire resources of the United States (under Roosevelt) are at our disposal," and "I haven't the slightest doubt that President Roosevelt would pardon anyone who killed him." On September 8, 1935, Long was shot in the State Capitol building and died two days later.

Much as we would see nearly thirty years later when John F. Kennedy was assassinated, the evidence in the Long murder was horribly mishandled. The gun allegedly used to shoot him was not subject to normal chain-of-possession protocol. The bullet that killed him was never produced as evidence. There were no X-rays of Long, and no autopsy was conducted. The closest the authorities came to an investigation was the coroner's inquest, which consisted primarily of handpicked testimony gathered by the district attorney, one of Long's many political opponents. A plan initially introduced into the Louisiana state legislature to independently investigate the assassination was canceled, according to Long's aide Gerald L. K. Smith, due to pressure from Roosevelt. Many people today question the official version of Long's death, which laid the sole blame for the shooting on young doctor Carl Weiss, who was conveniently blown away at the scene by a fusillade of shots (the most common number reported is thirty) fired into him by Long's bodyguards.[145]

In his 1986 book *Requiem For a Kingfish: The Strange and Unexplained Death of Huey Long,* journalist Ed Reed examined the medical procedures performed at Our Lady of the Lake Hospital operating room, and claimed the doctors had removed a second bullet from Long's body and never reported it, while leaving the other inside. Reed tracked down Merle Welsh, the funeral director for both Long and Weiss, who told him one of the surgeons had come to the funeral home that night and taken a bullet out. Reed also located the funeral home assistant who had supposedly kept the bullet on a key ring as a memento. One of the surgeons was notorious anti-Long Dr. Henry McKowen, who had recently remarked, "If I ever give Huey an anesthetic, I will put him to sleep for good." Although he did at least recognize his bias and requested that his every move be monitored. Long had been coherent enough after the shooting to personally request Dr. Urban Maes, but unfortunately, he was delayed by a minor car accident and didn't make it in time. Reed termed it "one of the most bizarre and unreal operating room settings that one could possibly imagine." Long biographer T. Harry Williams called it "one of the most public operations in medical history," and pro-Long Dr. Cecil Lorio, who was a scrub technician in the operating room, described it as "a vaudeville show." Another doctor, Long political appointee Arthur Vidrine, remarked after the surgery that, "It was nothing. It was just a perforation of the intestines." There were clearly a slew of medical irregularities involved in the Long case, but the fact that no autopsy was performed made clarifying the situation impossible. Reed concluded that the official theory of the shooting "must now be relegated to that graveyard of hoaxes, frauds, and fairy tales."

Although suspicion about the real motives behind the assassination began percolating while Huey Long's body was still warm, the first actual investigative piece on his murder didn't appear until

1963's *The Day Huey Long Was Shot,* written by Associated Press reporter David Zinman. While Zinman came to no real conclusions about who was responsible for the crime, he poked innumerable holes in the official narrative of events. In 1985, MONY Life Insurance finally released the report written by its Bureau of Investigation. The report noted that "documentary evidence had been destroyed," and also concluded that "there is considerable doubt that Weiss ever fired a gun."

There are several theories about who was really behind the assassination of Huey Long. An increasingly popular one holds that Weiss was a patsy, set up to take a punch at the Kingfish, which his bodyguards used as an excuse to not only fire some thirty bullets into him, but to shoot Long as well. Regardless, the fact is the most outspoken proponent of redistributing the wealth in this nation's history, a man who fought big oil, the Federal Reserve and the big banks, and Wall Street, was murdered at the age of forty-two, a month after announcing his candidacy for the presidency, as well as asserting on the floor of the United States Senate that powerful forces were plotting to assassinate him.

In 2005, former Louisiana State Police Superintendent Francis Grevemberg signed a sworn affidavit for author Thomas Angers, stating that troopers who had been at the scene of Long's shooting told him in the 1950s that Weiss had been posthumously framed with a planted weapon. These troopers would later deny saying this.[146] A 1992 episode of *Unsolved Mysteries* covered many of the unanswered questions behind Long's death, intimating that his bodyguards had shot him. There are good reasons to question any motivation Dr. Carl Weiss would have had; although his father-in-law Benjamin Pavy was one of Long's plentiful political opponents, the young doctor had a wife and infant son, and was scheduled to perform surgery the next morning. According to his family, he was happy that night and showed no signs of planning an imminent murder. Weiss's son, Dr. Carl Weiss Jr., has vigorously maintained his father's innocence for years. "I don't believe that he fired a fatal shot or that indeed that he carried a gun into the state Capitol that night," Dr. Weiss told a Baton Rouge symposium in 2010. An anonymous man told retired Winn Parish Deputy Sheriff Greggory Davies about attending a "Huey Long Assassination Club" meeting in his younger days, which were organized by "doctors, attorneys, businessmen—upper class folks."

While researching this book, I contacted Greggory Davies, who was still living. In a March 23, 2014, email, he clarified his story, telling me that "I hesitate to divulge the now-deceased's person who told me this story. When he told me this in the late nineties, he said he'd never told it before to anyone." His friend described being picked up by a prominent doctor, a hood was placed over his head, and he was taken to a meeting, with the security along the way being such that they had to go through several checkpoints and produce ID. They eventually wound up at "a remote location where he was led inside a barn. He was told he'd have to take an oath, which he did, and he was then released from the hoodwink. . . . He said the entire jest [sic] of the meeting was a discussion about killing Huey P. Long." So here we had a meeting of powerful Louisiana men, for the express purpose of plotting the murder of the most charismatic populist figure this country has ever known; they all were sworn to secrecy, and afterwards Davies' friend "was too afraid to tell a soul." According to Davies, "My guess on a time line would be only a short time prior to Huey's death."

In 1985, Ken Burns produced the intriguing documentary *Huey Long*. The film, striving to be somewhat impartial, had minimal narration, consisting primarily of Long's speeches and remembrances by supporters and detractors. The venom was still dripping from the tongues of journalist I. F. Stone and Betty Carter, mother of Jimmy Carter's press secretary Hodding Carter III, as they spoke about the man they clearly loathed. Hodding Carter II, Mrs. Carter's husband, was the editor of the Louisiana *Daily Courier*, and an avowed enemy of Long's who regularly called him a demagogue. He once said, "If ever there was a need for shotgun government, that time is now." This was not the only time Carter alluded to the assassination of Long; at another point, he wrote, "We hope to God that Louisiana men awake to these wrongs and to the sole remaining method of righting them." Without a trace of self-consciousness or guilt, Mrs. Carter admitted, "I can't remember any Saturday night that I went anywhere that we didn't talk about killing Huey Long." Stone chimed in, "I was really glad when they shot him." Cecil Morgan was featured prominently throughout the documentary and was misleadingly referred to as a former legislator when, in fact, he'd led impeachment proceedings against Long and went on to become an attorney for Standard Oil. One can gauge the vitriol normally expended against Huey Long in the establishment press by the fact that this documentary was probably their least biased effort.

Not everyone bought into the mainstream media propaganda that Huey Long was a dangerous demagogue and a corrupt dictator. Singer-songwriter Randy Newman dedicated a wonderful album of music to the Kingfish, 1974's *Good Old Boys*. Newman's mother grew up in New Orleans (his father, Lionel Newman, was a famous Academy Award–winning film composer), and young Randy became fascinated with the Kingfish, reading numerous books about him. He was especially interested in the tragic 1927 flood that covered much of Mississippi, Arkansas, and Louisiana, and would later be inspired to write the haunting song *Louisiana 1927* about it. Long stoked rural resentment against the big-city bosses in his first campaign for governor by making the flood an issue. The 1997 book *The Great Mississippi Flood of 1927 and How it Changed America,* by John M. Barry, revealed that the most influential business leaders in New Orleans had illegally dynamited the city's levees. People's properties were destroyed, and many were left homeless afterwards, all for the purpose of protecting the investments of the powerful.[147]

In his 2012 book, *The Rich Don't Always Win: The Forgotten Triumph Over Plutocracy That Created the American Middle Class, 1900–1970,* Sam Pizzigati gave full credit to Huey Long for pressuring FDR into doing something about workers' rights and instituting progressive taxation policies. But Roosevelt's actions weren't quite the same as what Long proposed; no fortunes were touched, and plenty of loopholes remained for the wealthiest Americans to take advantage of. However, the playing field did become more level, and thanks to the post-World War II economic boom, Vice President Richard Nixon could brag to Nikita Khrushchev during their 1959 "kitchen debate" that any American worker could afford a home of his own, equipped with all those dazzling new appliances and conveniences. Needless to say, no American leader can make such a boast now.

Long's words ring as clear and fresh today as they did more than seventy-five years ago. Of black Americans, this southerner declared, "Treat them just the same as anybody else; give them an opportunity to make a living and to get an education." In regards to Hitler (and contradicting the absurd attempts to compare the two men), Long said, "Don't liken me to that son of a bitch. Anybody that lets his public policies be mixed up with religious prejudice is a goddamned fool." Long described today's political world perfectly with his comment that, "They've got a set of Republican waiters on one side and a set of Democratic waiters on the other side, but no matter which set of waiters brings you the dish, the legislative grub is all prepared in the same Wall Street kitchen."

Long recognized the simple truth that it was preposterous and self-destructive to permit an elite handful to have more money than "he and his children and his children's children can spend or use in their lifetimes." Imagine a present-day politician uttering these words, as Long did in 1934 as part of his Share the Wealth proposals: "To limit the hours of work to such an extent as to prevent overproduction and to give the workers of America some share in the recreations, conveniences, and luxuries of life." His characterization of the elite's rationale for hoarding all the wealth, which appeared in his 1933 autobiography *Every Man A King*, cannot be improved upon: "This food and these clothes and these houses are mine, and while I cannot use them, my greed can only be satisfied by keeping anybody else from having them."

Just imagine what an inspiration Long would have been to the Occupy Wall Street movement. In that lengthy April 4, 1932, Senate speech referred to earlier, which Huey titled "The Doom of America's Dream," he provided figures that are chillingly familiar, regarding concentration of corporate power; 100 percent of aluminum controlled by the Aluminum Trust, 80 percent of the telephone industry controlled by the American Telephone & Telegraph Company (AT&T), 75 percent of the telegraph industry controlled by Western Union, were among numerous examples he cited of monopolies in various industries. Needless to say, with all the mergers we've seen over the past few decades, corporate power has been further consolidated into an even smaller number of hands. Huey also noted presciently in this speech, that the reason so few Americans were then paying income tax was due to the undeniable fact one has to have income in order to be taxed on it.

This is the logical response to the common present-day argument espoused by conservatives; that the top 40 percent of Americans pay all the taxes. Few counter with the fact that the bottom half of Americans have practically no wealth and little income. Everyone pays taxes of various kinds; only 17 percent of workers, for instance, had zero payroll tax liability in 2012, according to the Tax Policy Center. They also found that the poorest 20 percent pay a disproportionate average of 11.1 percent of their income in state and local taxes; in some states, the rate is an incredible 16 percent. Meanwhile, the richest pay only 2.8 percent in state and local taxes. Sales taxes, of course, hit everyone equally, as do gasoline taxes.

It is worth quoting more from Huey Long's great April 4, 1932, speech on the floor of the United States Senate: "Machines are created making it possible to manufacture more in an hour than used to be manufactured in a month . . . but instead of bringing prosperity, ease, and comfort, they have meant unemployment; they have meant idleness; they have meant starvation. . . . Whereas they should have meant that hours of labor were shortened, that toil was decreased . . . that they would have time for pleasure, time for recreation." What would Huey Long think of the further progress he could never have envisioned: the computer age, satellite technology, and other astounding advances, and how that has somehow translated into even-longer working hours and less leisure time for the majority of Americans?

In a 1941 speech on the Senate floor, populist Senator William Langer of North Dakota, in an effort to counter the continuous attacks on the late Kingfish's character, stated, "This is not fooling the farmer, the worker, the small businessman; it is not fooling the child who can read today because of the free textbooks that Huey Long obtained; it is not fooling the citizen who can vote today because Huey Long abolished poll taxes." Langer closed by calling Huey "the unmatchable champion of the common people."

The 2016 presidential campaigns of both Bernie Sanders and Donald Trump echoed different elements of Huey Long's populism. Considering how much each of their messages owed to the Kingfish, and how frequently both were compared to him by journalists and historians, it is somewhat surprising that neither of them ever mentioned Huey Long's name during their campaigns.

Huey Long would be mortified over the disparity in wealth we see in America today. We cannot even imagine how different the twentieth century might have been if this country's most sincere and well-known populist had not been assassinated just as he was on the threshold of attaining the highest office in the land.

7 DOES ANYONE EVEN CARE?

You don't make the poor richer by making the rich poorer.
—Winston Churchill

AUTHOR G. WILLIAM DOMHOFF, IN his classic 1967 book *Who Rules America Now?*, noted that the wealthy invariably give their maids every Thursday off. This is a textbook example of Groupthink, but while this ritual may be archaic, the clannish cohesiveness remains. Look behind the doors of almost any mansion, and you are likely to find a staff consisting exclusively of Spanish-speaking immigrants. This new tradition was first exposed in 1993 when President Bill Clinton nominated Zoe Baird for Attorney General. When it was revealed that Baird and her husband had hired illegal aliens as their nanny and chauffer, her nomination had to be withdrawn. Clinton's next Attorney General Nominee, Kimba Wood, had an identical problem; she'd used an illegal immigrant as a nanny for her child.

While Nannygate focused attention on the issue of wealthy Americans hiring undocumented workers and paying (usually significantly underpaying) household staff under the table, the practice appears to be firmly entrenched in the culture of the rich and sometimes famous. More recently, the revelation that Timothy Geithner, Barack Obama's first Treasury Secretary, had the exact same issue—"forgetting" to check on the immigration status of a housekeeper, showed quite clearly that this practice is continuing unabated. Geithner, by the way, was a uniquely "deserving" nominee for a position involving the overseeing of the nation's money, in that it was also revealed that he had failed to pay over $40,000 in federal income taxes.[148] As always, this issue knows no political partisanship; in 2001, Linda Chavez saw her nomination as George W. Bush's Secretary of Labor derailed when it was discovered she'd hired an illegal immigrant as housekeeper and nanny.[149]

When 2012 Republican presidential nominee Mitt Romney released his income tax records for 2010, they illustrated the fact that the wealthy aren't exactly generous with their household staffs. While claiming an income of $21.7 million, the Romneys paid a household staff of four a total of only $20,603.[150] (At least Romney paid some taxes; it has been documented that Donald Trump paid no taxes in multiple years, and when asked in a debate if he'd comment on how many years he paid no taxes, he simply responded "no.") While wealthy individuals might severely undervalue the worth of their staffs, the clueless nature of corporate America was exemplified by McDonald's 2013 online Holiday Etiquette Guide. The fast-food titan advised their lowly paid workers on how much to tip their au pairs, personal trainers, and pool boys. Employees must have been excited to learn that it was appropriate to give their housekeepers one day's pay as a holiday present. The previous month, McDonald's had come under criticism for suggesting its workers return unopened gifts as a way of paying down their holiday debt.

The Gilded Age plutocrats at least paid their servants relatively well. Today, wealthy families mimic one of the most disastrous trends in the corporate world and outsource their household staff. They are hiring outside contractors now for functions such as handyman chores, landscaping, and even child care. Their number one priority, even where their own children are concerned, appears to be paying the least amount of money possible to the help. Family cooks are often only paid when needed and have to supplement their incomes elsewhere. The days of providing room and board to housekeepers or other hired help, popularized in television shows like *Hazel* and *The*

Brady Bunch, are long gone. Meanwhile, California Governor Jerry Brown vetoed a bill in 2012 that would have required employers to pay overtime and give their servants meal breaks, offering the lame rationale that it would only cause the wealthy to hire fewer domestic workers. The next year, he did sign a bill mandating overtime pay, but needless to say, this would be a difficult thing to monitor.[151]

Hollywood is doing its own kind of outsourcing. The studios have found that it's far cheaper to fly their casts to Canada, New Zealand, or other locales, because otherwise they have to pay union dues to the domestic cameramen, technicians, sound engineers, set builders, etc. Pantelion Films, producers of the highly touted film *Cesar Chavez: An American Hero,* which extols the virtues of the former United Farm Workers union leader, has been criticized for "firing unionized workers and outsourc[ing] part of the entire production to Mexico," to quote from Chamba Sanchez's passionate rant on Facebook. The American Federation of Musicians held a rally to protest the outsourcing of scoring jobs to musicians outside the United States in April 2014. So-called below-the-line workers in the entertainment world, the grips, makeup artists, prop masters, and others, are facing the sort of problems employees all over America are confronting. Matt Greenstone, CEO of Angel City Studios, which specializes in titles and graphics for television, declared that "The jobs themselves were literally paying four hundred percent more" in 2001, when his company started, than they are now. "With the digital revolution, China, India, Japan, and a lot of Eastern European countries now, the cost of living is so cheap, they can pay workers pennies on the dollar compared to what we have to pay here," Greenstone observed.[152]

In recent years, there has been a concerted effort to convert rich people into "job creators" in the public consciousness. The notion that all wealthy people, by the very fact of being wealthy, create jobs is not based on any economic reality. Conservatives love to deify job creators and insist we must cut taxes on the wealthy and give them other generous incentives or all the jobs will simply vanish. Any wealthy person without ownership in a company is obviously in no position to create any jobs, except perhaps for their lowly paid, often illegal immigrant servants and aides. Even those entrepreneurs who own businesses are not the driving force behind job creation. As wealthy renegade investor Nick Hanauer has explained, it is a healthy economic ecosystem, starting with a company's customers, that is responsible for the actual creation of jobs. Without consumers to buy whatever goods or services a given company is producing, all the mystical job creators in the world couldn't salvage it.[153] "The annual earnings of people like me are hundreds, if not thousands, of times greater than those of the average American," Hanauer reasoned, "but we don't buy hundreds of thousands of times more stuff." As the news organization Truth-Out put it, "billionaires are not job creators, they are somewhere between symbiotes and parasites." Considering that the purchasing power of average Americans has been dwindling for over a decade, how well are any of these job creators doing?

Perhaps the biggest reason why the wages of working-class Americans have stagnated and effectively dropped over the past thirty years is the massive influx of immigrants into the country. Since passage of The Immigration Reform Act of 1965, according to the Census Bureau, the percentage of US population increase related to immigration went from 10 percent to over 33 percent by 1990. According to the Center for Immigration Studies, immigration—not live births—is now the largest factor contributing to population growth in America. Because most of the immigration came from Third-World countries such as Mexico, where the standard of living was so much lower than in the United States, the wealthy quickly seized upon it as a way to depress the wages of working-class Americans by paying them less for "jobs Americans won't do."

During the 1980s, there was a vigorous debate about the advisability of permitting so much immigration, especially illegal immigration, into this country. At that time, many conservative Republicans and independent-minded politicians like Colorado's Democratic Governor Richard Lamm strongly argued that the numbers of immigrants were a ticking time bomb, which was bound to sooner or later explode. There is now little public opposition to the millions of immigrants entering America annually. The right has been completely co-opted on this issue by powerful business interests who are happy with the way immigration has lowered their operating costs across the board, and the left will never argue against immigration because to do so would be racist in their politically correct world. Hispanics, especially, have been encouraged not to learn English by providing them with Spanish options on every phone menu, most signs in every building, most forms, with voter registration, etc. This senseless policy hampers assimilation and effectively keeps immigrants in their place, by limiting their own chances at upward mobility. The old conspiratorial mantra about order out of chaos certainly applies here; is there a better way to foment public fragmentation than to have people who must interact with each other being literally unable to communicate?

The American government is actively financing discord between Hispanic groups and US citizens. The National Council of La Raza—which means "the Race" in English—was given $15.2 million in federal grant money in 2005 alone. La Raza is overtly for the interests of Mexico first, even though they exist in the United States and are being heavily financed by American taxpayers.[154] This radical group and others like it are openly promoting "Reconquista," or the ethnic cleansing of the American Southwest, which they feel historically belongs to Mexico. Far from being concerned over these dangerous notions, high-profile leaders like George Bush, Karl Rove, Bill Clinton, John McCain, and Barack Obama have served as keynote speakers at past National Conference of La Raza gatherings. Not only has La Raza been given generous millions in taxpayer funds, the largest corporations have also contributed plentifully to it. Obama's domestic policy advisor Cecilia Munoz came from La Raza, as did Supreme Court justice Sonia Sotomayor. La Raza operates more than a hundred segregated, Latino-only charter schools across the United States, funded by American taxpayers.[155] La Raza has a board of directors of its own, and it is littered with the usual suspects from the top levels of the corporate world. The US leaders making such asinine, illogical allocation of tax dollars and expressions of support are not even worth minimum wage. In August 2014, it was revealed that the Department of Justice was funneling some of an estimated $16.6 billion settlement with Bank of America to the National Council of La Raza (among other groups), over alleged discrimination in lending.[156]

Judicial Watch disclosed, in December 2014, that it had received documents from the Department of Health and Human Services, which revealed that the Obama administration had paid Baptist Children and Family Services an incredible $182,129,786 for the purpose of providing basic shelter care to 2,400 unaccompanied alien children. This was just for a four-month period in 2014 at only two locations: Fort Sill, Oklahoma, and San Antonio's Lackland Air Force Base. Basic calculations found that at Lackland the illegal immigrant children had cost the taxpayers nearly $65,000 each during the period of May to September 2014. Some of the perks provided to these children included laptops and cell phones. At this astonishing rate, it would cost taxpayers nearly $200,000 annually for *each* of these immigrant children. Does it cost anywhere near $200,000 for basic shelter care of any underage American citizen? Even the most indulgent parents would find it difficult to spend that much money on their offspring. And, as always, juxtapose this excessive generosity against the hardline approach now favored by both liberals and conservatives when it comes to the poorest Americans. As an astute anonymous wit remarked on a conspiracy forum, "That is like $19,000 a month per illegal. How is that possible? Sounds like a lot of money being funneled elsewhere." IRS Commissioner John Koskinen finally admitted to Congress in 2015 that under Obama's executive amnesty decree, illegal immigrants will be able to get retroactive years of tax refunds, even though they paid no taxes![157] Perhaps most outrageously of all, an Obama administration memo allowed US Border Patrol and Customs agents not to arrest illegal immigrant drunk drivers. The memo actually specifies that this is an official policy even if they permit the driver to "continue down the road and they kill someone."[158]

In an op-ed piece published by the *New York Times* on October 11, 2011, Steven A. Camarota, Director of Research at the Center for Immigration Studies, demonstrated convincingly that, to quote the title of his op-ed, "More Immigrants, Lower Wages." Camarota revealed that the Economic Policy Institute had found that real, inflation-adjusted, hourly wages for men without a high school education were 22 percent lower in 2007 than they'd been in 1979, and 10 percent lower for those with a high school education. Camarota stated the obvious when he wrote, "Better compensation would go a long way in making it easier for employers to recruit and retain good workers." Common sense, and basic math, tell us that if you don't have enough jobs or resources for your citizens, you shouldn't keep allowing millions of immigrants to cross over your oddly unguarded southern border each year, and you shouldn't stress the need for more legal immigration on the basis of finding talent for certain jobs, which supposedly doesn't exist within the American populace. George Washington University economics professor Robert Dunn analyzed the situation thusly; "if there's an unlimited supply of labor facing this country from outside, from the South or wherever, at five dollars an hour, I don't care how fast this economy grows, the wage rate for such people is going to be five dollars an hour."[159] Another astute economist, Vernon Briggs of the Center for Immigration Studies, declared, "The low-wage strategy may work in the short run. . . . In the long run, we are not going to win a wage-cutting contest with the Third World."

The evidence of immigration's impact upon American wages is overwhelming; in July 1992, *Economic Geography* found that wage increases in cities with small immigrant populations were 48 percent higher than in cities with a large rate of immigration. No less a figure than former Clinton administration Labor Secretary Robert Reich admitted, "Undoubtedly access to lower-wage foreign workers has a depressing effect (on wages)." The Center for Immigration

Studies has concluded that between 40–50 percent of the wage loss experienced by lower-skilled Americans could be attributed to immigration. In just the state of New Jersey alone, the Federation for American Immigration Reform estimated that health-care costs for illegal immigrants amount to some $200 million annually. At the same time, many American citizens struggle to meet the astronomical costs of health care. President Trump's decree to build a wall along the southern border resonates with many Americans, frustrated by decades of inaction on the issue of immigration.

As the Federation for American Immigration Reform (FAIR) put it, in a 2010 article, "In short, the mass importation of low-skilled workers through immigration damages the job market for Americans, depresses wages for low-skilled natives, and costs the taxpayer billions a year—all for the benefit of businesses that have become dependent on cheap, foreign labor. An immigration system that admits too many people, without regard to their skill levels or impact on the labor force, is to blame." Donald Trump cited figures from FAIR during his 2016 presidential campaign that concluded illegal immigrants cost taxpayers some $113 *billion* annually. There are several classes of foreign workers that permit employers to bypass payroll taxes for them. Obviously, this impacts the Social Security and Medicare trust funds, already in sad shape from decades of neglect. Since illegal aliens tend to work in the underground economy and get paid under the table, they don't pay the taxes legal workers do. Former Arizona state treasurer Dean Martin reported his state alone lost between $1.3 and $2.5 billion each year on educating, incarcerating, and providing health care for illegal immigrants.[160] The Heritage Foundation estimated that it would cost American taxpayers $6.3 trillion over the next fifty years to legalize immigrants under the latest reform proposal.[161]

We don't need skilled immigrants any more than we need unskilled ones. American citizens should be given the first opportunity to fill any position, especially in this dreadful employment market, where we have far more willing workers than we have jobs. But advocating for American companies to hire Americans first is considered akin to being nativist or racist. Because our leaders allowed this situation to fester, that horse left the barn a long time ago. When combined with the distorted, slanderous notion that the poor and unemployed whose families have been in this country for generations are just lazy and unwilling to better themselves, these huge levels of immigration have provided a toxic mixture for the working conditions, wages, and benefits of everyone concerned (except, of course, the wealthy, who will never have to compete with Third-World executive compensation). The situation is similar in Canada, where one in four new jobs is being filled by a temporary guest worker. Our leaders are basically discarding the old adage that charity begins at home and are figuratively feeding the neighbors while their own family lacks food and water.

Despite all the evidence to the contrary, the *New Republic,* exemplifying the mainstream media's campaign to promote the latest Immigration reform act, would declare that, "Immigration has economically benefited U.S. workers."[162] The latest proposed reform bill would greatly increase the number of H-1B visas (given to foreign workers in specialty areas, utilized by companies because of a theoretical shortage of domestic talent), with the intention of doing to computer programmers and the like what was done years ago to the vast unskilled labor market. The fantasy that there is a crying need for foreigners to perform jobs countless Americans are begging for, and could easily do, is just another indication of how corrupt those making these mindless decisions are. Some 250 IT workers at Walt Disney World were given pink slips at the end of 2014 and were also informed that they had to train their replacements, mostly highly skilled immigrants brought in under the H-1B visa program by an outsourcing firm in India. "I just couldn't believe they could fly people in to sit at our desks and take over our jobs exactly," a man in his forties who was still unemployed several months later was quoted as saying.[163] Americans laid off in favor of foreign workers are routinely prohibited from criticizing their former employers, as part of their severance package.[164]

Writer David Seminara was one of the few public voices to make the point that notions like this country needs foreigners to fill jobs that Americans can't or won't do "are the kind of flawed assumptions that have led to the creation and rapid growth of the H-2B visa program, which has resulted in more than half a million jobs being filled being filled by foreign guest workers over the last five years." The H2-B visa program imports temporary or seasonal workers. Illustrating just how important these foreign workers are to the corporatocracy, the US Chamber of Commerce announced in 2009 that the H-2B program was one of its Policy Priorities.[165] As the Economic Policy Institute has noted, these guest worker programs especially impact the employment prospects of young Americans, as they are forced to compete not only with H-2B visa guest workers, but also young people from other countries who are in America under the J-1 Exchange Visitor Program, which involves visiting scholars and others in an effort to promote cultural exchange. In the words of critic Daniel Costa, "J-1 workers have also taken what used to be unionized jobs with decent pay and fringe benefits," in addition to positions at amusement parks and national parks that formerly went to high school or college students. According to Costa, "employers have tight control over guest workers, can pay them less than the prevailing wage, and aren't required to pay Social Security, Medicare, and unemployment taxes on their behalf." As of 2011, there were 320,000 participants of the J-1 program in the United States. Often unreported by the mainstream media is the glaring fact that sixty-six thousand of the H-2B visas go to foreigners with little or no education or for jobs that require few or no "skills."[166] This alone makes a lie of the oft-repeated mantra that these visas are crucial to the economy because US employers can't find the talent they need domestically to fill these jobs.

In May 2014, Department of Homeland Security deputy secretary Alejandro Mayorkas announced that the Obama administration was inviting an extra one hundred thousand foreign workers to fill jobs in the United States over the next four years. These additional foreigners boosted the total of guest workers in this country above 750,000. Already, since June 2012, the Obama administration had granted work permits to over 521,000 illegal immigrants. Jeff Sessions, a senator from Alabama at the time, recognized how foolhardy these policies were. "This will help corporations by further flooding a slack labor market, pulling down wages." Sessions continued, "It is good news for citizens in other countries who will be hired . . . for struggling Americans, it will only reduce wages, lower job opportunities, and make it harder to scrape by." According to Rochester Institute of Technology professor Ron Hira, there are roughly 650,000 university-trained guest workers with long-term visas, presently residing in the United States. This figure nearly equals the eight hundred thousand American citizens who have recently obtained degrees in such skilled areas as engineering, business, accounting, medicine, and software.[167] Perhaps this is why the number of college graduates in the United States working minimum wage jobs has risen nearly 71 percent over the last decade, according to Bureau of Labor statistics. The Institute for College Access and Success estimates that the average American college student graduating in 2016 was left with $37,172 in student loan debt.[168] This amounted to a $7,000 increase just from 2015.

An eye-opening article in US News & World Report on September 15, 2014, confirmed that the reality is, in terms of science, technology, engineering, and math (STEM) jobs, "ample supply, stagnant wages, and, by industry accounts, thousands of applicants for any advertised job." The story noted that average IT wages are the same as when Bill Clinton was in office, despite constant cries about a shortage of talent for job openings. On the contrary, "the growth of STEM shortage claims is driven by heavy industry funding for lobbyists and think tanks" and invariably there follows a plea for more guest workers to fill the jobs that Americans are mysteriously incapable of doing. Another damning statistic is the fact that two-thirds of all new IT hires are now foreign guest workers. Those exorbitant college costs, usually financed via backbreaking student loans, don't appear to be returning much of value, as the Census Bureau reports that only about one in four graduates with a STEM bachelor's degree has a STEM job.

Sometimes these immigrants confront management about their abysmal pay and benefits. One notable example of this was when some one hundred fifty workers (about three-quarters of the company's workforce) from Palermo's Pizza factory in Milwaukee, Wisconsin, met on May 27, 2012, and signed a petition to unionize. In response, Palermo's sent letters to eighty-nine immigrant workers, demanding they show documentation of their legal status. Ten days later, the company fired almost all of them. Obviously, the company could have, and should have, verified the papers of their employees when they hired them. The only time corporate America shows concern about the immigration status of a worker is when, as in this case, there was the perceived threat of higher pay and better benefits.[169] The US Chamber of Commerce steadfastly opposes any penalties for hiring illegal immigrants, even going so far as to fight such sanctions in Arizona at the US Supreme Court level. The AFL-CIO, once a powerful bastion for workers' rights, strongly supported the recent amnesty provisions in Obama's immigration reform bill.

The *Boston Globe* reported how the New England Patriots had hired a large number of illegal Guatemalan fugitives from deportation to clear snow from Gillette Stadium in Foxborough, Massachusetts. The Guatemalans were pulled over by the authorities on their way to the stadium.[170] California Attorney General Kamala Harris was elected to office despite an unbelievably irrational program she presided over as San Francisco District Attorney. The program, Back on Track, involved helping illegal immigrants avoid prison or deportation for any violent crimes they committed, opting instead to *train them for jobs.*[171] American citizens charged with violent crimes would love to have that kind of option. And while Americans are forcibly groped by TSA agents and subject to harassment at the hands of local, state, and federal law enforcement, ostensibly in the name of fighting terrorism, a story broke in 2007 about illegal immigrant Nada Nadim Prouty being hired for sensitive jobs at both the CIA and FBI, where she was caught stealing classified information.[172] One seemingly suspect group that is incomprehensibly permitted to bypass all the TSA measures is the Muslim Brotherhood. While they cannot be profiled, there are a myriad of videos online, chronicling TSA agents shoving their hands down the pants of small children and conducting intrusive searches of severely handicapped people. After initial denials, the TSA has admitted that illegal aliens are now permitted to board planes with only Notice to Appear forms, which have no photo and can be easily forged.[173] Whatever TSA director John S. Pistole is being paid, he's not worth it.

Long before the likes of Scott Baio and Ted Nugent came out in support of Trump and his proposed wall, a celebrity went against the establishment grain and blasted this nation's disastrous immigration policy. Actor Phil Hartman, on a 1997 episode of HBO's *Dennis Miller Show,* stated boldly that, "You cannot even discuss this subject without being considered a racist in this country." Hartman was very critical of America's capitulation on this issue, referring to our "insane policies" on immigration and asking "why we don't even have a cogent dialogue about the problem." Hartman showed amazing awareness of the subject, castigating both the Democrats, who were unwilling to anger one of their voting constituencies, and the Republicans, who were interested in keeping "a cheap labor pool." Hartman also noted that within the next five years, American taxpayers were going to be paying out over a billion dollars in entitlements to "foreigners who haven't put so much as a dime into the system." Calling our government a "giant corporation," Hartman summed up things by stating, "Immigration, illegal and otherwise, is good for business." A year after issuing these controversial remarks, on May 29, 1998, Phil Hartman was killed by his wife in a bizarre murder-suicide, leaving behind two small children.

In the almost twenty years since Hartman's untimely, unnatural death, taxpayers have obviously paid out more in various entitlements to immigrants than he could ever have imagined. If critics of the massive, mostly incomprehensible Affordable Care Act are to be believed, illegal immigrants may well be the only people in America who will be getting free health care under the law.

The mainstream media is just as awful on this issue as any other important one. The *New York Times* ran a propaganda piece in its June 22, 2011, edition, titled "My Life as an Undocumented Immigrant." The Filipino immigrant, Jose Antonio Vargas, who was the subject of the article, had the added politically correct bonus of being gay. We are informed that, somehow, Vargas got a job at the *San Francisco Chronicle* as a college student "writing freelance articles." Shortly afterwards, he won an internship at the *Washington Post*. In 2008, he would be part of that newspaper's coverage of the shootings at Virginia Tech, for which he shared a Pulitzer Prize. We also learn matter-of-factly that Vargas had met Ariana Huffington sometime earlier, and she subsequently recruited him to join her at the *Huffington Post*. There is an inherent bias that no one with a brain could fail to see in this article and in every piece the establishment press does on immigration. The media unthinkingly promotes the idea that more immigration is good. They don't factor in the damage done to the labor markets, and they drown out any token criticism with the rallying cry, "diversity is our strength!" An intelligent reader should not be motivated by the attempted emotional pull of this article, to somehow feel sorry for someone who has achieved far more—and enjoys a higher standard of living—than the vast majority of American citizens. Instead, the question should be, how does someone who is in this country illegally manage to get such prestigious jobs?

In 2013, a particularly odious immigration scandal was exposed, with little fanfare in most of the establishment press. Apparently, illegal immigrants have been benefiting from a tax loophole themselves for quite some time. Because they have no Social Security number, undocumented workers are provided with an individual taxpayer identification number, so they can file their tax returns.

The loophole they are using, the Additional Child Tax Credit, which gives a credit of $1,000 per child, permits them to claim multiple children living in Mexico as dependents. As a whistle-blower told Indianapolis TV station WTHR, "We've seen sometimes ten or twelve dependents, most times nieces and nephews . . . the more you put on there, the more you get back." This whistle-blower provided WTHR with thousands of examples where fraudulent deductions are made for children who not only don't live in the United States, but have never even been here. Several undocumented workers (the new politically correct term for what used to be called illegal aliens) told the station that they were informed it was legal.

This massive tax fraud still continues, in spite of warnings from the likes of the Inspector General of the Tax Department, Russell George, who declared, "The magnitude of this problem has grown exponentially," and charged that the IRS has known about it for years and that he himself had repeatedly warned them that this provision was being abused by undocumented workers. A report from the Inspector General concluded that the fraud was costing the taxpayers some $4.2 billion annually, a charge Donald Trump utilized during his 2016 presidential run. Incredibly, the IRS responded to this story by saying, "The law has been clear for over a decade that eligibility for these credits does not depend on work authorization status or the type of taxpayer identification number used. Any suggestion that the IRS shouldn't be paying out these credits under current law to ITIN holders is simply incorrect." George reacted thusly, "The IRS is not doing something as simple as requesting sufficient documentation from people seeking this credit."[174] Even more incredibly, the IRS admitted in 2016 that it *encourages* illegal immigrants to steal Social Security numbers to use for tax purposes, suggesting their job is strictly to process returns.[175]

No one should blame immigrants for seeking a better life. Those who are concerned about this issue are not racists. Immigrants have been used, in a very effective manner, to help drive down the wages and tear away the benefits of working-class Americans. They may have elevated their standard of living by immigrating here, but their presence has helped to lower the standard of living for all so-called unskilled American workers and many skilled ones as well.

8 How Failure Keeps Succeeding

I always knew I was going to be rich. I don't think I ever doubted it for a minute.

—Warren Buffett

IF CAPITALISM WORKED THE WAY it should, then incompetent executives would suffer some real financial consequences. Instead, we find that the most spectacular corporate failures aren't punished for poor performance and are often lavishly rewarded. As *Think Progress* put it, "The best-paid CEOs in American business have overseen companies that were bailed out, been fired, and been caught committing fraud at alarming rates over the past twenty years, a new report finds." The study in question was conducted by the Institute for Policy Studies. They drew upon the *Wall Street Journal's* annual list of the twenty-five highest-paid executives dating back to 1994. Of the 241 individuals who appeared on the list, 32 percent had overseen bailouts, had been fired, or had been kicked out for fraud. One example cited in the IPS study was Dick Fuld, former Lehman Brothers CEO, who raked in $466.3 million in eight years with the company. Lehman Brothers' 2008 bankruptcy precipitated the financial meltdown of our economy and was the largest one in history.

Investor Place ranked the "Worst 5 CEOs of 2013." One of the five was Lulumon CEO Christine Day, who was paid over $4 million in 2012, presided over a fiasco where the company's yoga pants were manufactured with too much transparency, and the founder and chairman of the company, Chip Wilson, exacerbated things by telling *Bloomberg TV* that, "quite frankly, some women's bodies just actually don't work for it." Wilson is worth $1.9 billion. Day didn't stay unemployed long after stepping down of her own accord, taking the CEO spot with fast-food company Luvo in January 2014.[176] Abercrombie & Fitch CEO Mike Jeffries caused an uproar in 2013 when he said publicly that his clothing was for "cool kids." He also stated that "we hire good-looking people in our stores. Because good-looking people attract other good-looking people, and we want to market to cool, good-looking people." Finally, he declared, "A lot of people don't belong in our clothes, and they can't belong." For the record, Jeffries is sixty-nine years old and hardly attractive or cool looking. He finally stepped down in 2014, walking away with a retirement package worth $27.6 million, despite a legacy of eleven straight quarters of lower sales.[177] In 2015, Sears CEO Edward Lampert adopted a public relations gimmick of taking only a $1 annual salary, but was actually paid $4.3 million in total compensation. By 2016, Sears teetered on the verge of bankruptcy, having closed numerous stores (as well as countless subsidiary Kmart stores).

Mergers are another way to reward those at the top of the business world; when Heinz was purchased by Warren Buffett's giant Berkshire Hathaway in 2014, their CEO William Johnson was gifted a $56 million golden parachute. Buffet's firm already has holdings in companies such as Geico Insurance and Dairy Queen, and owns a 9.1 percent stake in Coca-Cola. Although he criticized Coke's recent controversial executive compensation plan, which Evergreen CEO David Winters blasted as an "outrageous grab," Buffet abstained from voting on the issue. Buffet also strongly opposes public disclosure of CEO salaries. Buffet's longtime business partner, Charlie Munger, is predictably in lockstep, stating, "Envy is doing the country a lot of harm."[178] Coca-Cola was proposing to step up their executive pay scale significantly; in the words of David Winters: "We can find no reasonable basis for gifting management 14.2 percent of the share capital of Coca-Cola, worth $24 billion at today's share price. No matter how well a management team performs, it is unfathomable that they would require such astronomical sums of money to provide motivation."[179]

Chief Executive Officer, in fact, appears to be the one occupation where poor performance results in even greater financial benefits. Leo Apotheker, who had a short, disastrous reign as CEO of Hewlett Packard, became the third top officer in a row at the company to be fired with a multimillion-dollar termination package. His predecessor, Mark Hurd, slashed 6,400 jobs in 2009, a year in which he was paid $24.2 million, and was forced from the company after a sexual harassment allegation, comforting himself with a $40 million severance package. Hurd became a true rarity, a "double-dipping" beneficiary of a second golden parachute, when he and Safra Catz were given over $137 million *each* in 2016 by Oracle. In Apotheker's case, the company gave him a comparatively paltry $13 million. Experts defined Apotheker's golden parachute as "a fairly standard termination agreement."[180] A few years earlier, American International Group (AIG) CEO Martin Sullivan had been given an unbelievable $47 million when he was ousted for poor performance. AIG lost 47 percent of its market value during Sullivan's tenure.[181] The Institute for Policy Studies determined that "close to 40 percent of the highest paid CEOs in the U.S. have performed abysmally," while the average golden parachute doled out to failed CEOs was $48 million.[182] By 2016, if anything, the golden parachutes had grown even more mind-boggling. Both Steve Wynn, of Wynn Resorts, and David Simon, of Simon Property Group, received over $300 million when they left their respective companies.[183]

Thorsten Heins was ousted from his position as CEO of BlackBerry after less than two years at the helm for putrid performance; the phones he developed received mediocre reviews and his appointment of singer Alicia Keys as "creative director" failed to inspire anyone. Heins was given a $22 million severance payment in November 2013. I could find no information on how much BlackBerry paid Keys for what was surely a ceremonial title, or how much Polaroid is paying Lady Gaga to be their "creative director," or how much Intel pays will.i.am for the same role.[184] Keys' husband, Kasseem Dean, a.k.a. Swizz Beatz, went from global ambassador for a New York City hospital to Harvard Business School's management executive program to Reebok and finally, in July 2016, was appointed as Bacardi's "creative chief for culture." Justin Timbelake, for Bud Light Premium, and Nick Cannon, for Radio Shack, are other recent celebrity creative directors. One can be certain that none of them came cheap; it is probably safe to assume there were at least hundreds of thousands of dollars, if not millions, in these very special "swag bags."

While working-class people live in fear of layoffs, downsizing, and outsourcing, executives have no such concerns. The average worker would be fortunate to get paid for all his leave time upon being dismissed by a company and would be dumbfounded to be offered any kind of minimal severance package. Executives of all stripes fare much better, with the separation benefits increasing as one climbs higher up the corporate ladder. Exxon Mobil's Lee Raymond left his job in 2005 with a handsome $321 million severance package, while Gillette's James Kitts had to settle for $165 million. Target gave CEO Robert Ulrich $164 million when he stepped down in 2008. American Airlines CEO Gerard Arpley was in the distinct minority; when the company declared bankruptcy in 2011, he didn't collect any severance package, commenting that "It is not good thinking— either at the corporate level or at the personal level."[185] It is almost impossible to fail once one has attained a high-ranking executive position. None of the myriad of poor-performing CEOs have trouble getting other high-paid jobs in the business world. Even without a full-time position, they can maintain their One Percent status by attending a few annual board meetings, as almost all of them serve as directors for other big corporations. If a blue-collar worker had this kind of poor track record, his resume would be scoffed at by all employers and he'd be blamed for his own inability to find employment elsewhere.

CEOs often lay off large numbers of workers and then are rewarded with even bigger bonuses for "saving" the company money. Verizon, for example, laid off 1,700 employees in 2012, while giving CEO Lowell C. McAdam $22.5 million in total compensation for the year. The company apparently was not in financial straits, as the layoffs would indicate; it paid its top five executives some $350 million in the five years preceding 2012, according to the *Wall Street Journal*. More than half of McAdam's compensation was derived from performance awards. How can you have performed well if you're forced to lay off that many workers? Verizon, reflecting the new normal, also orchestrated an elimination of the company's pension plan, an increase in health insurance premiums, and a greater leeway in outsourcing jobs, among other austerity measures.[186] As the Minnesota Progressive Project calculated, McAdam's huge bonus for just that single year could have covered the salaries of all 1,700 laid-off workers.

On a smaller scale, but still involving numbers that boggle the mind of an average citizen, *Time* magazine managing editor Richard Stengel had overseen cuts to staff while being paid $700,000 and getting a $289,000 bonus in 2012. As *Time* moved to freeze pay and lay off hundreds of workers in 2013, Stengel was still in line to receive another bonus worth as much as $250,000. Stengel, epitomizing the way the line between government and journalism is often nonexistent, left the magazine afterwards for a job in the State Department. Edward J. Wasserman, dean of the University of California, Berkeley's school of journalism, said that such payouts reveal how much the media has learned from Wall Street. "It offends our sense of justice," Wasserman declared, "Some people are not just escaping, but walking away in terrific shape financially, whereas others get a fairly minimal severance and no safety cushion at all." In a follow-up to the *Washington Times* story about the *Time* magazine layoffs, it was revealed in early 2014 that *Time* Chief

Content Officer Norman Pearlstine has a contract that guarantees him at least $900,000 annually with a sign-on bonus of $1.4 million and a potential long-term incentive compensation of $500,000 per year. A spokesman for the magazine commented on the situation thusly: "Mr. Pearlstine is appropriately compensated for his role in the company."[187]

Chrysler CEO Lee Iacocca, who once said, "We've got to pause and ask ourselves: how much clean air do we need?" was a pioneer in the institution of layoffs and plant closings. In 1980, the Congress authorized a $1.5 billion bailout loan to his struggling company. Chrysler also received $2 billion in concessions from labor, dealers, and other creditors. The same year he begged the taxpayers to rescue his company, Iacocca made $868,000 (remember, this was in 1980). By 1986, his yearly compensation was up to $20.5 million, along with what *Forbes* called a boatload of options.

General Motors came crawling to the taxpayers in 2009, on the heels of the big banks, and our elected representatives dutifully doled out some $49.5 billion to them. Why did GM need help? Clearly, by any objective measure, it was due to years of manufacturing mediocre products and selling them at prices that corresponded to the far superior performing Japanese cars. In a truly competitive free enterprise system, the leadership at GM would have realized they needed to slash the sales prices of their automobiles significantly, cut down on excessive compensation to upper management, and investigate why they couldn't compete in terms of reliability and quality to other, similarly priced foreign brands. Instead, they refused to cut their sticker prices and demanded that the taxpayers lavish more corporate welfare on them. GM CEO Dan Akerson, who by 2012 was getting over $11 million annually in compensation, according to *Forbes,* had the gall to insist that the company should not have to pay anything back to the government. "I would not accept the premise that this was a bad deal," Akerson defiantly declared at the National Press Club. He also called the bailout "a positive for the US economy."[188] It certainly was a positive for *his* company, as indicated by his successor Mary Barra's 2015 compensation of $15.2 million.[189] The very fact that the phrase "too big to fail," contrived to explain the bailouts of the banks and General Motors, was accepted calmly by millions of people ought to tell us something about where the mind-set of America is. The reality is the vast majority of Americans have been sentenced to a life where they are "too small to succeed."

In May 2013 alone, the Bureau of Labor estimated that there were nearly 128,000 "mass layoff events" in the United States. They define a mass layoff as one involving fifty workers or more. As *CNN Money* reported in a March 5, 2013 story, layoffs were very uncommon even twenty years ago. The writer recounted attending an IBM conference in 1992, and how horrified and startled the attendees were that "Big Blue" had announced its very first layoffs. The story accurately summarized the situation: "The corporate movement away from job security coincided with the advent of big executive bonuses and the rise of global competition." *CNN Money* also pointed out the obvious; because of all the massive executive salaries and bonuses, in the unlikely event a corporate big shot is part of a layoff (even without getting any golden parachute), they almost certainly would have been able to save a very nice nest egg, making it easy to still live comfortably. The average worker, on the other hand, has little to fall back upon.

Huge layoffs often mean larger compensation for the CEOs and other executives who preside over them. Johnson & Johnson's William Weldon garnered $25.6 million in 2009, while eliminating nine thousand jobs. Weldon "earned" this tidy sum as he also faced a massive drug recall scandal. Another pharmaceutical executive, Fred Hassan of Schering–Plough, had a $33 million golden parachute bestowed upon him in 2009 after he cut sixteen thousand workers from the payroll. The Institute for Policy Studies calculated that the $598 million total compensation awarded to the executives who'd laid off the most workers in 2008–2009 was enough to provide average unemployment benefits to 37,759 workers for an entire year. American Express not only gave CEO Kenneth Chenault $16.8 million in 2009, the same year it begged taxpayers for money; the company also laid off four thousand workers since receiving $3.4 billion in bailout funds.[190] Hewlett Packard CEO Meg Whitman, with a net worth of $1.7 billion, was paid over $15 million in 2012, while her company was in such dire straits that it had to eliminate nearly thirty thousand employees. The HP board of directors justified Whitman's compensation through its pay for performance philosophy. Again, what kind of performance could result in slashing thirty thousand jobs? The HP Board is littered with all the usual suspects; an ex-chairman of Walgreens and McDonald's, a former vice president with General Electric, etc.[191] In late 2014, Whitman announced that Hewlett Packard would be splitting into two companies, which would result in a downsizing of an estimated fifty-five thousand employees.[192] Whitman has always been known for her executive "talent." During her tenure as CEO of eBay, she presided over the purchase of Skype; their payment was so excessive that it was sold to a group of investors four years later at a nearly $1.5 billion loss.

The new normal in the business world is to nitpick over absurd trivialities that affect only the lower paid workers. Goldman Sachs exemplified this curious philosophy in 2011, as it eliminated one thousand jobs and downsized its *drinking cups*. The megabank's London office removed potted plants, causing disquiet among the staff. In typical corporate copycat style, Morgan Stanley followed suit on the plant question, also opting to cut back on foliage in its offices. Undoubtedly, they have a hard-line attitude about missing pens and notepads as well. Of course, if these companies were truly in financial peril, they'd have to look at the question of executive compensation and bonuses, first and foremost. In that same year, the *New York Times Dealbook* reported that the largest banks set aside $65.69 billion for bonuses.

Even in the wake of the tragic BP oil spill in 2010, corporate America found a way to reward one of the executives at the center of it. As critic Bernard Goldberg recounted in an April 24, 2011, entry on his blog, Transocean Ltd. was the owner of the oil rig that exploded, killing eleven workers and perhaps forever polluting a major body of water and our whole ecosystem. Transocean's CEO Steven L. Newman's salary was actually raised after the massive mishap by some $200,000, to $1.1 million. Transocean released the following absurd explanation to the SEC, "Notwithstanding the tragic loss of life in the Gulf of Mexico, we achieved an exemplary safety record . . . we recorded the best year in safety performance in our Company's history." At least BP had the decency to deny its top executives additional bonuses for their performance.

While the business world seems to operate on the premise that the worse the executive performance, the more compensation should be offered, our government sometimes just allocates money for nothing at all—especially when it comes to the military. The Obama administration canceled plans in early 2014 for new US Army armored vehicles. In 2011, the army had begun doling out lucrative contracts for this program, which by the time plans were scrapped for the project had amounted to an estimated $1.2 billion. So defense contractors BAE Systems and General Dynamics received a huge windfall in return for nothing. Future Combat Systems, which was considered the most ambitious acquisition program in military history, was canceled in 2009 after the Pentagon had already wasted $19 billion on it. An Expeditionary Fighting Vehicle, envisioned as a swimming tank, was scrapped in 2011 after poor performance had already eaten up $3.3 billion. All told, the Obama administration alone has canceled programs that add up to approximately $50 billion in wasted funds.

Of course, unnecessary spending on the military is one of the last bipartisan issues. George W. Bush axed the Comanche helicopter in 2004, after pouring $7.9 billion into the project.[193] The army's biggest military lemon also came under Bush with the Future Combat System, which cost some $19 billion before being canceled. The Bush administration also frittered away billions on two separate space initiatives and an Airborne Laser Project.[194]

A report by the Treasury Inspector General for Tax Administration exposed that from 2010–2012, the IRS gave employees with disciplinary problems some $2.8 million in bonuses. Even more incomprehensibly, some 1,100 employees who *owed back taxes* were paid $1 million in bonuses and given more than ten thousand extra paid vacation hours. At least five of these employees were given performance awards, even after being disciplined for such transgressions as intentionally underreporting income and paying their taxes late. As an April 23, 2014, story in the *Washington Post* put it, "at the IRS, breaking the federal tax laws you were hired to enforce and running afoul of other agency rules aren't considered relevant to performance-based awards." While unions have seen their power and effectiveness all but disappear in the blue-collar private sector, the National Treasury Employees Union somehow got the IRS to agree that bad conduct would not be factored in when making performance-based awards. In defending itself, the IRS pointed out that their agency was hardly alone in following such a curious practice. "Of the 15 federal and 13 state policies we examined," the agency wrote in a letter to the Inspector General, "only one agency specifically prohibited granting an award if conduct issues were present." Evidently, the largest publicly known recent IRS bonus went to former commissioner Richard E. Byrd, who received $60,270. Performance bonuses to employees who have been reprimanded for important issues? And why is any government employee who has been caught cheating on their own tax returns permitted to keep working for the IRS, of all places?

According to the Urban Institute, as of 2010, some 3.5 million Americans, or about 1 percent of the population, had been homeless for a significant period of time. Meanwhile, Fox Business estimated that there were 18.9 million vacant homes across the country. While it would undoubtedly take some thought to develop a coherent plan to put those without shelter into some of these empty structures (something our leaders have never been good at), this is just one of many instances in which a chronic problem seems to have a convenient solution waiting with open arms. As Virgin Group founder Richard Branson observed, "No one benefits from an empty house."[195] The myriad of empty homes are primarily the result of the explosion in foreclosures; banks foreclosed on some eight million homeowners from 2007–2011. In Europe, the situation is even more damning, as there are eleven million empty homes, enough to house all the homeless across the continent twice over. Many of these homes were built in holiday resorts, as additional toys for the rich, before the 2008 financial crisis, and have never been occupied. On top of this, hundreds of thousands of half-constructed homes have been bulldozed. David Ireland, chief executive of the Empty Homes charity, called the situation a shocking waste and argued that the issue of wealthy buyers using houses as investment vehicles rather than residences needed to be addressed by policymakers.[196]

As long ago as the 1930s, Huey Long was rightfully chastising the government for its absurd practice of paying farmers *not* to grow food. One of the more baffling programs of FDR's New Deal was the Agricultural Adjustment Act, which instituted the payment of subsidies to farmers in return for not planting on part of their land and killing off excess livestock. The rationale behind the act was to raise the value of crops, but it made little sense to critics like Long, who liked to declare, "We have more food than we can eat," and thus there was no reason for anyone to be in want. In 2006, an investigation disclosed that a senseless agriculture program, approved by Congress, had resulted in some $1.3 billion being paid since 2000 to individuals who owned land that once was used for crops like rice but were presently doing no farming at all. And as might be expected, it is often the already wealthy who benefit from this truly nonsensical policy. For instance, Houston surgeon Frank Howell was paid $490,709 during one decade. As the *Washington Post* noted, this was merely a continuation of decades-old farm subsidies but on an even more outrageous level—and something that "benefits millionaire landowners, foreign speculators, and absentee landlords, as well as farmers."[197] This situation remained unchanged as of 2012, as a report from the Government Accountability Office found that the USDA had doled out millions to over two thousand farms that hadn't grown any crops since 2006, and to 622 that hadn't farmed at all since 2001. *Bloomberg* pointed out that due to pressure from powerful lobbies, "Congress is poised to funnel billions of dollars more to individuals who already are more prosperous than the typical American."[198] The US Senate passed a new farm bill in early 2014, which expanded crop insurance and other agribusiness benefits. The same bill, which passed overwhelmingly in a rare bipartisan vote, authorized the slashing of $8 billion in food stamps over the next decade. In the words of the *New York Times,* "Overall, farmers fared far better than the poor" under the legislation.[199] By 2016, farm subsidies had reached record levels of more than $25 billion every year.

According to the Government Accountability Office, celebrated figures such as Ted Turner, Bruce Springsteen, Jon Bon Jovi, and Scottie Pippin, each of them about as far removed from farming as can be, incomprehensibly have received farm subsidies. One of the world's richest men, Microsoft cofounder and present owner of the NFL's Seattle Seahawks and NBA's Portland Trail Blazers Paul Allen, gets government farm subsidies. So do fellow billionaires Charles Ergen, cofounder of the DISH network; Philip Anschutz, cofounder of Major League Soccer; Leonard Lauder, heir to and former CEO of Estee Lauder Companies, Inc.; Amway cofounder Richard DeVos; Cox Enterprises chairman Jim Kennedy; and Chick-fil-A founder S. Truett Cathy.[200]

The handouts aren't limited to farm subsidies. In a special report entitled "Subsidies of the Rich and Famous," by Oklahoma Senator Tom Coburn, it was revealed that musical impresario Quincy Jones, who is worth an estimated $310 million, and songwriter Johnny Mandel, both received a $25,000 grant from the National Endowment for the Arts. Some $1.5 billion in taxpayer funds from various states are channeled directly to big movie studios each year. Very rich real estate mogul Maurice Wilder, with a fortune of at least $500 million, who has no connection to farming, was paid some $200,000 over a four-year period. "From tax write-offs for gambling losses, vacation homes, and luxury yachts to subsidies for their ranches and estates, the government is subsidizing the lifestyles of the rich and famous," noted Senator Coburn. "Multimillionaires are even receiving government checks for not working."[201] This is even more outrageous than garden-variety corporate welfare, but few seem to be focusing attention on it, and neither liberals nor conservatives seem to care.

The adage that everyone rises to their own level of incompetence is often quoted, and the truth in it widely accepted, but like the often insightful *Dilbert* comic strip, which is routinely displayed in offices all over America, no one seems willing to confront a reality they are instinctively repulsed by.

9 THE THIRD-WORLD STANDARD

Normal is getting dressed in clothes that you buy for work and driving through traffic in a car that you are still paying for—in order to get to the job you need to pay for the clothes and the car, and the house you leave vacant all day so you can afford to live in it.

—Ellen Goodman

As DEPRESSINGLY TRUE AS THE above quote may be, such a state of existence may seem idyllic in another fifty years, if the elite get their way.

One of the most curious trends in the history of civilization are so-called micro-apartments, or apodments, which are already popular in Hong Kong, China, and Japan, and now being built in cities across the United States. These dwellings typically provide less than 370 feet of living space and are sometimes no bigger than a wealthy person's master bathroom. They basically provide the tenant with a place to sleep and watch television, and perhaps use a laptop. One of the leading members of the One Percent, New York's former mayor Michael Bloomberg, backed the development of the city's first all-micro-unit building. Those occupying these cramped quarters will certainly not be saving money by doing so; the rents are expected to run anywhere from $940–1800 per month. These absurdly small units are allegedly a response to overcrowding and cramped space. Trying its best to defend this downturn in living standards, *Psychology Today* intoned, "Organizing and living in a tiny house can clearly be a challenge, and many people really enjoy solving puzzles." Berkeley developer Patrick Kennedy told *The New York Times* that his bottom line was 160 feet "without causing psychological problems."[202] In New York's East Village, one can buy a 450-square-foot condo for $340,000. I suppose location *is* everything.

In San Francisco, deluded yuppies are paying $1,850 monthly rent for a 279-square-foot space. "We need to think outside the box in providing housing for our population," said San Francisco Supervisor Scott Weiner. Thinking outside the box while living inside a box; how ironic. While the standard studio apartment—previously the smallest place anyone could legally live—is normally 500 to 600 square feet, micro units are much tinier. At least Weiner is walking the walk; he lives in a 490-square-foot condo himself. Alan Mark, president of San Francisco's Mark Co., advises people to "think of your apartment as your bedroom and the neighborhood as your living room."[203]

The push for smaller quarters is part of the overall campaign to get the mass of human beings to lower significantly their expectations about life and to support austerity measures. Already, the new norm has accustomed young workers to accept no annual raises, few or no benefits, and no pension. Learning to quell any dreams of a single-family home, a townhouse, or even your own apartment is an essential ingredient of the drive to turn the United States into a Third-World nation. Carrying this campaign to the ultimate extreme, Hutson Tillotson University Professor Jeff Wilson began a well-publicized year living in a dumpster in the fall of 2013. The professor emphasized that dumpster living is enough to satisfy anyone (well, anyone in the target group of the bottom 80 percent of Americans), using the slogan, "less is more." The dumpster had a shower, toilet, kitchen, bed and Wi-Fi access. Call me cynical, but I think it's safe to bet that Professor Dumpster is no more living in a dumpster than reality shows like *Survivor* are legitimate. The good professor's project even utilized a Kickstarter campaign, in order to coax gullible citizens into financing it.[204]

There are still some voices of sanity left that argue against this obscenely reduced standard of living. "Are we saying it is acceptable to box people up in little tiny spaces?" Tommi Avicolli Mecca, director of counseling for the Housing Rights Committee, told the *New York Times.* "What standard are we setting here?" Such micro units would serve about as well as anything possibly could to identify human beings by class, bringing us closer to the Alphas and Betas from Aldous Huxley's *Brave New World.* As the website *Coexist. org* points out, these micro units aren't new, "they have just been historically illegal—and pretty terrible to live in." New York City had outlawed these kinds of miniscule dwellings back in the 1950s, deeming them inhumane and substandard. But clearly our concepts of inhumanity and relative standards of living have changed dramatically over the past sixty years.

So-called passive houses are being pushed by the powers that be as well. Already in Japan, these aesthetically ugly dwellings are popping up elsewhere; they are being heated and cooled by body heat or refrigerators, rather than conventional electricity or gas. In 2010, *Infowars* published a copy of a new resolution passed by the European Union banning the construction of ordinary single-family homes which fail the "zero-energy" standard of matching the amount of renewable energy created on-site with the amount of energy used on-site, starting in 2020. A July 26, 2011, story in *Forbes,* headlined "California Wages War on Single-Family Homes," and an April 24, 2015, article titled "Kiss Single-Family Homes Goodbye," on the Seattle Bubble website, trumpeted the new normal in this regard. Meanwhile, the palatial estate where environmentalist guru Al Gore lives burned more than twenty times the national kilowatt hour average in 2006, according to the Tennessee Center for Policy Research. And Hollywood activists commonly fly by private jet, even when they're traveling somewhere to lecture the unwashed masses about conserving energy and generally making do with less.

The advice offered by celebrities to the uncelebrated riffraff is often truly ridiculous. They hold concerts for causes like Live Aid, Farm Aid, or Comic Relief, whereby they donate their valuable services while demanding working-class fans fork over the actual dough. Singer Sheryl Crow proposed that "a limitation be put on how many squares of toilet paper can be used in any one sitting." Crow suggested that only one square be used per visit and even joked that her brother had proposed going even further, and "washing the one square out."[205] Crow is a typical hypocritical celebrity; according to *The Smoking Gun,* she routinely demands four tour buses, three tractor trailers, and six cars when she performs, adding up to quite a collective carbon footprint. Brad Pitt's ex-bodyguard claimed that Brad Pitt doesn't use *any* toilet paper, in an effort to save the environment. He apparently defends the practice by noting that "people in Third-World countries do it all the time."[206] If this is true, at least Pitt is walking the walk. But it would be a really disgusting walk. One of the most obnoxious celebrities imaginable, Bill Maher, offered up the following gem: "if every American just gave up eating meat and cheese one day of the week, it would be the equivalent of saving ninety-one billion driving miles in a year."[207] Lowering your standard of living is really cool, as long as you aren't part of the wealthiest 20 percent of Americans. Actress Jennifer Aniston rivaled Crow by making the dubious claim that she brushes her teeth in the shower, and since two minutes of showering uses as much water as an African uses in a day, she restricts herself to a three-minute shower.[208]

The essential message is: you, the average person, must sacrifice in order to save the planet. Therefore, according to Jason Mattera's *Hollywood Hypocrites,* the ultra-diva Barbra Streisand lectures people about conserving water, while she spends $22,000 a year on watering her own lawn and gardens. In April 2013, actor Ben Affleck launched a well-publicized campaign to feed himself on $1.50 a day for five days, to bring attention to the estimated 1.4 billion people around the world who live below the extreme poverty level. The message here was clear; Americans spend too much on food, when all over the world people are starving. So you should eat less, as that will somehow feed people somewhere else, to use typical celebrity logic. After his five-day diet, Affleck undoubtedly went back to eating lobster, filet mignon, or whatever else he wanted and still managed to feel good about himself.

Food prices have risen sharply over the past few years, which again severely impacts the 80 percent of Americans suffering to one extent or another financially. Wholesale beef prices alone rose 23 percent from 2013 to 2014. More incredibly, the Bureau of Labor reported that the cost of shrimp had risen 61 percent during the same time period. "Living standards will suffer as a larger percentage of household budgets are spent on grocery store bills," commented economist Chris Christopher of HIS Global Insight.[209] We also see increasing shortages of various essential items, what "conspiracy theorists" call artificial scarcity. In George Orwell's *1984*, the unavailability of formerly plentiful goods was a key component of Big Brother's authoritarian state.

One of the most persistent themes in modern politics is that of shared sacrifice. In a July 2011 speech, President Obama urged Democrats and Republicans to engage in shared sacrifice to break the customary budget impasse. High-profile Catholic bishops advised GOP leaders that balancing the budget "requires shared sacrifice for all" a few months later.[210] During August 2011, Obama sounded the same theme, declaring "If everybody took an attitude of shared sacrifice, we could solve our deficit and debt problem."[211] Multibillionaire Warren Buffet told his fellow plutocrats, "When we are asking for shared sacrifice from the American people, I would at least make sure that the people with these huge incomes get taxed at a rate that is commensurate with the rate they got taxed at not long ago." Buffet's company, Berkshire Hathaway, defeated a claim by the IRS that it owed taxes dating back to 2002 in a 2015 court decision.[212] Goldman Sachs CEO Lloyd Blankfein, who revealed his limitless chutzpah with a 2009 comment about doing "God's work" as he garnered some $70 million in compensation, wrote in a November 13, 2012, *Wall Street Journal* op-ed that, "Any political agreement to cope with the 'fiscal cliff' will require flexibility and shared sacrifice."

The entire debate over taxpayer debt is a distortion of reality. American taxpayers did not accumulate or authorize this monstrous debt, which was accrued primarily through unwise loans and the unaudited machinations of the Federal Reserve System. Yet virtually every politician in both major parties, and every mouthpiece in the mainstream media, harp on the notion that we must pay down this debt. We could repudiate the interest on this debt and force the Fed to deal with the situation it created when it was allowed to monetize the debt, instead of lecturing the already struggling average taxpayer about fiscal responsibility and declaring that, once again, we must sacrifice things we've come to expect, such as Social Security, unemployment insurance, Medicare, etc. These sober, elected officials will never sacrifice one penny of their impressive compensation packages or their lucrative pensions.

Americans have seemingly always been asked to sacrifice for the common good, which in reality means complying amiably with a corrupt system that bestows almost all the rewards on a small percentage of the population. Huey Long is the only politician I know of who advocated giving to the common people instead of sanctimoniously asking them to give up more of the little they possess. Surprisingly, this call to sacrifice has been a consistently successful strategy for politicians in both parties. "Americans are ready to sacrifice, and they have a whole history of doing it," pollster John Zogby noted, in the midst of the 2008 presidential campaign between two candidates (Obama and McCain) who were competing to see who could ask more of the American people.[213] This, again, was one of the attractions of both Bernie Sanders and Donald Trump as candidates. Their rhetoric swirled around making life better for the average citizen.

President Obama certainly did not stop living what the *Washington Times* called "the 1 percent life" during his time in office.

While the White House canceled all public tours due to a shortage of funds during one of those countless budget impasses, the Obamas have taken numerous lavish vacations all around the world. As the paper noted, while it cost $74,000 a week to run the White House tours, the cost alone for using Air Force One for all those vacations is an astounding $180,000 per hour. In the first three months of that year, the Obamas had already taken three vacations, including the president's golfing trip with Tiger Woods, and First Lady Michele's ski excursion to Aspen, Colorado. In December 2015, the Obama family took another vacation to Hawaii; the cumulative cost of their Hawaiian trips alone was estimated at $85 million.[214] Vice President Joe Biden was keeping pace, bilking the taxpayers for such extravagances as a $585,000 one-night hotel stay in Paris and a $321,000 London limousine tab. This is hardly a partisan thing; George W. Bush, by most accounts, spent an incredible 32 percent of his presidency on vacation. Ronald Reagan was also renowned for spending huge chunks of his time in office at his Santa Barbara ranch.

The Affordable Care Act, or Obamacare, has been criticized by right-wing opponents as some kind of massive government handout. Nothing could be further from the truth. In reality, it seems to be a typical sort of bureaucratic nightmare. The insurance companies basically wrote the law, as *Forbes* pointed out, in an October 1, 2013, article headlined, "Obamacare Enriches Only the Health Insurance Giants and Their Shareholders." The article blasted the Obama administration for giving "a free ride for the health insurance industry" that would permit massive premium hikes on consumers. Obamacare doesn't provide free health care to anyone, outside of perhaps illegal immigrants. It does mandate that everyone buy health insurance, and the rates are still outrageous. Those who opt not to buy it must pay a penalty, which increases every year. Even more ominously, Obamacare included a $3,000 incentive for each illegal alien a US firm hires over a native-born worker. This nonsensical loophole was surreptitiously attached to the disastrous Obama amnesty plan, whereby the president autocratically declared some five million illegal immigrants to be lawful residents eligible for work permits.[215] By the end of 2016, even the Obama administration was acknowledging the substantially increased premium costs of his "affordable" act. Articles like the one appearing in *CNN Money* on October 15, 2016, detailed the horrific experiences of everyday people. Plans can cost $1,200 a month with deductibles of $6,000. The article reported that some ten million Americans were buying individual coverage through the exchange system without receiving any federal subsidies. Donald Trump's frequent 2016 campaign references to Obamacare as a disaster struck a chord with many for good reasons.

Unpaid penalties for not buying Obamacare are taken out of any tax refunds. The penalties more than tripled in 2015, spiraling to $325 or 2 percent of a person's income. Even children under the age of eighteen aren't exempt, as they will have to pay half the new adult rate, or $162.50, if they are uninsured. Senior insurance analyst Laura Adams had predicted this on a November 12, 2014, *CBS News* report. Adams had pointed out that "It's a big penalty for the middle-class for not having insurance." What other product has ever been a mandatory purchase for the American public? And Obama, in an interview with NBC, refused to rule out *jail time* for those Americans who don't buy health insurance. The contempt our leaders hold for the average citizen was captured clearly in the comments of MIT professor Jonathan Gruber, another of the primary architects of Obamacare. Gruber acknowledged that lack of transparency had been a huge political advantage, in conjunction with "the stupidity of the American voter," in getting the Affordable Care Act passed.[216]

Ezekiel Emanuel, brother of powerful Chicago mayor Rahm Emanuel, lobbied for this new Third-World-style, "less is more" standard in a widely circulated article in the September 17, 2014, *The Atlantic*. It was titled tellingly, "Why I Hope to Die at 75: An Argument That Society and Familes—and You—Will be Better Off if Nature Takes its Course Swiftly and Promptly." The man who was one of the architects of Obamacare evoked the ugly specter of science fiction films like *Logan's Run* with his eugenics-like rejection of life extension or quality health care for the elderly who have outlived their usefulness. Ezekiel was supposedly the inspiration for the "death panels" associated with Obamacare. In his 2009 paper, "Principles for Allocation of Scarce Medical Interventions," Rahm's brother advocated a system "which prioritizes younger people who have not yet lived a complete life" and also maintained that "allocation by age is not invidious discrimination." The AFL-CIO passed a resolution criticizing the Affordable Care Act, claiming it would "drive the costs of . . . union-administered plans, and other plans that cover unionized workers, to unsupportable levels." The Manhattan Institute for Policy Research claimed that in most states, health insurance rates will continue to rise dramatically because of Obamacare, by as much as 160 percent. Healthy young adults will be especially hard-hit; in senior fellow Avik Roy's words, "to pay for insurance that is even costlier than the coverage they already can't afford."[217]

Despite Republican efforts to replace Obamacare, health care is rapidly becoming another privilege that only the wealthy can afford. With its spiraling costs that no one is doing anything to control, it may well be the exclusive province of the wealthiest 20 percent of Americans in the near future. Rush Limbaugh, in a disturbing 2009 interview on William Shatner's *Raw Nerve* television program, argued that the poor have no inherent right to health care, any more than they'd have a right to a house on the beach. Limbaugh seriously suggested they should settle for a bungalow instead, meaning an even lower-quality version of health-care than the sloppy, incompetent medical industrial complex normally provides. Libertarian economist Tyler Cowen was blunt in sounding the same theme, recommending "A rejection of health care egalitarianism. . . . We need to accept the principle that sometimes poor people will die just because they are poor."[218] And Medicaid is hardly the answer, as Dori Hartley revealed in an article headlined "Too Poor for Health Care, Too Rich for Medicaid" published in the January 19, 2014, *Huffington Post*.

Because she made more than $241 a month, she didn't qualify for Medicaid assistance. You'd have to be virtually destitute to qualify for this kind of medical assistance aimed to help the poor.

One of Obama's most visible acts of instituting shared sacrifice was to raise Social Security taxes back up to 6.2 percent on January 1, 2013. The sacrifice from this, of course, fell solely on those making $119,000 per year or less, as the regressive Social Security tax is only imposed on the *first* $119,000 of income. It also only further exacerbated an unworkable situation; a Boston College study found in 2013 that there was now a $6.6 *trillion* "retirement deficit" in America—meaning the difference between what workers have been able to save for retirement and what they will actually need. For once, Rev. Al Sharpton asked a pertinent question in a December 5, 2012, blog entry: "If we did not share in the prosperity, why should we have to share in the sacrifice?" Of course, the good reverend has prospered quite nicely, as shown by his $5 million net worth, but the point is well taken. For only the third time in the past forty years, Social Security recipients received no cost-of-living adjustment in 2016.[219]

The wealthiest Americans don't worry about Social Security; the CEOs that sit on the powerful Business Roundtable hold an average of $14.6 million in their retirement accounts, or enough to pay them $86,043 every month once they retire. To cite just one example of these unfathomable retirement accounts, David Cote has $134.5 million in his Honeywell pension, which would pay him $795,134 per month! How many people work an entire lifetime without earning that much money? By contrast, the average American worker has saved up so little in retirement that he or she can expect a measly $71 per month during their golden years.[220]

Another exorbitant pension was even blasted by *Forbes.* McKesson, the nation's largest drug distributor, was allotting a $159 million pension for CEO John Hammergren, only fifty-four years old at the time. "Hammergren has pulled down hundreds of millions in compensation," Harvard Law Professor Jesse Fried noted,

"Even without the pension, it would very hard for him to spend all his money before he died." (In 2012, Hammergren was the highest-paid CEO in the nation, with a compensation package of $131 million for just that one year.) The only pension that has ever come close to the one Hammergren can get when he retires is the lump-sum pension benefit of $126 million paid to Richard Grasso, the former chairman of the New York Stock Exchange. The *Wall Street Journal* cited a 2012 study that revealed 60 percent of CEOs at the top S&P firms still get conventional pensions, with an average value of $11 million.[221] By 2016, the retirement assets of the richest one hundred CEOs equaled that of 41 percent of all American families.[222]

All these admonitions about sacrifice are not meant for the One Percent, or the top 20 percent. They are directed exclusively at the 80 percent of Americans who are either living paycheck to paycheck, or who are unemployed and facing the untold consequences associated with that. Ohio Democratic Senator Sherrod Brown attempted to get his peers in Congress to join in on all this shared sacrifice when he introduced the Shared Retirement Sacrifice Act of 2011. The bill would have required lawmakers to wait until age sixty-six to collect retirement; under the present system, they can get full pensions at the age of fifty. Brown explained his rationale behind the bill, saying, "I hear lots of members of Congress, particularly conservative members of Congress, say we should raise the retirement age for Social Security." As of October 2014, 601 retired members of Congress were collecting a pension based fully or in part on their service in Congress; the average pension amount was $72,660 for the older members who do not collect Social Security (Congress didn't pay into the Social Security system until 1984), while the other group was getting an annual pension of $41, 652, in addition to their Social Security checks.[223]

Almost fifteen thousand public retirees, including former Congressional leaders and a university president, are receiving six-figure pensions from a system that has a $674.2 billion shortfall. On average, one of every 125 retired federal civilian workers collects more than $100,000 in annual benefits, including ex-Speaker of the House Newt Gingrich. As the Third Way, a Washington, DC, research organization put it, "There are some pensions that make you question the system as a whole." Meanwhile, according to the Employee Benefit Research Institute, about half of all private-sector workers have no retirement plan other than Social Security. Irving K. Jordan Jr., former president of Gallaudet University, was the largest beneficiary, with $375,900 per year in retirement pay. Former Republican congressman Robert Michel collects $211,452, which is more than he was ever paid while in office. "Oh, for heaven's sake," Michel exclaimed when informed of his generous retirement, "I didn't realize it was up there." Former Vice President Dick Cheney's pension started in 2009, paying him $132,451 annually.[224] Al Gore was receiving $120,378 in the same year, while President George W. Bush was getting $196,700.[225] Unlike Social Security recipients, these wealthy public servants are unlikely to ever miss a yearly cost-of-living raise.

In many states, the situation is similar. California, for instance, was paying almost nine thousand retirees at least $100,000 annually in benefits as of 2011. The median state income there, meanwhile, is only $56,000. Police, firefighters, and correctional officers can receive 90 percent of their peak salaries for life upon retirement. One particularly egregious example was retired police chief Roy Campos, who was paid an unfathomable $594,000 in 2009 after cashing out his 3,300 hours of sick and vacation time.[226] Recently, it was reported that both Chicago and New York were paying more retired police officers and firefighters than active ones.[227] Much like the Social Security crisis, whereby there will be not be enough workers to pay all the baby boomers once they retire, this is an impossible mathematical equation that our leaders are avoiding with their customary brilliance.

So while those who already accrued fortunes during their working years collect lucrative retirement pay, employees in that unlucky 80 percent sector of Americans must learn to accept, at best, a 401(k) plan to which they largely contribute themselves. In April 2014, the *Associated Press* published the results of a survey that found a sadly familiar figure: 80 percent of Americans are struggling at a "near poverty" level. Oxford University Press concluded that 76 percent of white Americans are plagued by economic insecurity—defined as having experienced unemployment, a year or more of being on food stamps or other government aid, or having an income below 150 percent of the poverty line. The figures for minorities are even higher, although the gap is narrowing. Based on present trends, by 2030, around 85 percent of all working-age adults will experience bouts of economic insecurity. Earlier this year, it was widely reported that one in three Americans have *zero* retirement money.[228] Social Security itself estimates that at least 4 percent of workers are "never beneficiaries," or those who never made enough money to collect anything at retirement. With the rush to eliminate old-fashioned guaranteed pensions, and fewer younger workers even receiving a 401(k) plan, it is obvious that a continually increasing percentage of Americans will be fully dependent upon their Social Security income. And they want to raise the retirement age, and either cut Social Security or eliminate it.

Once again, shared sacrifice is only shared among those at the bottom.

10 NATURAL TALENT

Everything in life is luck.

—Donald Trump

SOMETIMES THOSE WHO MAKE IT do so despite not growing up in a stable, financially comfortable family, or being related to someone with influence. However, these persons usually succeed for one of two reasons: either they are exceptionally good looking, or they are physically large and strong.

The most popular spectator sport in America is professional football. Not far behind are college football, professional basketball, and college basketball. Pure genetics goes a long way in determining potential success in these sports. Someone like Shaquille O'Neal, for example, had such limited athletic skills that he would probably not have made his high school team if he had only been six feet tall. But the fact he was over seven feet tall, with a wide, powerful build, enabled him to prosper at basketball even though he couldn't dribble, shoot, or run very well. Even if one considers playing a game for a living "work," O'Neal never honed his skills at all (just look at his laughable free-throw shooting) and relied exclusively on overpowering the opposition in close proximity to the basket. Most dominant, big men in the history of basketball were dominant because they were big, not because they were exceptionally talented.

To play at the higher levels of basketball, one must be very tall. No matter how well you can shoot, or dribble, or pass, if your genes limit you to a height of five-foot-six, you are going to be very fortunate to make a high school team. This doesn't mean that every tall person is going to be a successful basketball player, but clearly most successful basketball players are tall. In football, the same thing applies to important positions such as wide receiver, tight end, offensive line, and defensive line. Most quarterbacks are well over six feet tall as well nowadays. So again, no matter how well you might be able to play the game of football, you'll be limited to beer leagues with your friends if your genes max you out at five-feet-five inches in height. Linemen, especially, possess virtually no special athletic skills at all beyond their abnormal size, which provides them with greater strength.

Because of the fact the marketplace compensates professional athletes in an extravagant way, enabling them to accrue more wealth in their short careers than most Americans can accumulate in fifty years of full-time employment, it's fair to ask if they are worth what they're being paid. Since genetics is purely random and is such a crucial factor in athletic success, isn't it fair to acknowledge its contribution? Pro sports pensions are the best in the business, outside of the ones devised by CEOs for themselves. Using numbers provided by *Investopedia,* an NBA player qualifies for a full pension after only three seasons of play. Where else can one collect retirement on three-years-worth of work? And the pension they get is pretty lucrative; the minimum yearly benefit presently is $56,988 upon retirement at age sixty-two. If one plays eleven seasons, it grows to $195,000 annually. NBA players also get a 401(k) plan, but it's probably a lot different than yours; the league matches player contributions at the rate of 140 percent. The NFL's pension plan is not nearly as good, but it still compares favorably to most in the private sector; players get $470 per month for every season they played and can start collecting full benefits at age fifty-five. Their 401(k) plan is great, though, as the league matches 200 percent of player contributions.

Nothing tops the pension that Major League Baseball players get. A major leaguer is eligible for the pension plan after only *forty-three days* of play, for which he would get an incredible $34,000 per year in retirement. One day on an active roster qualifies a player for full comprehensive medical benefits. The pension is so lucrative that numerous players with less than ten years in the league are receiving over $100,000 a year in benefits beginning at age sixty-two. NHL players do pretty well, too, as they can start collecting retirement at age forty-five, and if they played 160 games or more in the league (which is barely two seasons), they get $45,000 annually. The PGA is more hit or miss, as pension benefits are tied to success in tournaments, but the top players have millions in their retirement accounts.

Athletes are also able to supplement their millions with autograph signing sessions or speaking engagements, and all too often, they treat their adoring fans with disdain. The even wealthier team owners have effectively priced most of those adoring fans out of the sports market. As the *Chicago Sport and Society* put it, "in case you didn't notice, attending pro sporting events has become a pretty elitist activity. Right up there with lipoplasty and lunch on the veranda." This particular article focused on Chicago teams, but they mirror what is transpiring in every part of the country. The Chicago Cubs announced they were raising season-ticket prices by 20 percent following their 2016 World Series championship. The average price for a family of four to attend a Chicago Bears game in 2016 was nearly $528, without even factoring in any wildly overpriced items from concession stands. To illustrate how inflated these prices are in comparison with salaries, the article noted that in 1911, ticket prices for a Chicago White Sox baseball game ranged from 25 cents to $1, which would be about $6 to $24 today. The poor and working class could attend forty to fifty home games easily in those days, and afford the nickel sodas and ten-cent hot dogs as well.[229] In 1980, while working a relatively low-paid blue-collar job, I was spending $160 for season tickets to the Washington Capitals hockey team for good seats. I was able to console myself during the awful performances the Caps invariably put on in those days with large cups of beer that cost less than $2. In 2016, the Fan Cost Index estimated the average price of four adult tickets, two small draft beers, four small soft drinks, four hot dogs, parking for one car, two game programs, and two adult-size adjustable caps at each Major League Baseball park. The Boston Red Sox were the most expensive team to see in such a scenario, at a cost of $360.66, while the cheapest deal was with the Arizona Diamondbacks, at a mere $132.10. Needless to say, no working-class family (and obviously no poor family) could responsibly waste such an amount of money on a regular season baseball game, which are often relatively meaningless since teams play a 162-game schedule.

It costs an average of $103.27 to attend a Los Angeles Lakers regular season NBA game in 2016, and if you wanted to watch the New England Patriots play in 2016, the average ticket price was $347 to $596, depending upon the opponent. NFL tickets in general make it impossible for parents to take their kids out to the ball game in the traditional American manner. The supposedly fan-friendly, publicly owned Green Bay Packers charge $77 for the cheapest seats in legendary Lambeau Field. Two parents with two children would have to shell out $308 for seating alone to attend a single, regular season NFL game in Green Bay, often in frigid, inhospitable conditions. And parking is outrageous wherever you go. In Chicago, fans pay $46 to park at a Bears game, and each beer costs $9. Like so much else in our society, what used to be an event everyone could enjoy has become the province of the wealthiest 20 percent of our citizens. Corporations are largely responsible for artificially propping up attendance figures, doling out tickets to their employees as perks, and buying up the lavish box suites to impress their fellow elitists.

In November 2014, when Buffalo experienced a tremendous snowstorm, the Bills of the NFL had the audacity to ask fans to help shovel the four feet or more that covered their football stadium so that they could play a scheduled home game against the Jets. To quote a November 19, 2014, *Associated Press* report,

"The Buffalo Bills are looking for anyone with a snow shovel and plenty of spare time." Evidently, the notion of hiring professionals with huge plows didn't occur to these penny-pinching executives. The team's Twitter account indicated that the pay would be a less-than-scintillating $10 per hour. A public relations nightmare was averted when the ensuing criticism forced the NFL to veto the proposal. Much as these plutocratic owners expect taxpayers to build their stadiums for them, they expect their fanatical supporters to perform physical labor for them at bargain-basement rates. This idea was hardly new. Minnesota Vikings fans once trudged proudly into snow-covered stands at the University of Minnesota stadium to clear them in time for a rare NFL game there. In December 2013, Green Bay Packers fans turned out in droves to help remove snow from Lambeau Field. This is a long-standing tradition in football-crazy Green Bay, and according to a June 2, 2014, story from *Fox News,* the pay rate is an identical $10 per hour. As John D. Rockefeller said, competition is a sin.

The other way in which genetics helps determine success is in the area of natural physical attributes. Especially considering the present-day obsession over "hot" males and females, being born with the genetics of a well-proportioned body, attractive features, and above-average height go a long way in assisting one's career path. Trophy wives are an accepted part of our civilization, after all. As *Business Insider* acknowledged, "Studies have shown that attractive people are usually hired sooner, get promotions more quickly, and are paid more than their less-attractive coworkers." Professor Dario Maestripieri explained in *Psychology Today* that, "Good-looking people are more appealing as potential sex partners, and other people choose to interact with them, to spend time near them, talk with them, buy insurance from them, and hire them as employees." Attractive people have other desirable traits, such as supreme self-confidence and self-esteem, which are directly related to their good looks. Studies at Rice University and the University of Houston found that those interviewing for jobs who had facial blemishes or any disfigurement (birthmarks, scars, etc.) were more likely to be rated poorly by the interviewers. The interviewers also tended to recall less-information about these less attractive job candidates.[230] Does anyone, can anyone, earn being attractive?

As an article on *AOL Jobs* put it, "In this tough economy, it appears that one of the things beauty does is get you a job." There are even special websites devoted to beautiful job seekers everywhere, with taglines like "More Beauty! More Business!" as they strive to match up attractive job candidates with physically discerning employers. Even the CEOs of larger companies, yet another study found, are considered more attractive than the CEOs of smaller ones. There is no federal legislation against employers hiring on the basis of physical attractiveness. Abercrombie & Fitch, for instance, has a "look policy," which survives despite a lawsuit alleging it was racially discriminatory. Now the company simply looks for good-looking people of all races. The *Economist* has referred to this "attractiveness discrimination," or the practice of "hiring hotties."

Certainly, everyone can make themselves appear more attractive, and most of us strive to look as good as we possibly can. But there is no denying that the task is much easier if one is just born good-looking. Are good-looking people worth more than average-looking and below-average-people? Do they deserve to be paid more, and treated better, simply because of their genetics? Dr. Gordon Patzer, in his book *Looks: Why They Matter More Than You Ever Imagined,* argued that, "Physical beauty comes with tremendous power, and tremendous benefits. Those who possess it are generally luckier in love, more likely to be popular, and more apt to get better grades in school. . . . Recent studies document that people blessed with good looks earn about 10 percent more than their average-looking colleagues. They are also more likely to get hired and promoted at work." Penelope Trunk, author of *Brazen Careerist: The New Rules For Success,* is more blunt, declaring that those who aren't blessed with beautiful genes must work out regularly, get plastic surgery, dye their hair, and fix their teeth, just in order to compete. Anyone who has watched movies, or television shows, or listened to talk radio, in the past few decades, understands just how essential sexually attractive women, especially, are to our culture. They are overtly used to sell everything from beer to car insurance. Look at the way decidedly unattractive men rate females on a scale of one to ten, and imagine how empty those who are rated a four or lower must feel. Could anything be done to boost their self-esteem? Is it fair that the women who have done nothing other than be blessed with a fortunate gene pool earn almost limitless compliments, and benefit from nearly risk-free chances at success, while their plain-looking female peers are relegated to second-class citizenship?

"An honest employer will tell you that it pays to hire good-looking staff," according to Greg Hodge, managing director of BeautifulPeople.com. This sort of very real discrimination is just about the only form of discrimination these days that not only is permitted but is openly boasted about. This whole area is problematic; after all, who wants to be classified as ugly or unattractive, and who would be willing to claim discrimination based upon that?

A 2014 study by Princeton University gave more detailed statistics on the "attractive" gap in employment. According to this research, attractive people have a better than 72 percent chance of getting a callback after a job interview, earn approximately $230,000 more than their plain peers during the course of a lifetime, and have an average salary of just under $79,000 annually (versus $50,323 for those unlucky, non-"hot" workers). The height gap alone is appreciable; people who were six feet tall at age eighteen earned an average of nearly $12,000 more per year than those who were only five-foot-one at age eighteen. No statistic is more glaring than the fact the average Fortune 500 CEO is six feet tall, while 90 percent of all CEOs are above the average male height of five-foot-ten. Swedish research showed that taller people, on average, get a better education.[231] "The truth is," declared Arianne Cohen, author of *The Tall Book,* "tall people do make more money." This advantage exists even with teenagers, as researchers determined also that a taller male at age sixteen will wind up making more money as an adult than a shorter peer, regardless of how tall they each become as adults. Many studies show that overweight women, especially, face discrimination in hiring, pay-rate levels, and receiving raises.

The superficial nature of our society is revealed in nearly every study done on these subjects. A 2010 study by Queensland University of Technology found that blonde women are paid more than 7 percent higher than their non-blonde female peers in the workforce. The study correlated this difference to the same gap one would see from getting an entire extra year of education. Did these women earn the genes that gave them blonde hair? A study funded by Proctor & Gamble, Harvard Medical School, and others concluded that women who wear makeup earn as much as 30 percent more than their female coworkers who don't, and are also ranked as more trustworthy and competent. Yale University research found that beautiful workers earn an average of 5 percent extra for their looks, while those deemed unattractive can make as much as 9 percent less because of their physical appearance.[232] How do you earn the genes that solely dictate how tall you'll be? Did the tall and the attractive work hard to get these kinds of advantages?

When I was a volunteer at a local organization that helped disabled adults lead productive lives, I was impressed with how they would kick off their annual banquet by playing the full clip of Susan Boyle's 2009 appearance on the *Britain's Got Talent* television program. Listening to her sing *I Dreamed a Dream*, and watching the startled reactions from host Simon Cowell and everyone else in the crowd, was truly inspirational. But the very fact that Susan Boyle, a woman with all her mental and physical faculties intact, could shock the world with her vocal abilities is very telling. The reason she became such a huge story, of course, was because of her ordinary, not terribly attractive, physical appearance. Audiences have been conditioned to think that only beautiful women have this kind of talent. Boyle understandably struggled with her newfound notoriety, and much of the public probably still blanches when they see the person behind that beautiful, powerful singing voice. As always, there is a double standard here, as male singers have never had to be, and still don't have to be, exceptionally good-looking in order to succeed.

Female journalists, even at the local level, and virtually all the on-air reporters, are, almost to a person, very attractive physically. They often appear indistinguishable from aspiring actresses or models. The few who aren't good-looking are so rare they stand out like sore thumbs. It's astonishingly common for former NFL cheerleaders to gravitate to the seemingly incongruous world of journalism; there are a myriad of examples of this on the website *UltimateCheerleaders. com* Discussion of women in broadcasting invariably reverts to the question of their lack of representation, not the disproportionate number of exceptionally attractive female journalists.

However we look at it, no one can deny that physically attractive people are treated preferentially by nearly every individual and every institution in our society. Hard work has nothing to do with that, and it isn't something that can be earned. Like so many good and bad things in life, it's purely a matter of luck. The same thing can be said for athletes whose success is directly tied to their physical stature, which is solely dictated by genetics. They may have put their noses to the grindstone and perfected their skills. But as Barack Obama said, they didn't build their success without some help.

11 The Good Old Days

Every time you raise the minimum wage, the people who are hurt the most are the most vulnerable.

—Ted Cruz

As far back as 1832, the New England Association of Farmers, Mechanics, and other Workingmen condemned the practice of child labor, declaring, "Children should not be allowed to labor in the factories from morning till night, without any time for healthy recreation and mental culture."[233] By 1836, Massachusetts required that children under fifteen years of age working in factories attend school at least three months out of the year, and in 1842, the state limited children's workdays to ten hours. In 1892, the Democratic Party adopted a plank in their platform to ban children under fifteen from working in factories. It wasn't until 1938, when the Fair Labor Standards Act was passed, that minimum age and hours of work for children were regulated by federal law.

Americans of my generation took for granted such things as the forty-hour workweek, vacation and sick leave, and pensions. Few realize how important the Fair Labor Standards Act was, and how the rules it established are being gradually torn away. Walmart, for instance, has regularly flouted the requirement to pay overtime to workers who put in more than forty hours a week, or eight hours a day. In the first of dozens of similar lawsuits, a federal jury found in 2002 that Walmart had forced employees in Oregon to work unpaid overtime from 1994–1999. In 2007, the Department of Labor announced that the retail giant had agreed to pay $33.5 million in back wages, plus interest, to settle a federal lawsuit accusing the company of violating overtime laws for 86,680 employees.[234] Employees working in Walmart warehouses filed lawsuits as well, alleging they were paid for fewer hours than they worked. The latest Walmart settlement included a $463,815 civil penalty imposed by the Department of Labor, for "the repeat nature of the violations."[235]

Despite all this controversy, Barack Obama nominated former Walmart Foundation President Sylvia Mathews Burwell to head the Office of Management and Budget in 2013.[236] Obama then infuriated what remaining labor activists there are in America by showcasing Walmart's advances in energy efficiency. Former Labor Secretary Robert Reich reacted indignantly, posting on Facebook, "What numbskull in the White House arranged this?"[237] Fast-food workers in three states accused McDonald's of similar practices, including forcing workers to clock out but remain at work, docking pay for the purchase of company-required uniforms, and failing to pay employees overtime.[238]

With the transformation to a global economy, and the disastrous trade deals that led directly to companies relocating factories in Third-World nations, it's fair to assume that many of the products we buy every year have been made by the estimated seventy-three million children between the ages of ten and fourteen who are part of labor forces around the world. Using statistics from the International Labor Organization, in India, 14.4 percent of children fourteen and younger are employed as child laborers. In Bangladesh, it's an astounding 30 percent, and Kenya leads them all with 41 percent of its children working. Altogether in Asia, over forty-four million children are forced into labor, while Africa has twenty-four million and Latin America five million children in the workforce. The economic reasons for forcing industry to remain in the United States should be obvious to all. Add to this the pure immorality of contributing to the sickening spread of child labor in the twenty-first century, and you have another sound reason to passionately oppose the concept of free trade. Much of President Trump's populist appeal centers around the issue of trade and differs from normal party rhetoric. As Trump explained in one of the 2016 presidential debates, "I did disagree with Ronald Reagan very strongly on trade. I disagreed with him. We should have been much tougher on trade even then. I've been waiting for years. Nobody does it right." Trump referred to NAFTA as "the worst trade deal maybe ever signed anywhere."[239]

Project Censored reported in 1995 that child labor was alive and well again in the United States. "Child labor today is a point where violations are greater than at any point during the 1930s," Jeffrey Newman of the National Child Labor Committee said. An NBC Bay Area investigative unit found, in 2012, that dozens of children were working the fields in the San Joaquin and Sacramento Valleys, some as young as eight years old. The reporters were able to determine the children often worked as many as ten hours per day in temperatures over one hundred degrees. The unit further discovered that these youngsters were working all over the country, from North Carolina to California. A perplexing exemption in the 1938 Fair Labor Standards Act permits children twelve, or even younger in some circumstances, to legally work in agriculture. An effort by the Department of Labor to end this practice met with strong opposition from growers, large food processors, and producers.[240] A similar report about these child migrant workers in Oregon appeared the following month in *The Oregonian*.[241] The Economic Policy Institute recently reported that four states have lifted restrictions on child labor. Wisconsin, with austerity measure devotee Scott Walker as governor, abolished a previous law limiting sixteen- or seventeen-year-olds to no more than five hours of work on school days. The same report noted that Mississippi had adopted a law that bans cities and counties from "adopting any minimum wage, or paid or unpaid sick leave rights for local workers." In December 2016, Ohio's state legislature banned cities from raising local minimum wages.[242] Ohio joined Idaho and seventeen other states in recent years that have passed such "preemption laws."

CNN aired a report on October 1, 2012, about the prevalence of child labor in China. Many of these Chinese sweatshops manufacture goods that are shipped to the United States and sold in our stores. Reporter Leslie Chang spent two years cultivating relationships with factory workers in south China. These young workers labored long days, sometimes for weeks on end; the most lenient factory gave them one day off per week. The mandated Chinese workday is eleven hours, but this was routinely ignored, as was the minimum wage. Pay was withheld for the most minor of infractions, and she noticed countless safety violations. Workers often had to sleep ten to fifteen in a room, with fifty people sharing a single bathroom. According to a 2016 investigation, China's Pegatron Corps., one of the largest factories assembling Apple's iPhones, pays workers so little that they are forced to work excessive overtime just in order to eke out a living.[243] A 2016 report from Verisk Maplecroft warned companies that they run "an extreme risk" of associating with modern forms of slavery by doing business in both China and India.[244] *This* is the regime America and other purportedly "free" nations are so anxious to do business with, and, increasingly it seems, to emulate.

IMF Managing Director Christine Lagarde praised China for its efforts to "rebalance its economy" that same year.[245] The Hoover Institution advertised the establishment's fondness for the world's largest totalitarian state with a March 22, 2012, article entitled, "Importing China's Economic Model." The Institution acknowledged that American business leaders are growing more and more smitten with "Chinese authoritarian chic." Only a depraved media like ours could even attempt to make authoritarianism seem cool. The story quoted an earlier *Wall Street Journal* article by retired Microsoft COO Robert Herbold in which he gushed over China's fiscal soundness and old-fashioned Communist five-year plans. Herbold cautioned that the United States was losing ground to China in the global competitiveness arena and declared that big changes were needed. As the Hoover Institution noted, these changes include fixing the budget and the burden of entitlements, implementing an aggressive five-year debt-reduction plan, and moving beyond political gridlock to approve some winning plans. We can easily envision just how this debt reduction would work; more of the same austerity measures, with the wealthy always exempt from them. The mantra of pay more and get less. And, of course, we are all-too aware of how concerned our leaders are about those dastardly entitlements that benefit the common riffraff. Coca-Cola's CEO Muhtar Kent echoed these sentiments, as the article informed readers that he, "believes that in many respects, the United States is a less friendly place to do business compared to China."

As noted previously, the Fair Standards Labor Act of 1938 first established a federal minimum wage. States are free to have a higher minimum wage, but the present federal rate of $7.25 was established in 2009. In most areas of the country today, it would be necessary to have a minimum, full-time wage of at least $15 per hour for a single person just to eke out a halfway decent existence in a one-bedroom apartment. The present minimum wage would come to $15,080 per year, or $3,400 below the federal poverty line for a family of three. In 2015, Seattle passed a law mandating a $15 hourly minimum wage. In 2016, both New York and California passed laws mandating a state minimum wage of $15 per hour. Both measures will be implemented incrementally and easily overtake Minnesota's $9.50 state minimum wage, which was previously the highest in the nation. President Obama issued an empty Executive Order in February 2014, which raised the federal minimum wage for government contractors only to $10.10 per hour. But even this was too much for many Republicans. Tennessee's Senator Lamar Alexander publicly declared that he doesn't believe in the concept of a minimum wage during a June 2013 Senate debate. The most common argument against raising the minimum wage is that businesses will then just pass the cost on to consumers. Panera Bread CEO Rob Shaich, a big Obama supporter who has publicly advocated a minimum wage increase, nevertheless predictably told *Fox News* in a May 2014 interview that such an increase would mean higher prices for consumers.

Without any government interference, nearly all businesses would eliminate vacation and sick time, yearly raises, pensions, and any other employee benefit. There would be terrific abuses in terms of health-code violations and worker safety. Almost all businesses routinely pass along the costs of increased taxes, health and safety regulations, minimum wage increases, and now Obamacare, to the consumer, because there is nothing to stop them from doing it. There is no logical economic rationale behind this, but since all sacrifice has to come from the 80 percent of those outside even the periphery of the inner circle, and all the well-paid experts maintain these are ironclad rules of the marketplace, everyone just accepts it. These costs are never passed on to upper management, in terms of decreased or eliminated bonuses or salaries, and their gargantuan increases in compensation over the past few decades somehow did not automatically impact consumers. Just as salary freezes apply strictly to the common workforce, every small gain in wages by the lowest-paid employees usually results in price increases for everyone, thereby mitigating much of the increase. Any minimum wage is relatively worthless anyhow without a corresponding maximum wage, in my view.

Just about half of all the states in the union misleadingly call themselves right-to-work states. This law ostensibly gives workers the right to decide whether or not they want to join a union, but in reality, it empowers the corporate campaign to strip unions of their influence. The law certainly doesn't guarantee anyone employment, as the name implies. In 2000, the already weakened AFL-CIO made the point that right-to-work laws lead directly to lower wages and deteriorating conditions for employees. Wisconsin Governor Scott

Walker created great controversy with his 2011 budget repair proposal that would have mandated additional contributions from state and local government workers to their health-care plans and pensions. The proposal would have led to an estimated 8 percent decrease in average take-home pay. The bill would also have eliminated many collective bargaining rights. In a brazen political move aimed at what he perceived as a sympathetic voting bloc, Walker exempted police and firefighters from the law.

Yet another way in which businesses have cut costs is in the rise of unpaid internships. These internships were historically almost always reserved for college graduates, or at least those pursuing a college degree, and in the past they generally paid a nominal salary. As the *New York Times* reported, "No one tracks how many college graduates take internships, but employment experts and intern advocates say the number has risen substantially in recent years." The article chronicled the plight of interns who couldn't break free from the unpaid cycle.[246] The new norm is that in many industries, the bottom of the job pyramid is no longer entry level but unpaid internship. Some unpaid interns are fighting back; a lawsuit victory by interns working for Fox Searchlight Pictures on the movie *The Black Swan* has resulted in similar complaints against Conde Nast, Warner Music, and Gawker Media. A Fair Pay Campaign is lobbying for the White House to pay its interns. Former child stars Mary-Kate and Ashley Olsen have built a $1 billion fashion empire, but they were sued for nonpayment by forty past and present interns in 2015.[247] Unpaid internships enable companies to employ workers without having to give them any financial compensation; is this really all that different from indentured servitude, or even slavery? New guidelines issued by the Department of Labor in 2014 somewhat improved the situation, as they banned interns from being used in sales, and decreed that they couldn't be used to displace paid workers.

While implementing a disastrous, failed drug war, our ruling elite have tolerated, and probably enabled, the laundering of billions of drug money through the largest banks imaginable—like Bank of America, J. P. Morgan, and HBSC. The FBI publicly disclosed the fact that the brother of a Mexican drug cartel leader had used a Bank of America account to buy and sell horses with the ill-gotten proceeds.[248] According to *Forbes*, Bank of America CEO Brian Moynihan was paid over $16 million in 2015, an increase of 23 percent from the previous year.[249] Wachovia and Wells Fargo (with Warren Buffet being a notably large investor), which bought Wachovia in 2008, also provided bank accounts for Mexican cartel drug lords.[250] In late 2016, Wells Fargo CEO John Stumpf left the company after thirty years, with a staggering $130 million package.[251] The average worker with that many years serving one company would be fortunate to be given a farewell luncheon. This astounding payoff came in spite of the massive scandal, exposed earlier in 2016, involving the creation of over two million phony bank accounts, which resulted in Wells Fargo firing some 5,300 employees.[252] It is an acknowledged fact that 8 percent of all international trade is connected to the drug business. Meanwhile, the marijuana industry, now legalized in Colorado, is unable to access essential banking services.[253] The failure to prosecute these too-big-to-fail institutions, when untold numbers of poor persons are languishing in prison for decades after being caught with small amounts of these same drugs, underscores the point that there are dual standards of justice in America.

Apparently debtors' prisons are making a comeback. Fox News ran a report on December 28, 2013, that, "As if out of a Charles Dickens novel, people struggling to pay overdue fines and fees associated with court costs for even the simplest infractions are being thrown in jail across the United States." The jails, known as debtors' prisons, once flourished in the United States and Europe but were thought to have been eradicated long ago. "It's a waste of taxpayer resources, and it undermines the integrity of the justice system," a staff attorney for the ACLU's National Prison Project told Fox News. A new, more extensive set of such fines are being imposed by states and counties, in a supposed effort to deal with budget deficits. Of

those who owe these fines, not surprisingly, around 80 percent qualify as indigent. Some of these fees, which people are being dragged
into court over, actually involve costs incurred while the individual was incarcerated; this could be everything from toilet paper to
the bed in the inmate's cell. As the story further reported, "Many
jurisdictions have taken to hiring private collection/probation companies to go after debtors." Pamela Dembe, president of the First
Judicial District of Pennsylvania, told reporters that an estimated
four hundred thousand residents owed the city of Philadelphia
money. Attempting to justify these new authoritarian fines and the
truly draconian debtors' prison-type punishment, Dembe stated,
"If the defendant doesn't pay, law-abiding taxpayers must pay these
costs." The ACLU studied eleven different counties and found that
seven were operating what they termed "de facto debtor's prisons."
In Huron County, Ohio, a full 20 percent of all arrests in the second half of 2012 were for failure to pay fines. In a similar vein, debt
collectors have started working with state and local governments to
suspend drivers' licenses, block registration renewals, and assess fees
that can carry an interest rate of 100 percent for unpaid tolls.[254] In
some cases, violators can be sent to jail.

The *New York Times* ran an editorial on July 13, 2012, headlined, "Return of Debtors' Prisons." The flagship newspaper of the
establishment stated, "judges routinely jail people to make them pay
fines even when they have no money to pay. Felony offenders who
have completed their prison sentences are often sent back to jail
when they cannot pay fees and fines they owe because they could not
earn money while locked up." The problem has grown more severe,
according to the *Times,* because of "budget-strapped state courts
looking for sources of revenue and ever more poor people becoming
ensnared in the court system." The paper cited a ridiculous example
of a woman convicted for a drug offense, being charged for things
such as postage and using judicial computers. Marie Diamond,
writing for *Think Progress* in December 2011, also noted that some
debtors are now required to *pay* for their time spent in jail, which

would, of course, exacerbate their precarious financial situation and make it even more unlikely that they'd have the wherewithal to pay any more "fines" upon release. In late 2015, both CNN and the The *Huffington Post* ran separate stories on the rising prevalence of these draconian institutions, thought to have been abolished by our more enlightened forebears.

These kinds of barbaric measures are not even cost effective; the ACLU and the Brennan Center estimated that counties are losing thousands of dollars each year directly from locking poor people in these unofficial debtors' prisons. And outsourcing plays a vital role here, as it does now throughout the business world. Many municipalities are utilizing the services of Georgia-based Judicial Corrections Services, a private probation firm that boasted $13 million in revenue in 2009 through its handling of debt collection. This company's practice of piling additional fees on top of the defendants' debt was blasted by one Shelby County, Alabama, judge as "a judicially sanctioned extortion racket."[255] *CBS News* reported, on April 5, 2013, that "Roughly a third of US states today jail people for not paying off their debts, from court-related fines and fees to credit card and car loans." With more and more financially strapped consumers unable to pay their bills, a whole cottage industry of collection agencies and firms dedicated to buying what they refer to as junk debt has been born. This is very similar to what has been a staple of the real estate industry for decades; loan companies buying and selling mortgages. Debtors' prisons, like regular ones, will never include any wealthy inmates.

There are companies all across America specializing in lending money to those who are in such hopeless situations they're willing to pay sinfully usurious interest rates. A story in the January 20, 2011, *Texas Observer* described these predatory loan shark companies: "Cash America and other payday lending companies advertise heavily on street corners in low-income neighborhoods and offer easy cash on the Internet to borrowers in financial crisis. These 'easy' loans carry jacked-up fees and exorbitant interest rates. In Texas, an eight-day payday loan carries a 1,153 percent annual rate." The Center for Responsible Lending found that the average payday loan carries an effective interest rate of *391 to 521 percent,* while the typical payday borrower remains in debt for 212 days.

Former NBA star Magic Johnson, who is worth $500 million, became a spokesman for Rent-a-Center. As consumer advocate Edmund Mierzwinski told *Daily Finance,* "There is nothing good about rent to own. . . . People will never get ahead with it. Rent to own promises the dream of ownership and then takes it back with a one-hundred-week contract. It's very difficult to meet the terms of the contract and when you don't meet the terms, they may come and violate the debt collection laws. I thought Magic Johnson made enough money playing for the Lakers." In 2009, the Washington State Attorney General sued Rent-a-Center, charging them with an assortment of anticonsumer, illegal practices. Johnson also served as a pitchman for Jackson Hewitt's tax refund anticipation loans, which only appeal to those in true economic despair and carry an annual interest rate of 100 percent in some cases. Like Eastern Motors and similar companies, Rent-a-Center and what Mierzwinski accurately labeled the "predatory lending industry" have a long, documented history of targeting low-income minority communities.[256] Gary Rivlin, author of the book *Broke, USA: From Pawnshops to Poverty, Inc.,* added, "The brilliance of rent-to-own is they figured out how to sell a person a TV for $1,500 that would cost something like $600 with a credit card. Really, Magic? I loved you, I rooted for you, and that's what you're lending your name to?" Magic Johnson, like George Lopez, Russell Simmons, and Kim Kardashian, also lent his name to a prepaid debit card, which always carries excessive fees and again appeals only to the poorest people in America. When *BuzzFeed* asked Magic Johnson Enterprises to comment on these issues, they declined. Every year, the NBA gives out a special Magic Johnson Award, which is supposed to go to someone of especially reputable character, a genuinely good guy.

Businesses taking advantage of the most economically vulnerable people in our society is hardly a new phenomenon. This subject was covered extensively in an eye-opening piece by Stephanie Mencimer, in the *Washington City Paper,* on March 19, 1999, headlined: "LemonAid—The Car Might Quit on You, But the Loan Never Will." In one case Mencimer cited, a woman was sold a lemon, and wrecked the car when the brakes failed, but despite the fact the vehicle was totaled, Credit Acceptance Corporation sued her and won a judgment permitting them to garnish from $250–300 out of every paycheck. She'd been ripped off from the outset, having been charged a 22 percent interest rate, and was effectively paying $8,000 for a car that had a blue book value of only $3,000 in pristine condition.

Incredibly, the poor even pay more for insurance. A 2012 study by the Consumer Federation of America found that "Low-income drivers are routinely charged higher auto insurance premiums than well-heeled car owners." This is because the insurance industry factors in elements such as occupation, credit history, education, and residence location, resulting in the poor being routinely labeled higher risks and thus subject to higher rates. The report found that the exorbitant costs of insurance made driving effectively unaffordable for many low-income households, leaving them at a further disadvantage in the rat race by restricting where they can work, shop, find day care, or go to school. The study also exposed the inconsistency of the industry; it apparently doesn't factor in the fact that the poor drive only about half the annual miles the richest 20 percent of Americans do, due to the cost of gas and car maintenance, which should theoretically lower their risk. Estimates vary on how much more the poor have to pay for the privilege of driving, but various comparisons estimate the difference as at least $300 annually, with perhaps as much as $1,000 per year.[257] And *America Online* reported on January 28, 2013: "Even if they have better driving records, researchers found that drivers in lower-and-middle income brackets were charged higher premiums than well-to-do drivers in

66 percent of the cases studied. . . . In more than 60 percent of cases studied, the safer driver was charged at least 25 percent more than the one with a checkered driving record." Once again, we see the marketplace charging those who have the least means to afford it more than anyone else for a product that is practically mandatory in our society.

Even twenty-five years ago, would anyone have believed we'd see movements to abolish the minimum wage, to eliminate overtime, or to bring back debtors' prisons? The return of child labor? What would Charles Dickens or any other truly liberal nineteenth-century reformer think of our world?

12 Why What Pays What

When somebody says it's not about the money, it's about the money.

—H. L. Mencken

ALL OF US UNDERSTAND THAT the modern capitalist marketplace has determined that employees in upper management are worth tremendous salaries and unlimited perks and benefits. No one is considered more valuable to our society, according to the marketplace, than CEOs of large companies. Depending on the source, it appears that the average Chief Executive Officer makes as much as 475 times the compensation of the average worker. Japan, on the opposite end of the spectrum, pays their CEOs on average only eleven times what they pay workers. The next closest country to the United States is Venezuela, where CEOs make a comparatively paltry fifty times what average employees make. Research from *Bloomberg* indicates that the ratio of CEO-to-worker pay has increased an incredible 1,000 percent since 1950. And that 1,000 percent figure uses a much more conservative present estimate of a 204 to 1 CEO-to-worker ratio. The AFL-CIO puts the ratio at 354 to 1. Whatever it is, it's clear that the gap is huge, growing larger all the time, and the extreme difference is a uniquely American phenomena. A particularly egregious case was that of JCPenney's CEO Ron Johnson, who had been making 1,795 times the pay of an average worker at his company before being ousted for poor performance.[258]

So what is it that makes a CEO worth such astronomical sums? Normally, we hear vague rhetoric about leadership, vision, or changing the culture, in terms of desirable executive traits. As noted, there are those persistent references to some talent they possess, which is impossible to define or quantify. We know they go to a lot of meetings, some of them held in swanky resorts. They very rarely produce anything of substance, such as a valuable product or innovation that results in the quality of life improving for everyone. They are normally shrewd only in the sense that they have manipulated the system—often through insider knowledge and almost always with valuable connections—and have accumulated a great deal of money in the process. When we meet a CEO, or hear one speak, we don't shake our heads in awe; they aren't that impressive in any way, other than in the astronomical financial compensation they command. Certainly, they are self-confident, but great wealth cannot help but inspire supreme self-confidence. They certainly aren't renaissance men or women.

Every year, *Parade* magazine runs a cover story on "What People Earn." It's always attracted my attention, because it unintentionally exposes what an unfair system of income distribution America has. From the April 15, 2016, issue, we learn that a bridge operator in Seattle earns $53,575, the International Olympic Committee Chairman $242,000, a Wisconsin Walmart sales associate $20,615, a legal videographer in Colorado $9,865, an Arizona blogger $150,000, an Arizona professional dog sitter $7,895, a Michigan teacher $52,000, a Pennsylvania high school cafeteria worker $4,636, an Oklahoma Uber driver $42,000, a Florida corrections officer $36,900, a middle school special education teacher in Colorado $46,400, and a Virginia payroll technician $36,000.

This is juxtaposed against the $1.7 billion a Chicago hedge fund manager made, CNN's Anderson Cooper's $11 million, actor Leonardo DiCaprio's $29 million, race car driver Dale Earnhardt Jr.'s $23.8 million, rapper Jay Z's $56 million, Lady Gaga's $59 million, chef Gordon Ramsey's $60 million, and Taylor Swift's estimated $80 million. They all pay the same price for food and other necessities of life.

The salaries for ESPN's talking heads are unbelievable, considering their job consists of talking about sports, something most fans do every day around the watercooler. Tony Kornheiser and Michael Wilbon were paid $1.5 million each per year for their *Pardon the Interruption* program, as of 2010.[259] They both signed extensions in 2016 for an undisclosed sum. Dan Patrick pulls down a nice $5 million annually from ESPN. CBS Sports pays announcer Jim Nantz the same yearly salary, and Fox broadcaster Joe Buck makes $5 million as well. Bob Costas and Al Michaels get $5 million each, leading me to believe this is some kind of a standard top-tier announcer's salary. Jim Rome, between his radio and TV shows, makes an incomprehensible $30 million a year, and has built a $95 million fortune. These figures all came from Celebrity Net Worth. It's become common once a high-profile (or even a mediocre) athlete retires to instantly be handed a lucrative deal by ESPN or another network to provide on-air sports commentary. Most of them do little more than yell or laugh hysterically at each other. Yet they're getting millions, while the boys at the barbershop or the local bar are spending what little extra cash they have for the privilege of discussing the same subjects with each other.

What makes an ESPN talking head worth so much more than a teacher, who is paid an average of $77,957 in New York (the highest state average)? Why do high-profile journalists, sports, and otherwise, get their impressive compensation, while physical laborers cannot earn more than a minimum wage or slightly higher? Those who have the money make the rules, and the rules they've established decree that the hardest jobs by any measure, the ones that require a lot of standing, moving, and lifting, almost always pay far less than the jobs that mandate the ordering and overseeing of all that labor. A disinterested observer would have to conclude that those who clean the toilets and scrub the floors are doing much harder, and more valuable work, than the vice presidents, analysts, managers, and directors being paid at a much higher rate. The explanation "I'm paid for what I know, not what I do" was a defense mechanism invented for just this reason.

"Big wheels," as they used to be called, or "suits," don't ever appear to be doing much of anything. And based on the CEOs we've examined, they often don't appear to know much, either.

If millions of red-blooded American males all over the country are at least as expert in their knowledge of sports and have shown a propensity for making educated observations, flavored with wit and passion, in countless discussions at home, in bars and parties, or around the workplace, then shouldn't we question why the few who do make it into this much desired profession are compensated so generously? There are only so many people who have the aptitude to be a brain surgeon, for instance, and it is one of the most important jobs imaginable. It stands to reason, therefore, that brain surgeons ought to be compensated accordingly. If a skill is rare, it is normally deemed more valuable by the marketplace. By any measure, sports commentary is not rare, requires no special education or training, and can be done proficiently by literally millions of people. So why, then, does it pay so well? Should a Bob Costas or an Al Michaels really be making more than a brain surgeon? How does that make sense, in terms of the marketplace always being right?

How do we logically explain Don King's incredible success story? King started out as a two-bit numbers runner and was convicted twice of murder; in the second case, he was imprisoned for stomping an employee to death who owed him $600. As King would later describe it, "These are the things that happen."[260] The judge nonsensically reduced King's second-degree murder conviction to "nonnegligent manslaughter," and he served just four years in prison. Exactly how does one go from being a common thug incarcerated for murder to positioning one's self to promote the fights of Muhammed Ali, the most celebrated sports figure of his era? Even the mainstream media has sometimes wondered about King's connections. During a 1992 Senate investigation, King invoked the Fifth Amendment in response to questions about his ties to mobster John Gotti. Predictably, King has reacted to any allegations of Mafia ties by calling them racist.

King's sordid story was covered in Jack Newfield's book *The Life and Crimes of Don King: The Shame of Boxing in America.* This decidedly uncouth character has somehow managed to build a $150 million fortune.

King's primary rival in the world of boxing promotion was Bob Arum. Arum's success is almost as dubious as King's; while he came from a totally different world, attending Harvard Law School and working as a Justice Department attorney in the 1960s, he inexplicably gravitated to the shady, mob-infested field of prize fighting.[261] In 2004, the FBI investigated Arum for being involved in fixing a fight against his own fighter. Arum has made even more money than King from his sordid business, with an estimated net worth of $200 million. How can anyone maintain that he has earned this kind of wealth? Boxing has always been, in my view, only a few steps ahead of cockfighting or dogfighting.

My friends and I used to play a game at parties called "Why are they famous?" Everyone would take turns coming up with names that had achieved notoriety without any clear reason behind it. I remember Dick Clark was always one of the first to be mentioned. When Clark died in 2012, he left behind a $200 million fortune. That's pretty good for someone working in show business that couldn't act, sing, direct, write, or dance. Ryan Seacrest seems destined to be an even more successful version of Dick Clark; he has already accumulated an incomprehensible $250 million, with a similar skill set. Simon Cowell is the British version of Seacrest and has amassed some $400 million. Paris Hilton, already destined for great wealth as an heiress to the hotel fortune, has earned $100 million on her own doing . . . well, mostly posing for paparazzi. Sean Combs, known variously as Puff Daddy, P Diddy, or just plain Diddy, is the biggest name in the rap industry without even having the talent of a rapper. In one of those unexplained gaps in the narrative, Combs formed Bad Boy Records, in conjunction with industry giant Arista, after he'd been fired by his previous company. Combs was a poor kid from Harlem; his father was a criminal who was shot to death at a young age. So how does this all add up? Why would a corporate giant like Arista offer someone of his background and limited skills an opportunity to jointly own a new rap label?

Robert Mapplethorpe was a photographer who burst into prominence in the 1980s with pictures of himself with a bullwhip inserted in his anus and the like. He died in 1989 of AIDS, but the Robert Mapplethorpe Foundation in New York is thriving quite well; 2014 public documents indicate it has over $232 million in assets. Another noted photographer is Andres Serrano whose most famous work was *Piss Christ*, a picture of a crucifix submerged in a glass of his own urine. No figures are available on his net worth, but there are online references to Serrano being well-off financially. Ironically, Serrano still proclaims himself to be a Christian. Pablo Picasso amassed a fortune of $500 million dollars at his death, and helped lead the art world down this disastrous cultural path. Andy Warhol left an estate of some $220 million. His pop art and pretentious manner made him famous for . . . well, being famous. No modern artist appears capable of painting the Sistine Chapel or something like *The Last Supper*. Whether they have any artistic talent at all is debatable. Why, then, are they more valued by our society and much wealthier than blue-collar workers who are putting in forty hours a week for their employers?

The average full-time administrative assistant earns $14.98 an hour, as of October 2016, according to Payscale.com The median income for all certified public accountants is just over $62,000. The positions a rung below this—the staff accountant, accounts payable and receivable type of jobs, exemplify the new normal in corporate America. Most accounting positions never required a college degree of any kind even ten years ago, and paid much better than the ones that now do require one. Those who can afford the ever-increasing college tuition costs are now offered jobs at a lower rung on the employment ladder and are paid less to perform them. Meanwhile, those who don't graduate from college, for whatever reason, are relegated to an even lower rung on the employment ladder. The dwindling number of file clerks usually makes around $20,000 per year, keeping them just above the poverty level. The average wage for all construction workers can often be over $20 an hour, but it involves real physical labor and some danger, and it tends to be temporary and/or seasonal in nature, with no benefits. As of 2014, the average electrician made $51,110 annually, using Bureau of Labor statistics. As unions continue to have less power and influence, electricians will become more and more nonunion, and make less money with fewer benefits as a result. The average fast-food worker makes around $16,000, according to Glassdoor.

Consulting has become a lucrative field. *Consultants Mind* reported that MBA graduates who majored in Consulting at the top colleges, like Harvard, Virginia, or Duke, can make $130,000 with a $25,000 signing bonus as soon as they enter the workforce. Big strategy consulting firms pay over $200,000 annually, five to seven years post-MBA. But what exactly does a "consultant" do to earn that much more than construction workers and accounting clerks? What are they studying, exactly, at institutions of higher learning, about "consulting?" On the surface, it would seem ludicrous for any corporation to pay an outsider a huge consulting fee to advise them about anything. After all, these same companies are bestowing enormous salaries and benefits on their own executive staffs; why can't all of their in-house talent make the right decisions on their own? George Mason University Professor Robin Hanson asked this same question, stating, "The puzzle is why firms pay huge sums to big name consulting firms, when their advice comes from kids fresh out of college, who spend only a few months studying an industry they previous knew nothing about. How could such quick-made advice from ignorant recent grads be worth millions? Why don't firms just ask their own internal recent college grads?"[262] Consultants seem a lot like critics; the old adage of "those who can, do; those who can't, teach" seems to apply. At any rate, how can the marketplace justify paying these kind of glorified advice-givers more than individuals performing arduous, physically demanding tasks?

The 1979 film *Being There,* starring Peter Sellers as a simple gardener whose innocuous, television-inspired remarks are mistaken for profundity, provided a refreshingly satirical view of all consultants. The biggest consulting firm in America has long been McKinsey & Company. Consulting firms were used as far back as the 1930s, primarily to combat the power of unions. As the *New York Observer* put it, "Anyone who has worked in the corporate milieu knows that the arrival of McKinsey on the scene tends to not be a sign of good news for the rank and file." The article makes the case that McKinsey can be credited with starting the whole executive compensation explosion: "In 1951, General Motors hired McKinsey consultant Arch Patton to conduct a multi-industry study of executive compensation. The results appeared in *Harvard Business Review*, with the specific finding that from 1939 to 1950, the pay of hourly employees had more than doubled, while that of 'policy level' management had risen only 35 percent." *Harvard Business Review* went on to publish a yearly report about executive compensation. Corporate thinking has always been distinguished by its unoriginality, so it was predictable that Pan American World Airways would quickly use McKinsey's services to explore the issue of stock options for its management team. McKinsey's consultant Arch Patton specialized in this area and would go on to later write the books *Men, Money and Motivation: Executive Compensation as an Instrument of Leadership* and *What is an Executive Worth?,* both published by giant McGraw-Hill. Patton was considered a management guru and was named chairman of a presidential commission on legislative, judicial, and executive branch salaries in 1973.[263] Consultants, like well-paid corporate leaders themselves, never delve into the excesses of executive compensation, and perpetually search for ways to cut the emaciated bottom of the workforce, while ignoring all the fat at the top. No wonder the marketplace values them so highly.

The money doesn't stop flowing for the wealthiest individuals once they retire. Not only do they draw lucrative pensions that pay them more than many active workers earn, or sit on various boards of directors and garner additional easy income, they can always fall back on consulting themselves. As of 2006, about 25 percent of retired CEOs had some kind of consulting arrangement with their old firm. Elite executives like Samuel Palmisano, IBM's retired CEO, can still make $20,000 *for any day he spends four hours* advising his former company. Less than four hours means Sam will have to console himself with a mere $10,000. IBM was also paying a million dollars annually to staff and furnish their retired chief's office. The total value of Palmisano's retirement package was some $271 million, which stunned even the corporate world.[264] This consulting, no doubt, could be done in a fancy restaurant or on a golf course. As the *Wall Street Journal* generously describes this practice, "Many former executives enjoy lucrative consulting gigs at their old companies. Boards dole out these agreements to guarantee smooth leadership transitions and prevent former bosses from joining rival, poaching staffers or filing suit against the company."

According to the business world's favorite newspaper, sixteen former CEOs from the nation's one thousand largest companies are being paid at least $500,000 in consulting fees. Even when the company doesn't want to continue to receive consulting from their retired executives, the money keeps rolling in; ex-Acxiom CEO Charles Morgan was promised $500,000 annually as a consultant for three years, but even though the company stopped calling for his services after two months, he still received the full $1.5 million. Boeing's Scott Carson was paid $1.5 million after retirement for no more than seventy-five hours of consulting per month. Carson acknowledged that he never worked the full seventy-five hours in any month, and that "in the last six months, it was nothing," but he was still paid in full. The paper reported that Carson continues to work the system well as chairman of the Board of Regents at Washington State University. Phillip "Rick" Powell has consulted with First Cash since he stepped down as CEO nearly a decade earlier. His initial yearly fee was $500,000, subsequently raised to $700,000 annually, in a contract that the company's Board extended through 2016.[265]

Retired Swift Transportation Co. CEO Jerry Moyes was set to be paid $200,000 monthly after his retirement at the end of 2016, more than he received when working.[266]

I'm not going to compare and contrast the average salaries of every occupation in the labor force. But I wanted to provide some glaring examples of how the marketplace seems to wildly overvalue seemingly unimportant occupations, while greatly undervaluing other, extremely crucial ones. The Bureau of Labor Statistics tells us that the average retail worker makes just over $21,000 per year, while the average 2015 yearly salary for all American workers was $48,098. The average CEO, including all small companies, makes $759,189 per year. As noted earlier, the average Major League Baseball player or NBA player makes more in one season than the average American worker, even with a college degree, will accrue working fifty-plus years. At the same time, the one hundred highest-paid CEOs made at least $2.5 billion in 2015, roughly equivalent to the annual economic output of a nation like Sierra Leone.[267]

What kind of marketplace permits this? What kind of economic system enables it? What kind of leadership is content with it?

13 PROFITS BEFORE PROGRESS

"The paradise of the rich is made out of the hell of the poor."
—Victor Hugo

JIMMY CARTER TALKED A GREAT deal during his presidential campaign, and throughout his four years in office, about developing new, alternative forms of energy. Carter's comment back then that "We must start now to develop the new, unconventional sources of energy we will rely on in the next century" seems laughably ironic now. The next century is here, and we haven't progressed one iota in this respect since the 1970s.

We have to ask ourselves, considering how vested the very wealthy are in the present arrangement, how any intrepid inventor could hope to break up the oil monopolies and utility barons. According to their filed financial reports, the big five oil companies—BP, Chevron, ConocoPhillips, Exxon-Mobil, and Shell, garnered a combined $93 billion in 2013. As the Center for American Progress noted, this amounts to $177,000 per minute. Incredibly enough, this astronomical amount was 27 percent lower than their profits from the year before. The oil companies will no doubt use the decrease in profits—due primarily to lower prices at the gas pumps—as an excuse to demand an extension of their $2.4 billion annual tax breaks. According to the Congressional Joint Committee on Taxation, another loophole will save them approximately $7.5

billion over the next decade. Seth Hanlon, former Director of Fiscal Reform at the Center for American Progress, called it, "a subsidy for foreign production by US oil companies."[268] Even with lower prices at the pump, the Energy Information Administration estimates that the average US household spent $1,962 on gasoline in 2015, equivalent to nearly 5 percent of the average household income.[269] The American Petroleum Institute and the oil companies are also lobbying to lift the ban on exporting crude oil, which would allow them to sell their domestically produced oil at the higher world price, thereby increasing their profits. These sound remarkably like the kind of counterproductive deals that Huey Long fought against in Louisiana.

In 2011, the oil industry made $375,000 million per day in profits. The CEOs of the five big companies received an average compensation of $60,110 per day that year, as their pay rate jumped an astonishing 55 percent from 2010. Exxon-Mobil's CEO Rex Tillerson, President Donald Trump's choice for Secretary of State, was paid nearly $100,000 a day in 2011.[270] Oil Change International estimates that the federal government provides the oil companies with as much as a *trillion* dollars annually in subsidies, which block clean energy alternatives. So exactly how are the titans of Big Oil earning such unfathomable profits? They have invented nothing, created no innovations beyond the move to unleaded gas, which through political pressure became mandated in 1986. Fuel efficiency is only marginally better than it was in the late 1970s— when the push for higher mileage vehicles began—if you leave out the hybrid vehicles and electric cars, which are still beyond most poor and working-class budgets. They are not displaying any talent in presiding over an industry that sells a product everyone is inescapably dependent upon; their profits are assured, since they set the price at the pump, and no matter how high it goes, the public has no choice but to pay it. The ruminations over why the price of gas rises and falls with the prevailing winds are pointless because the issue is purposefully confusing. Usually it boils down to a mantra that we must curb our dependency on foreign oil. Another variation on this theme is that Americans shouldn't be complaining because compared to the rest of the world, our gas is cheap.

A typical story of this kind appeared in the June 25, 2013, *International Business Times,* and was headlined, "Gas Prices at the Pump: Europeans Pay Almost Twice as Much as US Residents." This was keeping in line with what is, or at least was, apparently official Obama administration policy. In 2008, Secretary of Energy Steven Chu told the *Wall Street Journal* that he wanted to increase gasoline taxes over the next fifteen years until they were consistent with European rates. "Somehow, we have to figure out how to boost the price of gasoline to the levels in Europe." Chu declared. Four years later, when grilled by Congress regarding this controversial statement, Chu hesitated and eventually stammered out, "I no longer hold that view." The general public continues to be at the mercy of both corporate and government leaders who clearly don't have their interests at heart. Not only are these plutocrats definitely not worth the riches they've accumulated, they have grown exceedingly wealthy at the direct expense of the public interest.

Nikola Tesla was one of the greatest scientific minds the world has ever known. He was partially or directly responsible for radio, alternating current, one of the first X-ray machines, and a directed energy weapon that supposedly could put an end to all war, among other things. He also claimed to have devised an earthquake machine and was obsessed with developing wireless power. Rumors persist that he had invented a way to distribute free, limitless power to the world, but that J. P. Morgan and other backers withdrew his funding. Needless to say, such a universal, wireless power would probably have been impossible to monitor, therefore making it impossible for a corresponding fee to have been assessed to consumers. Within hours of Tesla's death, all his papers were confiscated by the government and some still remain classified. Ironically, Tesla gets a good deal of credit even from the establishment now, which refers to him as "the patron saint of modern electricity." But his most dangerous notion, that of providing free, clean power to everyone, is only discussed by those deemed conspiracy theorists. The ultimate proof that our predatory capitalist system penalizes real ingenuity and value is demonstrated by the fact that despite all his incredible achievements, Nikola Tesla died virtually penniless.

Another similarly brilliant, original man was psychoanalyst Wilhelm Reich. He was initially a disciple of Sigmund Freud but broke off to become one of the most radical minds the world of psychiatry has ever seen. Shortly after arriving in New York in 1939, Reich coined the term orgone, which he defined as a powerful cosmic energy derived from human orgasms. A year later, he began constructing what he called orgone accumulators and treating his patients with them. The mainstream media of the day, led by vicious attacks on him in the *New Republic* and *Harper's,* reacted as they always do toward new and revolutionary ideas. The Food and Drug Administration accused Reich of fraud and banned the interstate transport of his orgone accumulators. He was charged with contempt in 1956 and sentenced to prison, and afterwards over six tons of his publications were burned by order of the court. He died in jail a year later. Reich made many fantastic claims, among them being able to cure cancer with orgone energy, and to also be able to shoot down UFOs. Many have wondered, of course, about why the FDA was so interested in a psychoanalyst's unorthodox treatment methods to the point of burning his records and imprisoning him. Reich's most valuable book was probably the fascinating *The Mass Psychology of Fascism.*

In the 1980s, an inventor named Stanley Meyer developed the first water-powered car. Meyer's death was exceedingly strange; after a meal on March 20, 1998, at a Grove City, Ohio, Cracker Barrel restaurant with his twin brother Stephen and two Belgian investors, Meyer suddenly grabbed his neck and bolted outside. His brother described what happened in the parking lot: "I ran outside and asked him, 'What's wrong?' He said, 'They poisoned me.' That was his dying declaration." After an investigation by the Grove City police, the cause of death was predictably determined to be from a brain aneurism. When Stephen Meyer told the Belgian investors about his brother's sudden death, he was amazed at their response. "I told them that Stan had died and they never said a word," he recounted, "absolutely nothing, no condolences, no questions. I never, ever had a trust of those two men ever again." Stephen Meyer, although fully knowledgeable about his brother's work, was supposedly so frightened by his death that he refused to continue the research. An obscure online reference from 2007 makes the claim that Stephen Meyer "wants $7 million before he is willing to talk to anyone." Meyer's work was credible enough that the 1995 BBC documentary, "It Runs on Water," narrated by science fiction legend Arthur C. Clarke, focused on his "water fuel cell" invention. Meyer's neighbor Charlie Hughes would later report to independent investigators how he'd seen both "limousines [from which] men in turbans stepped out" and military vehicles with "army brass," in Meyer's driveway. Hughes also claimed that Meyer told him, "The Arabs wanted to offer me $250 million to stop."[271]

Joseph Newman began demonstrating his own energy device back in the 1980s. Newman's device is a DC motor that purports to produce more energy than it consumes, a supposed scientific impossibility, dismissed as a perpetual motion machine and rejected by the US Patent Office. Dr. Robert E. Smith, an official with NASA, stated, in regards to Newman's invention, "If the manner in which Joseph Newman conducted his experiments and the results were made known to the industrial or engineering community then, in my opinion, several companies and/or individuals possess the expertise and capabilities to construct the hardware required to fully exploit the apparent capability of his new concepts."

The elite are just as anxious to keep alternative health products off the market as they are to keep alternative energy from replacing our antiquated, profit-laden fossil fuel industries. The medical establishment fought the very concept of "you are what you eat" for a long time, preferring instead to push their low-calorie diet based on artificial foods, such as margarine instead of butter and saccharine in place of sugar. While they have begrudgingly admitted, in recent years, that perhaps fresh fruits and vegetables are more valuable to human beings than potato chips and diet soda, they still hold a real animus against vitamins and other natural products.

In December 2013, the *Annals of Internal Medicine* published the results of three separate studies, which examined the effects of multivitamins. This mouthpiece of the medical establishment commented on the entirely predictable findings in an editorial titled "Enough is Enough: Stop Wasting Money on Vitamin and Mineral Supplements." The antennae of all intelligent men and women should be fully raised by this; the medical industry has certainly never done anything to convince anybody that they are the least bit concerned about people wasting money. The editorial summarized the conclusions of these carbon-copy studies: "The message is simple: Most supplements do not prevent chronic disease or death, their use is not justified, and they should be avoided." A month later, the mainstream media trumpeted the findings of a New Zealand study, which determined that vitamin D is not effective in fighting disease. Vitamins and natural supplements are in direct competition with the medical industry, of course. It is certainly in their vested interest to claim there are no beneficial effects to be gained from these cheaper, non-pharmaceutical products.

The FBI and FDA have far too frequently resorted to armed raids on natural-care clinics and health-food stores in their lust to eliminate the competition. Alternative outlets like *Natural News* have documented many of the numerous FDA raids on raw milk farmers, dietary supplement makers, and natural medicine practitioners. While the FDA is seemingly far removed from a military agency, its armed raids are often conducted SWAT-team style. In another example of extreme overreach, the FDA has gone to the extremes of claiming that walnuts are, in fact, a drug! They sent a strong letter to California's Diamond Foods, wherein they insisted that any alleged health benefits be removed from the label or that the company apply for a new drug application. As William Faloon, editor of *Life Extension* magazine, put it, "The FDA's language resembles that of an out-of-control police state where tyranny reigns over rationality."[272] Michael R. Taylor, the Food and Drug Administration's food safety czar under Barack Obama, responded to very mild criticism of the FDA's tactics at a press conference by maintaining, "We believe we're doing our job," and described the campaign against raw milk producers as a public health duty.[273]

The medical-industrial complex should be anxious to try new methods of dealing with cancer and other deadly diseases. After all, their own methods have not eradicated anything substantial since the days of yellow fever and diphtheria. The American Medical Association has a powerful financial motive to continue their slash-and-burn ways; their doctors are trained to prescribe the highly toxic drugs produced by the pharmaceutical industry, despite the potentially deadly side effects inherent in virtually all of them. In 2010, the Department of Health and Human Services admitted that bad hospital care contributed to the deaths of 180,000 patients annually on Medicare alone. A study by patient safety researchers, released in 2016, found that some 251,000 deaths every year can be attributed to "medical errors" in medical facilities. If these numbers are true, they would make establishment medical care the *third* leading cause of death in America, behind only heart disease and cancer.[274] The latest figures available from the Centers for Disease Control, in 2014, revealed that doctors are responsible for some twenty-three times more deaths than guns. Even more damningly, a March 2004 article in *Life Extension* magazine reported that medical negligence from doctors or hospitals was, in fact, the leading cause of death in America. As has been demonstrated numerous times over the years, whenever doctors have gone on strike in any particular country, the death rate there has dropped. One recent study was published in the academic journal *Social Science and Medicine* and found "all the different studies report population mortality either stays the same, or even decreases, during medical strikes."[275] Even the *Wall Street Journal* cites startling statistics like the fact that surgeons operate on the wrong body part as many as forty times per week in America, and that roughly 25 percent of all hospital patients will be harmed by an error of some kind. Medical specialists, surveying their own fields of expertise, have concluded that 20 to 30 percent of all medications, tests, and procedures are unnecessary.[276]

The news—even in the establishment press—is full of articles with titles like "How Hospitals are Killing E.R. Patients," "Hospitals are Still Killing Patients With Needless Mistakes," "Medical Errors Harm Huge Numbers of Patients," and "How Hospitals Can Stop Killing so Many Patients." Doctors, and especially surgeons, are very, very well paid. A general surgeon, on average, makes $260,000 per year. The lowest paid medical practitioners, pediatric physicians, make $156,000 on average. Many specialists, like cardiologists, orthopedic surgeons, and radiologists, average over $300,000 annually. If you've ever been to a psychiatrist, or know someone who has, you probably realize how much they're earning their average salary of $170,000. With the awful track record of hospitals, and doctors in general, why are they worth such lavish compensation?

The reason we are still driving the same gas-guzzlers our grand-parents were, and still awaiting all the magnificent advancements the futuristic films and World Fairs sixty years ago predicted for us, is because no advance in technology can be permitted if it interferes with the finances of the plutocrats who have hoarded all the wealth. Cancer won't be cured until another disease comes along that will ensure enough patients to keep the medical industrial complex's profits high. Just imagine what a cure for all cancer would do to the business of establishment medicine. The same thing goes for new forms of energy; as long as the big oil companies are making the sinful profits they are from the present system, how can anyone believe they'd just roll over and allow new energy sources that would cost the average citizen comparatively nothing to be marketed? The utility companies are in the same situation. None of those who run these huge conglomerates is ever going to sacrifice their own riches for the benefit of all people. In this unfair world we live in, progress can never come at the expense of profits.

14 Keeping the Masses Down

If you want to know what God thinks of money, just look at the people he gave it to.

—Dorothy Parker

THOSE SEEKING WORK IN TODAY'S job market are well aware of how much things have changed since the 1990s or so. The lowest-paying jobs, especially in retail, have become the most difficult and time-consuming to apply for. Gone are the days when a job seeker could drive around, knock on enough doors, and eventually get hired on the spot by an employer anxious to fill a position. All applications must be submitted online now, and if you don't have a computer, they will ask you to come in and use theirs. Frequently, you will have to take a long, tedious test, which can consist of as many as two hundred questions, all of them psychological in nature and very difficult to answer correctly. In most cases, you will be competing with a hundred or more people for each opening. The Bureau of Labor announced in July 2013 that there were now more than three unemployed persons for every job opening in the country. The Bureau of Labor also acknowledged that unemployed workers outnumber job openings in every sector of the economy.[277] In March 2015, *The American Prospect* reported that there were six unemployed construction workers for every construction job opening. Yet, we persistently hear conservative talking heads and business owners claim they can't find people to work.

As the voice of corporate America, the *Wall Street Journal* acknowledged in a October 24, 2011, article entitled, "Why Companies Aren't Getting the Employees They Need," the new norm is employers expect workers to come in right away and do the job without any training or "ramp-up time," to use their words. The newspaper stated, "In other words, to get a job, you have to have that job already." In the past, businesses often promoted from within, and there was always a buffer period to permit workers to adapt to their new responsibilities and learn by firsthand, on-the-job experience. "Working your way up the ladder" is yet another dead slogan from the past. The staffing company Manpower Group reports that 52 percent of employers surveyed claim they have difficulty filling positions because of talent shortages. This is, of course, completely contradicted by the statistics cited earlier that illustrate there are far more job seekers than jobs. The qualifications demanded of employees are often totally unrelated to the job description. It wasn't always this way; as recently as the 1990s, only 10 percent of workers who were a part of the Silicon Valley tech boom had IT-related degrees. Addressing another element of this twisted new marketplace, the newspaper stated, "The shortage of opportunities to learn on the job helps explain the phenomenon of people queueing up for unpaid internships, in some cases even *paying* to get access to a situation where they can work free to get access to valuable on-the-job experience." Perhaps that's what we'll ultimately come to; people paying employers for the right to be considered as eventual paid employees.

One way in which the elite flex their muscle and manipulate the system they control is through legal strategies like bankruptcy and civil lawsuits. Bankruptcy has long been a tool that the rich employ, and the laws are such that it invariably works to their benefit. Few people know, for instance, that Abraham Lincoln declared bankruptcy twice in his life. Many celebrities have utilized this tool, including singer Willie Nelson, who owed the IRS over $16 million in 1990, and released an album titled *The IRS Tapes: Who'll Buy My Memories,* using the proceeds to pay the government. Donald Trump's businesses have declared bankruptcy numerous times. Trump worked the system as only an insider with great assets can in order to, in his words, "renegotiate the debt." Bankruptcy is not for the unwashed masses, however. For them, it destroys their credit rating and ability to get any kind of loan. But at least until recent years, it was a last resort that was available to desperate people. The bankruptcy laws were first changed in 2005, and the changes, not surprisingly, adversely affected those at the bottom of the economic ladder. As CNN described it in an October 17, 2005, story, "A new bankruptcy law goes into effect today, making it harder for consumers to prove that they should be allowed to clear their debts in what's known as a 'fresh start'—or Chapter 7—bankruptcy." On top of that, those filing for bankruptcy "will be paying much higher fees to bankruptcy attorneys, who are expected to raise their rates by as much as 100 percent." The law also mandated that those seeking to file bankruptcy must meet with a credit counselor and attend money management courses at their own expense.

Since those filing for Chapter 7 normally have less-liquid assets, credit card companies and other creditors often received nothing under previous bankruptcy agreements. The consumer credit industry lobbied relentlessly for nearly a decade to get the 2005 Bankruptcy Abuse Prevention and Consumer Protection Act passed by Congress. Those lobbying for the new law argued that it would prevent "consumers from abusing bankruptcy laws" by using it to clear their debts. That kind of thing isn't for the average American, you see, but it is part and parcel of Donald Trump and his ilk's arsenal. They apparently aren't abusing anything, because they've earned their great wealth and all the endless perks that go along with it. Under Barack Obama, the bankruptcy screws were tightened further in 2010, making it even harder for working-class Americans to take advantage of a perk rich business leaders don't hesitate to exploit. If we had honest elected officials, the credit card industry would be the ones experiencing reform, with strict limits imposed upon their usurious interest rates. Instead, though, as always, it's the 80 percent of Americans left out of the inner circle that must sacrifice once again.

Tort reform sounds like a good thing. After all, we've heard about so many of these outrageous lawsuits and extravagant jury awards, illustrating a system that is seemingly crying out for some kind of reform. Perhaps the most famous "frivolous" lawsuit of all time was the 1992 case of Stella Liebeck suing McDonald's for being burned by their coffee. This story has been badly misrepresented by the media and politicians alike. As the Consumer Attorneys of California summarized it, in reality, Ms. Liebeck was not driving at the time, nor was her car even moving. She had the cup between her legs when it tipped over and spilled on her lap. The coffee was dangerously hot, enough so that she suffered third-degree burns that required skin grafts. This was not an isolated case as McDonald's had received some seven hundred previous complaints about excessively hot coffee and had paid settlements in some cases. Ms. Liebeck initially offered to settle for the $20,000 she owed in medical expenses, but the fast-food giant only offered her $800. The popular consensus holds that Liebeck was awarded millions, but the jury's original punitive damage award was reduced 80 percent by the judge, and resulted in a figure of $640,000, although the case actually settled out of court for an undisclosed sum.

Medical incompetence, as was noted, has shamefully become at least the third leading cause of death in America. Because of all the widespread malpractice, it's imperative to provide viable ways for individuals and groups to confront the problem legally. However, due to heavy lobbying by the medical and insurance industries, our elected representatives and most of the mainstream media treat the issue of malpractice as if the doctors and insurance companies were the victims, instead of the patients who've been harmed (and often killed) by their mistakes. Over the past several years, a number of medical malpractice laws have been passed all over the country, each of them designed to weaken the accountability and liability of health-care providers. In 2010, the Obama administration, pressured by the medical industrial complex, allocated $23 million to study "new patient safety initiatives." These new initiatives were in reality lame proposals whereby doctors and hospitals would confront patients who'd been injured through negligence and offer them a paltry sum of money after apologizing. Many people, especially grief-stricken relatives, are ripe for the picking in such circumstances and could easily be bamboozled into accepting a partial payment instead of the much larger compensation they should be entitled to.[278]

Civil lawsuits are often the only remedial action average people have at their disposal, and they're a powerful way to protect the rights of consumers and workers. The corporate world has co-opted the word *reform* in an Orwellian way, and twisted its meaning beyond recognition. In reality, all the reforms the business world and many politicians and lobbies push for would permit it to more easily discriminate against, harass and bully employees, rip off consumers, and pollute the air, water, and land. Pension reform, for example, means nothing more than decreasing or eliminating the amount of money companies contribute toward workers' retirements. Tax reform means slashing rates for the wealthiest Americans, as well as corporate, inheritance, and capital gains taxes. Entitlement reform means privatizing or eliminating Social Security, Medicare, and other programs that benefit the working-class and poor Americans. Prison reform means privatizing more prisons so that filling cells becomes the primary business model for the profiteers in charge of them.

A truly unique defense was postulated during the trial of Ethan Couch, a wealthy sixteen-year-old that killed four people and injured two others while driving drunk. Couch's defense was that he suffered from "affluenza," meaning that his entitled upbringing made the spoiled youngster incapable of judging right from wrong. Not surprisingly, given his family's economic status, Couch's preposterous argument prevailed, and he was sentenced to ten years of probation. In the wake of the incredibly light sentence, five civil lawsuits were filed against Couch. The doctor that took the stand testified that Couch was better off in rehab than in prison.[279]

Celebrities and wealthy defendants are inevitably directed toward rehab clinics after their arrests for drugs, while poor defendants are just as inevitably directed toward prison. The rich need help, while the poor need to learn a lesson. Celebrity repeat-drug offenders such as actor Robert Downey Jr., who once was caught sleeping naked in a neighbor's bed, are always given more rehab in lieu of prison time. In Downey's case, he eventually did serve time in the California Substance Abuse Treatment Facility and State Prison, but it was only after he'd been arrested multiple times, and I would be shocked if he didn't receive the most comfortable accommodations possible. Downey has bounced back quite nicely from his troubled days; by June 2013, he'd become Hollywood's highest-paid star.[280] According to Forbes, Downey brought home $80 million in 2016.

The most glaring example of the double standards in the drug war are the disparate punishments accorded users and sellers of crack cocaine versus those caught possessing or selling powder cocaine. The Anti-Drug Abuse Act of 1986 established much harsher, mandatory penalties for crack cocaine usage. While the Drug Enforcement Administration makes nearly twice as many arrests for powder cocaine as it does for crack cocaine, the crack cocaine sentences are 43.5 percent longer than the powder cocaine sentences, and their average length of imprisonment is nearly forty months longer.[281] Congress passed the Smarter Sentencing Act in January 2014, which was designed to decrease these glaring differences, often obviously racial in nature, and reduce the federal prison population. The so-called Three Strikes and You're Out laws, which were passed beginning in the 1990s, likewise penalize the poorest defendants. In reality, it is just another way to dole out harsh penalties for often petty crimes and to keep filling our prisons. The third felony that could cause someone to be locked away forever has been as insignificant, in actual cases, as the theft of a pair of work gloves, pilfering small change from a parked car, or passing a bad check.

Often even more unjust are the mandatory minimum sentencing laws, which can result in life-without-parole sentences doled out to nonviolent offenders. The crimes for which individuals are sentenced to life are often relatively minor in nature; the ACLU provided multiple examples in their report "A Living Death: Life Without Parole for Nonviolent Offenses." In one case, a defendant was sentenced to life for stealing a $159 jacket; in another, the unlucky soul was the middleman in a $10 marijuana deal. These life-without-parole cases don't include the nonsensical beyond-life sentences that are sometimes applied, such as a punishment of 350 years for a series of nonviolent drug sales. In yet another unbelievable case, two poor sisters in Mississippi were given life sentences for committing a robbery in which no one was hurt, and $11 was stolen. Joe Sullivan, a mentally disabled thirteen-year-old boy, was sentenced to life without parole in Florida for sexual battery; an older boy who was with him at the time accused Sullivan, and was himself only sent for a short period to juvenile detention. Before the Georgia Supreme Court finally struck down the policy, "sex offenders" in the state who failed to register a second time had been subject to mandatory life in prison sentences. Most people have no idea that *sex offender* is a blanket term that can extend from monstrous pedophiles to someone who is caught urinating behind a tree.

A poor or working-class youth of eighteen can receive a substantial prison sentence for statutory rape, which by definition could be something as innocuous as having sex with his seventeen-year-old girlfriend. On the other hand, the then thirty-four-year-old rock star Mick Jagger could proudly announce he was spending a summer in Paris with young Jodie Foster, who was all of fifteen at the time, and no one thought any more about it. Another member of the Rolling Stones, Bill Wyman, admitted to having sex with his teenage wife when she was thirteen and he was forty eight, and he actually talked to the police about it. Amazingly, they weren't interested.[282]

Republican congressman Mark Foley was embroiled in an ugly 2006 scandal, which involved sexually suggestive instant messages and emails to underage boys. The Florida Department of Law Enforcement closed its investigation less than two years later, citing insufficient evidence. There were similar allegations against another Republican representative, Jim Kolbe, that went unpunished as well. Ironically, the conservative Foley had been chairman of the House Caucus on Missing and Exploited Children, which had been responsible for legislation urging more stringent measures regarding sexual predators. In 1983, a previous congressional page scandal exposed both liberal Democrat Gerry Studds, who admitted having a relationship with a seventeen-year-old male page, and conservative Dan Crane, who had an affair with a seventeen-year-old female page.

The Who's Pete Townshend was caught using his credit card to download child pornography on the Internet in 1999. Townshend's ridiculous defense that he was conducting research was accepted by the authorities, who slapped him with a caution.[283] Paul Reubens, better known as Pee Wee Herman, had an unusually lenient settlement arranged for him by the California legal system. Police had found materials that "appeared to depict children engaged in sexual activity" during a 2001 search of his home. Three years later, he was allowed to plead guilty to a misdemeanor charge of obscenity. Reubens' representative told the press that the images in question were part of his "extensive historical art photography collection." At almost the same time, California authorities sentenced actor Jeffrey Jones, best known for his role as the principal in *Ferris Bueller's Day Off*, to five years of probation for a felony charge of hiring a fourteen-year-old boy to pose for explicit photos. In an oddly worded aside in the magazine article reporting the sentence, we learn that the judge "also prohibited Jones from possessing child porn." Isn't everyone, by law, prohibited from possessing child porn?[284] Singer and producer R. Kelly has been accused of raping underage girls several times. Journalist Jim DeRogatis received a video in 2002 depicting

R. Kelly having sex with an underage girl, and told the *Village Voice* that, "Dozens of girls—not one, not two, *dozens*—and not just one videotape, *numerous* videotapes. And not Tommy Lee/Pam Anderson, Kardashian fun video. . . . He orders her to call him Daddy. He urinates in her mouth and instructs her at great length on how to position herself to receive his 'gift.' *It's a rape that you're watching.*" [Emphasis original]. DeRogatis bitterly noted that all of Kelly's victims "settled because they felt they could get no justice whatsoever. They didn't have a chance."[285]

Rock stars like Iggy Pop and Ted Nugent (now a right-wing darling, someone of whom Sarah Palin would say, "If it's good enough for Ted Nugent, it's good enough for me") and groups like Kiss, Motörhead, the Beastie Boys, and Mötley Crüe wrote songs in the past about "jailbait," or having sex with girls as young as thirteen. And many stars went beyond just singing about it. Jerry Lee Lewis, Elvis Presley, and Led Zeppelin's Jimmy Page famously had relationships with young teenage girls. Aerosmith's Steven Tyler persuaded the parents of his underage girlfriend to sign *custody* over to him. In 1980, Don Henley of the Eagles was arrested when police found a drugged, naked sixteen-year-old girl at his Hollywood home. A fifteen-year-old girl was found there as well. Henley got off with a $2,000 fine and two years' probation. The underage girls didn't fare so well; the older girl was arrested for prostitution, and the younger one was charged with being under the influence of drugs.[286] Peter Yarrow, of the iconic folk trio Peter, Paul and Mary, pleaded guilty to taking "indecent liberties" with a fourteen-year-old girl in his hotel room when he was thirty-two. He served a three-month sentence and was *pardoned by President Carter* on his last day in office. In another of those endless intertwining power connections, Yarrow was married at the time to the late Senator Eugene McCarthy's niece.[287]

Apparently, if one is wealthy enough, it doesn't matter how heinous the offense is. Robert H. Richards IV, heir to the Du Pont family fortune, was convicted in a Delaware court of raping his three-year-old daughter. Richards was also convicted of sexually assaulting his infant son. While both charges had initially been for second-degree child rape, the Du Pont scion's top legal team worked out one of those deals that only the rich can, whereby Richards pled guilty to a single fourth-degree count of rape—while admitting that he had sexually assaulted his own children. Predictably, Richards was not sentenced to a single day in jail. According to Delaware state law, a second-degree child rape conviction carries a mandatory ten-year prison term for each count. So if Richards had been a janitor, or a truck driver, or a file clerk, or a computer programmer, he would have had to serve a mandatory twenty years in jail because such heinous charges would never have been subject to negotiation. Even so, the presiding judge, Jan Jurden, still had the latitude to impose a prison sentence. Instead, Jurden declared that Richards would not "fare well" in prison, and would benefit more from a sex offender program.[288] It would be astounding if Jurden or any of the other myriad of brain-dead judges that pollute courtrooms in every state of the union ever determined that a single poor or average defendant wouldn't fare well in prison. Does anyone fare well in prison? Again, we see the ironclad dual standards applied to those accused of sexual and drug offenses; the rich and celebrated must be helped and enrolled in treatment programs, while everyone else is beyond hope and must spend long, hard years behind bars.

In a just world, our leaders would value the right of all Americans to sue for damages if they're victimized by the medical industry or anyone else. The laws would apply equally to all; sex with underage partners would either be considered a horrific offense in all cases, or all cases would be treated as minor offenses. The same consistent legal and social standards would apply for drunk driving, drug possession, or anything else.

15 THE BEST AND THE BRIGHTEST

There is no distinctly American criminal class—except Congress.
—Mark Twain

POPULIST ACTOR/PHILOSOPHER WILL ROGERS WAS fond of criticizing the politicians of his day with witty quips like "This country has come to feel the same when Congress is in session as when the baby gets hold of the hammer." Rogers, like the equally famous and more dangerous Huey Long, died before his time unnaturally, less than a month before the Kingfish, in a 1935 plane crash. The very fact that our representative body has always been the butt of so many jokes should be cause for concern to all Americans. Why are our senators and congressmen such laughingstocks, such figures of ridicule that Mark Twain could proclaim long ago, "Suppose you were an idiot, and suppose you were a member of Congress; but I repeat myself," and everyone would chuckle and nod in agreement? While it has seemingly always been this way at least since the mid-nineteenth century, the situation has grown even more shameful in recent times. And, of course, there is the inexplicable paradox of this universal disdain for those who represent us, juxtaposed against the reality that more than 90 percent of them are regularly returned to office in every election by these same supposedly exasperated voters.

Sheila Jackson Lee has been in the House of Representatives for nearly twenty years. She has become notorious for expressing her astonishing lack of knowledge in public, despite an educational background that includes a BA from Yale and graduation from the University of Virginia law school. In the mid-1990s, after the Pathfinder spacecraft landed on Mars, Lee, who represents the district in which NASA's Mission control is located, during a visit to the Jet Propulsion Laboratory, asked whether or not the rover would be able to see where the astronauts had planted the American flag. In an October 2013 speech touching upon the partial government shutdown, Lee declared, "We have martial law." It was unclear if this was just a curious slip of the tongue—if Lee didn't understand the meaning of the term or if she was advocating for it. In a March 2014 speech from the floor of the House, Lee remarked that the US Constitution, which was first ratified by some states in 1787, was four hundred years old. Lee has been accused of treating her staff miserably, with some privately labeling her the boss from hell. Predictably, any criticism is met by charges of racism from this public servant who has referred to herself as a "freed slave." Former aide Michael McQueery tried to excuse Lee's behavior by maintaining that it wasn't uncommon on the Hill. "I've worked for two other members. They did the same thing," he explained.[289] Like so many of our tenured public servants, Lee has faced little competition since first being elected to office, and has only been challenged once in the Democratic Party primary system.

Lee is hardly alone in her magnificent ignorance. We all heard quite a bit about Dan Quayle's gaffes, especially his inability to spell potato correctly. But how many recall the C-SPAN broadcast, live from Thomas Jefferson's Monticello, where then-Vice President Al Gore gestured toward a bust that was clearly the easily recognizable owner of the property and author of the Declaration of Independence and asked the host, "Now who is this?" Gore's incredible quote, "I was recently on a tour of Latin America, and the only regret I have was that I didn't study Latin harder in school so I could converse with those people," somehow slipped past the late-night talk-show hosts and other supposed social satirists. We are supposed to believe that Gore, son of longtime United States Senator Albert Gore Sr. legitimately got into Harvard. Another vice president, Joe Biden, urged a paralyzed supporter at a 2008 campaign rally, who was sitting in a visible wheelchair, to "stand up and take a bow" without any ridicule from the establishment press. During the same campaign, Barack Obama made an infamous claim that he'd visited "all fifty-seven states," again with universal silence from the mainstream media. Sarah Palin's comment that she could see Russia from her house in Alaska received a lot more attention, but was actually a quote from comedian Tina Fey who impersonated Palin regularly on *Saturday Night Live*. George W. Bush's malapropisms, from being the "decider," to "fool me once—shame on—shame on you; fool me—you can't get fooled again," to the "Internets" to "is our children learning" are the stuff of legend. Yet, like an inarticulate athlete, he somehow finagled his way into Yale, became a governor, and then the two-term president of the United States. How did we allow people like these to become our leaders?

Georgia Representative Hank Johnson apparently thinks that land masses can "tip over." He expressed just this concern about the American territory of Guam to the admiral in charge of the US Pacific fleet during a 2010 congressional hearing. In Johnson's words, "My fear is that the whole island will become so overly populated that it will tip over and capsize." Conservative commentator Mark Steyn lambasted Johnson but also declared, "But it's business as usual in Congress." The blog *Left Coast Rebel* termed the incident, "a new low, a new 'tipping point'—even in the halls of Congress, if you will." Johnson scrambled to defend himself, claiming that he'd only been joking.[290] New York Republican Rep. Michael Grimm, already embroiled in a federal investigation into irregular campaign fund-raising, physically threatened reporter Michael Scotto after he was asked about the issue. Grimm, in a profanity-laced tirade, threatened to throw Scotto off the balcony and warned him, "You're not man enough. . . . I'll break you in half. Like a boy." Grimm doesn't hesitate to use his former status as a Marine for his political advantage. In 2010, a Republican primary opponent accused him of wearing ribbons he hadn't actually earned, and Grimm responded, "You sleep under a blanket of freedom that I helped provide. You should just say, 'Thank you.' What I've done in my life, you see in the movies."[291] This over-the-top bully had been promoted as a "rising star" in the Republican Party. In December 2014, Grimm pleaded guilty to one count of tax evasion and resigned from Congress the next month. He was sentenced to eight months in prison although his offenses carried a potential sentence of thirty months.[292]

Democrat James Moran has been representing northern Virginia in Congress since 1991. Over the years, he built up a formidable, old-fashioned-style political machine, which critics dubbed the "Moran Mafia." Two erstwhile opponents, who under state law had to get one thousand signatures on a petition to be placed on the ballot, had their petitions torn up and destroyed by Moran supporters. One of them was subsequently charged with three felony counts of forgery when he tried to make the now illegible signatures legible again, and after a two-year legal fight, he was forced to perform community service. Moran started building his career of public service during his days on the Alexandria, Virginia, City Council, from which he was forced to resign because of a vote-peddling scandal. According to the *Daily Kos,* when Moran was mayor of Alexandria, he "so frequently engaged in bar brawling that the local constabulary learned to ignore complaints that he had broken chairs, jaws, arms and legs in the town. When Moran and his wife fought at their marital home, the neighbors soon learned to ignore the noisome ruckus." Moran's official political motto became, "I like to hit people." Moran had a reputation on Capitol Hill as "the biggest crook in Congress." The Stop Trading on Congressional Trading Act was supposedly inspired by his sordid history of insider trading. Moran has been caught in numerous improprieties, including using campaign funds to buy himself a new Toyota Avalon. In April 2010, Moran became incensed when he saw an eight-year-old black boy staring at his ill-gotten automobile. Several witnesses reported seeing a "red-faced" Moran yelling and cursing at the child. The boy told the *Washington Times,* "He choked me and then cussed at me. I thought he was going to kidnap or kill me . . . All I told him was that I liked his car." Moran responded to the allegations by saying, "It's all lies." Moran never apologized, and actually questioned in the press the kind of parenting the child was receiving.[293] In 1995, Moran physically scuffled with another corrupt Congressman, Republican Duke Cunningham, as they were leaving the House chambers. During a 2002 congressional hearing, Moran screamed, "I'll break your nose!" at Republican Dan Burton. This is the man voters in northern Virginia, to their eternal shame, kept returning to Congress for over twenty years, until he finally resigned in 2015.

Conservatives in Congress, especially those who specialized in pious pronouncements against gays and sex in general, have often been caught in uncompromising moral situations themselves. Vocal Christian David Vitter, who advocated "teaching teenagers that saving sex until marriage and remaining faithful afterwards is the best choice," was of course caught with a prostitute associated with Deborah Jeane Palfrey, the so-called "DC Madam" who allegedly killed herself shortly after adamantly assuring talk-show host Alex Jones that she would never commit suicide.[294] Senator Larry Craig was caught literally with his pants down, trying to play footsie with another male in an airport bathroom in 2007. Craig had been hounded by rumors of cocaine usage and sex with teenage male pages as far back as 1982. Predictably, Craig was a member of the House "Ethics" Committee. Conservative Republican National Committee Chairman Ken Mehlman, who had proposed a constitutional amendment to ban gay marriage, admitted that *he* was gay in August 2010.[295] Rep. Mark Souder had the audacity to film a video preaching abstinence, as the married female staffer he was committing adultery with was standing alongside him.[296] Senator Brock Adams was accused of sexual misconduct, including rape, by *eight* different women.[297] With wildly incapable representatives like this, is it any wonder that so many problems never even get addressed, let alone solved?

Veteran House member Luis Gutierrez was asked in March 2014 about President Obama changing major portions of the Affordable Care Act without congressional authorization, and why businesses, but not individuals, were being granted exemptions. The video of this confrontation has to be seen to be believed; Gutierrez first shouted, "Don't touch me" in an animated, violent manner, and then he began humming or singing some indecipherable song to himself in a blatant attempt to avoid questions. The previous year, it had been reported that Gutierrez had paid a Chicago lobbyist more than $500,000 in taxpayer funds for over a decade to work with his congressional staff. "It looks like classic Chicago cronyism," observed Kathy Kiely, managing editor at the non-profit Sunlight Foundation. "It's really tantamount to a political patronage job."[298] In 2008, Gutierrez wrote to Treasury Secretary Henry Paulson, pleading the cause of Puerto Rican bank Banco Popular. The good representative forgot to note that the bank had contributed generously to his campaigns and that his wife had been a senior vice president there until 2007. Guiterrez's daughter also appears to have benefited from a sweetheart real estate deal, according to an investigation by the *Chicago Sun-Times*, through an affordable-housing program she was hardly qualified for. This same daughter apparently was one of the beneficiaries of notoriously corrupt Illinois Governor Rod Blagojevich, who was accused of assisting thousands of people to get state jobs, transfers, or promotions. *The Chicago Tribune* additionally reported that Gutierrez seemed ensnared in real estate zoning scandals of his own. Do the voters in his district really feel this is the best they can do in terms of representation?

Real estate scandals aren't relegated to the lower house of Congress. In April 2014, a Waco-like standoff between Nevada rancher Cliven Bundy and a host of federal authorities, led by the Bureau of Land Management, was covered in a predictably distorted fashion by the mainstream media. In reality, powerful Nevada Senator Harry Reid's close connections to a Chinese Energy Company, and their plans to build solar panel power stations on the land in question, appeared to be the real motive behind the government's actions. Also undisclosed by anyone in the establishment press was the fact the director of the Bureau of Land Management was a former senior advisor to Harry Reid. Harry Reid clearly was miffed when a group of brave Bundy supporters, riding on horseback like cowboy heroes of yore, caused the government forces to back down. A few days later, Reid publicly whined that "They're nothing more than domestic terrorists. I repeat: what happened there was domestic terrorism."[299] Here we have the Senate Majority Leader, earning $193,400 each year from taxpayers, who felt comfortable labeling a group of constituents that merely defended what they believed were traditional grazing rights as terrorists.

Another long-term New York congressman, Gregory Meeks, has been embroiled in a series of scandals as well. Among the improper gifts he has accepted while in office, according to Citizens for Responsibility and Ethics in Washington (CREW), is a home obtained at a below-market rate, major loans that he failed to disclose for years, and discounted rent on his district office. He also received at least six free trips to Caribbean resorts from a business backed by a convicted financier. He's been tied to several dubious nonprofit groups, including one that lost thousands of dollars intended for Hurricane Katrina victims. Senator Robert Menendez intervened in Medicare billing disputes in order to help a longtime big campaign contributor and friend, and he took two trips to the Dominican Republic on board this wealthy associate's private jet. Scott DesJarlais, despite his checkered career as a physician twice accused of having sexual relations with patients, nevertheless parlayed his experience into a seat in the House of Representatives. DesJarlais is hypocritically pro-life in that it was revealed he pressured his mistress into getting an abortion and that his then-wife had undergone two herself.[300]

Most Americans probably don't realize that recent Presidents Reagan, Clinton, and George W. Bush were all accused of *rape* at some point in their political careers. Naturally, nothing ever came of the charges against any of the men, and in Bush's case, the purported victim, Margie Schoedinger, died mysteriously as an alleged suicide.[301] Former Vice President Al Gore was accused, in great detail, of sexually assaulting masseuse Molly Hagerty. The alleged victim claimed that Gore had "acted like a crazed sex poodle" and bluntly called him a sexual predator. Hagerty was said to have a witness corroborating her story and more importantly, Gore's DNA on her pants. Hagerty charged that once she rebutted Gore's advances, he became "verbally sharp and loud" and discarded what Hagerty, who had voted for Gore in the previous election, termed his "Mr. Smiley Global Warming Concern persona."[302] Shockingly, prosecutors determined there was not enough evidence to pursue the case against Gore, even when two other masseuses accused him of the same thing.[303]

We never see any working stiffs serving in Congress—for even one term. There are no "Mr. Smiths" about to come to Washington any time soon. Our federal legislators have always been overwhelmingly lawyers or already rich, successful businessmen. High school graduates are almost unknown in the halls of Congress; 99 percent of the Senate and 93 percent of the House hold at least a bachelor's degree. While the establishment would no doubt scoff at the notion that a construction worker, a file clerk, or a gas station attendant could ever be qualified to serve in Congress, some occupations far removed from politics or the law seem to be automatic tickets to elected office. Retired athletes like former Major League baseball pitcher Jim Bunning and ex-NFL wide receiver Steve Largent were welcomed into Congress with open arms after their playing careers were over. Bill Bradley, longtime NBA player, had a lengthy Senate career and ran for president. Ex-AFL quarterback Jack Kemp enjoyed a nearly identical political career. Another NBA player, Tom McMillen, served three terms in the House. How did participating in games for a living qualify them for such a prestigious position, while no blue-collar position does?

Actors like Fred Grandy, who starred on the insipid television show *The Love Boat,* have also had lengthy careers in Congress. It would have been ridiculous enough for Grandy to be qualified for a spot on a cruise ship based upon the character he portrayed onscreen. Al Franken, a writer and sporadic performer on *Saturday Night Live,* somehow parlayed that into a United States Senate career. Arnold Schwarzenegger as Governor of California? Would anyone have ever believed that twenty years ago, even after Ronald Reagan took the same path from Hollywood to the White House? Sonny Bono, half of the singing duo Sonny and Cher, was a respected member of the House. And now the first reality television star, Donald Trump, is president of the United States.

Members of Congress in the past lived a rather austere existence, usually renting a room in local Washington, DC, boarding houses. Things have improved considerably for them. One of the many little publicized perks members of the House of Representatives receive is the use of an automobile—gas included—completely paid for by taxpayers. Longtime New York Democrat Charles Rangel is one of the most outrageous abusers of this system, as he permitted the public to fund his $777.54 monthly lease on a seventeen-foot-long luxury vehicle that, as Rangel described it himself, is "one of the bigger Cadillacs. I've got a desk in it. It's like an airplane." Rangel went on to rationalize the ostentatious nature of his vehicle, invoking his loyal constituents in the process, "I want them to feel that they are somebody and their congressman is somebody." There are few restrictions on the type of car public servants can choose, and no limits on how much they can spend. Rangel reacted to reporter Jason Mattera questioning this by advising him in a videotaped confrontation to "mind your goddamned business." Rangel is a veteran of scandals; first elected in 1970, one of the founders of the Congressional Black Caucus, he was censured by the House in 2011 for eleven counts of violating House ethics, including failure to pay rental income on his villa in the Dominican Republic. Rangel also benefited from getting apartments in New York at half price.[304] This car perk is about as thorough as it comes; those who elect to take it not only get free gas, they also don't have to worry about the costs of registration, maintenance, or insurance. The Senate, to its credit, does not extend members this particular benefit.[305]

Members of Congress get other innumerable perks that sometimes boggle the mind. Most of the time, congressmen fly commercially for free. They don't ever have to pay to park at any airport, either, with reserved spots always conveniently located directly next to their landing terminal. They have the opportunity to work out in a world-class on-site gym, complete with flat-screen TVs, swimming pool, sauna and steam room, basketball and paddleball courts, at no charge. As of 2015, Congress was working an average of 137 days per year. In addition, congressmen get the entire month of August off, two weeks at Easter, and are never scheduled to work weekends.

Congressmen also get their health insurance largely subsidized by the taxpayers. Their 401(k) plan charges fees of just 0.03 percent, as opposed to the average 401(k), which typically charges $5 for every $1,000. Members only pay 20 percent into their accounts; the remaining 80 percent is paid by their "employers." Their families receive more lucrative death benefits than the families of soldiers who are killed in action. The free franking privileges permit incumbents to mail as much literature as they want to their constituents, giving them a huge advantage over any potential political opponents. Members of Congress have their own elevators, parking spaces, and dining rooms, and they can use special underground trolleys to save tread on their shoes and shelter them from the elements. They get subsidized day-care services.

Until 2006, all these perks remained available to past members as well. The very weak reform passed that year banned ex-congressmen who had become lobbyists from using these facilities. An obscure provision entitles the Speaker of the House—presently paid $223,500 per year—to garner up to $1 million annually for up to five years, in order "to facilitate the administration, settlement, and conclusion of matters pertaining to or arising out of" his tenure in office, whatever that means. Former Speaker Denny Hastert accumulated $997,000 over three years to "document materials," according to the Center for the Public Integrity. This seems especially offensive in light of the scandal that broke in 2015, tying Hastert not only to financial irregularities, but also to a series of inappropriate relationships with the high school boys he had mentored as wrestling coach. By 1992, in wake of the House banking scandal, which involved members overdrawing their congressional checking accounts with impunity, a series of new reforms ended another amazing perk representatives had been receiving—free prescription drugs.[306] They also used to get subsidized meals, which makes even more laughable the recent admonitions that poor children who get subsidized meals in schools should learn there is "no such thing as a free lunch." By 1993, free medical checkups on-site and free prescription drugs were gone, too. Still, there are more than enough perks left so that, combined with a base annual salary of $174,000, our representatives are provided with a pretty enviable compensation package.

The president, meanwhile, is paid $400,000 per year, especially generous considering that taxpayers cover all official expenses. The First Family essentially lives in the most luxurious hotel imaginable, with a special pastry chef, twenty-four-hour cooking staff, valets and butlers, an on-site personal physician, a special beehive to cultivate fresh wild honey, as well as a new garden, so that the occupants of the White House can enjoy healthy, non-GMO food while they insist the rest of us eat the poisoned products of Monsanto while denying us even the opportunity to have GMO ingredients labeled.[307] To top it off, in addition to the salary, the president gets a tax-free $100,000 yearly travel expense budget and $19,000 for personal entertainment. Ex-presidents get a hefty pension, along with a paid staff and office space, phone services, and office supplies. A little-known historical fact is that until 1959, presidents left office with no pension or other perks. The most hilarious benefit is the paid, pompous state funeral, which spares the president's family the ordeal of paying what the industry indelicately refers to as final expenses. Is this lifestyle all that different from the reign of a monarch, which George Washington and the other Founders were anxious to avoid?

News broke in June 2014 that US taxpayers were spending nearly a million dollars annually to support former president Bill Clinton's lifestyle. Like the other living ex-presidents, Jimmy Carter, and both George Bushes, Clinton is paid a $201,000 yearly pension. In 2014, the government doled out $157,000 for staff salaries and benefits, $414,000 for office space, and $9,000 for phone bills incurred by Clinton. Meanwhile, the government is inexplicably subsidizing things like George W. Bush's portrait painting. In fact, Bush is getting even more annually from taxpayers than Clinton, with a total of $1.28 million in subsidies in 2014. The General Services Administration budgeted an unfathomable $102,000 for Bush's telephone expenses, leading one to ponder just who and where the great "decider" is calling.

In 2012, *ABC News* had reported that taxpayers were footing bills in the amount of $15,000 for Jimmy Carter's postage, $579,000 for Bill Clinton's office rent, and $80,000 for George W. Bush's phone bills (apparently, this guy really loves to use the phone). In 2011, taxpayers paid for Clinton to install at least ten televisions in his New York offices, equipped with top-tier DirectTV content packages. Jimmy Carter's office billed taxpayers for a much more modest Dish Network programming package. Both Bill Clinton's and Jimmy Carter's offices have subscriptions to the *New York Times* covered by taxpayers.[308] In 2016, the annual pay for ex-presidents was increased to $205,700.

Hillary Clinton, in the run-up to her 2016 presidential run, laughably informed the press that she and her husband were "dead broke" when they left the White House. She also claimed they still weren't "truly well off," despite Bill's estimated $80 million fortune and her own additional $21.5 million. Like other members of the One Percent, she added a reminder that "we've done it through the dint of hard work." NBC's Chuck Todd overtly attempted to defend

Hillary Clinton, helpfully (and inaccurately) pointing out that being in the public limelight was "not a bubble she chose."[309] Bill Clinton made other ridiculous references to how they were in touch with average people because they visited the local grocery store.[310]

Like many wealthy people, Bill Clinton has a foundation, which comes in handy at tax time. To those still recalling the myriad of scandals and allegations of corruption that have swirled around the Clintons ever since they entered public life, it's no surprise to learn that the Bill Clinton Foundation has been used for non-charitable purposes. The establishment's flagship newspaper, the *New York Times,* published an illuminating August 14, 2013, article on the subject. The article revealed that the foundation had been used to promote Bill Clinton's business ventures, as well as Hillary Clinton's political aspirations, and it was "supervised by a rotating board of old Clinton hands . . . threatened by conflicts of interest. It ran multimillion dollar deficits for several years, despite vast amounts of money flowing in." One example the paper cited was former Clinton personal assistant Douglas J. Band, whose lucrative corporate consulting firm boasts the ex-president as a paid adviser, being tapped to oversee the "Clinton Global Initiative," which brought up obvious conflicts of interest. Band's company, Teneo, charges client fees of up to $250,000 per month, often to those who were also Clinton Foundation donors. The Better Business Bureau had concluded in 2012 that the Clinton Foundation had failed to meet the standards of an accountable charity on six counts. Previous stories had listed other cases, such as New York developer Robert Congel donating $100,000 to the foundation in 2004 and shortly thereafter garnering millions in federal assistance for his mall project, courtesy of Senator Hillary Clinton.[311]

Bill Clinton's prolific paid-speaking career got off on the right foot with $125,000 payoffs from both Morgan Stanley and Credit Suisse in early 2001, coincidentally right after he'd signed the Commodities Future Modernization Act, which legally forbid the regulation of derivatives. Clinton would later get huge speaking fees from his friends in the banking world, such as Citigroup, Goldman Sachs, Lehman Brothers, and Deutsche Bank.[312] Hillary Clinton spoke to the same groups; she received $675,000 for three speeches to Goldman Sachs alone. Investigative reporter Carl Bernstein told CNN that it defied belief that she took such fees without considering the ethical ramifications.[313] The 2016 WikiLeaks disclosures amounted to a continuous exposure of the Clinton Foundation's conflicts of interest. The book *Clinton Cash*, by Peter Schweizer, detailed how much foreign governments and businesses had helped the Clintons. Donald Trump called the Clinton Foundation "a criminal enterprise" during the 2016 presidential campaign.

While the perks of the executive and legislative branches get media attention, those serving in the judicial branch of the government have a pretty sweet deal, too. Talk about power—imagine literally holding someone's fate in your hands, as judges in every courtroom do daily across this country. How can someone not develop a monstrous ego when all in attendance are required to rise when you enter a room, and the slightest challenge to your authority carries the threat of contempt? The Supreme Court justices are paid slightly over $200,000 annually, and have the position for life. As Supreme Court historian Lucas "Scot" Powe acknowledges, "In many ways, it's the cushiest job in the world." Clerks themselves do much of the actual work for the justices, summarizing the thousands of petitions and helping to write actual opinions. "There's also not that much required work," Powe said, "and they've made it less over time." Over the past thirty years, for instance, the court's workload has diminished, with 2016 consisting of the fewest decisions in at least seventy years. The Court has a nine-month term, giving them summers off, and many take advantage by traveling to give all expenses-paid "legal seminars" in some prime vacation locale. "They're not flying coach and they're not paying a cent for their travel or accommodations," according to Powe. There are also generous opportunities to earn extra cash, as justices can accrue thousands from speaking fees, professorships, and book deals. As *ABC News* admitted, the justices are "well off financially. Many also come from wealthy families or are married to high-earning spouses."[314] Those judges that opt to retire are eligible for a wonderful pension that pays them their highest salary for the rest of their lives. Federal judges can make as much as $145,000 in base salary, depending upon their location, and receive the same kind of superior benefits most government workers do. They also work fewer hours than the vast majority of employees, have job security for life, and like the Supreme Court justices, their pension plan allows them to retire at age sixty-five with full pay.

Does anyone really imagine that this is the best we can do? Embarrassing figures like Bill and Hillary Clinton, the Bushes, John McCain, Lindsay Graham, Nancy Pelosi, John Boehner, Dianne Feinstein, Barack Obama—trotted out as the heirs to George Washington, Thomas Jefferson, and the like? What has any political figure ever done—at least since the death of John F. Kennedy— to earn an exalted status in our society? With their overt tendency toward corruption, their visible lack of intellect and skill, and their frequent lapses into incompetent buffoonery, how can we claim that they are worth what *we the people* are giving them? Look at any old campaign speeches from nearly any period in our country's history, and you'll find the same tired arguments about nothing, the same empty promises that are inevitably broken. Few, if any, real issues, the ones that effect the 80 percent who remain forever outside the gates of power and influence, are even cavalierly broached. The choices we are given by these glorified welfare recipients are usually akin to choosing our means of execution. Invariably, we hear more condescending compliments to the American People, how we're the greatest country in the world, how we're always willing to sacrifice anything, how nothing can hold us down or defeat us, how we always bounce back again, and endless calls for new wars.

It is extremely difficult to find any brilliant speeches, any true moments of eloquence, in the collective political record of the modern era. Perhaps this is why some of John F. Kennedy's articulate, stirring speeches stand out so dramatically, and still resound with the public. Politicians from both major parties litter the landscape with self-serving rhetoric, largely meaningless sloganeering about children or education or leadership or jobs. In reality, they are concerned with one thing: pleasing the powerful forces that permit them to stay entrenched in their envious positions. They are no more deserving of their riches, their celebrity, and their place in history than the typical CEO, athlete, or entertainer is. What makes them worse than all the others, in many ways, is the fact *we* make them wealthy. We choose to keep re-electing them when they've proven conclusively over and over again that they are decidedly not deserving of being returned to office. The biggest individual welfare cheat in the country cannot hold a candle to your standard, unprincipled, elected representative. Their cost to taxpayers is the ultimate case of not getting our money's worth, and because they actually are given great powers, they have the ability to negatively impact all our lives with their decisions. If we are to eliminate taxpayer-funded entitlements, we need to start by looking at the entitled members of the government.

16 No Admissions, No Gratitude

Experience demands that man is the only animal which devours his own kind, for I can apply no milder term to the general prey of the rich on the poor.

—Thomas Jefferson

Two truly curious traits the very rich continuously exhibit are the inability to admit to being wealthy and a collective ungratefulness for their wealth. Republican Congressman John Fleming caused a small uproar when he complained, "Well, $500,000 a year might sound like a lot, but I'm hardly rich" during a September 2011 appearance on MSNBC. Fleming's comments were made in response to President Obama's proposed tax increases on the wealthy, or as Fleming and others call them, job creators. Fleming invoked the rallying cry of the elite, at one point declaring, "Class warfare has never created a job."[315] According to *ABC News*, Fleming's net worth is $9.5 million. Longtime Democratic Senator Charles Schumer echoed these sentiments, moaning that "It is hard to ask more of households making $250,000 or $300,000 a year. In large parts of the country, that kind of income does not get you a big home or lots of vacations or anything else that is associated with wealth." If that kind of income doesn't get you those things, one wonders what the average household income of $51,017 will get you.[316]

Bill and Hillary's daughter Chelsea Clinton told *Fast Company* magazine in a May 2014 interview that "I was curious if I could care about [money] on some fundamental level, and I couldn't." Despite her antipathy for wealth, Chelsea forced herself to accept a $600,000 annual salary for extreme part-time work as an NBC special correspondent. In 2013, she earned $26,000 per *minute* in a crucial, historically memorable interview with Geico's ridiculous gecko character. "I will always just work harder and hopefully perform better," Chelsea declared. She and her husband, former banker Marc Mezvinsky, purchased a $10.5 million Manhattan apartment in 2013.[317] Another presidential offspring, Jenna Bush Hager, daughter of George W. Bush, was hired by NBC as a sporadic correspondent. She managed to get a young-adult novel published by giant HarperCollins, with an incredible initial print run of five hundred thousand copies, and was hired as an editor at large by *Southern Living* magazine. She then had a second book published, cowritten with her mother.

Actor Ashton Kutcher, worth $140 million, also portends not to care about money. "If I don't make money, but what we deliver to people is love and happiness and connectivity and friendship and health, and whatever it is ultimately leads to people's happiness, I'm fine with losing my money," Kutcher was quoted as saying on the *Daily Stab.* Gwyneth Paltrow has uttered so many clueless statements that websites have compiled them. Paltrow has claimed, "I don't want to be rich and I don't want to be famous." Chronicling a lifestyle that few can comprehend, *Harper's Bazaar* stated, "Having survived her 10th London winter . . . with a visiting Italian chef, Japanese anime screenings, and hand-rolled sushi lessons . . . Paltrow admits that her dreams of relocating her family to . . . Brentwood, California, are becoming ever more urgent." She bragged to *Harper's* that women "come to me because they know I'm very loving and nonjudgmental and I'm not competitive, and I've been through a lot." One can only guess at what Paltrow could possibly mean by having been through a lot. Paltrow worked her way up the Hollywood ladder after being born to well-known actress Blythe Danner and Bruce Paltrow, a film producer and director.

The problems of the wealthy are difficult for the common riffraff to relate to. "Going to those parties," wrote David Patrick Columbia, editor of the *New York Social Diary,* describing all the charity galas for the upper crust, "a woman can spend $10,000 or $15,000 on a dress. If she goes to three or four of those a year, she's not going to wear the same dress." *Sex in the City* author Candace Bushnell, whose net worth is $40 million, expressed empathy for the very wealthy, which of course includes her, by saying, "People inherently understand that if they are going to get ahead in whatever corporate culture they are involved in, they need to take on the appurtenances of what defines that culture." Another celebrated novelist, Holly Peterson, who grew up the daughter of a founder of the equity giant The Blackstone Group, chimed in as well, "bankers who are living on the Upper East Side making $2 or $3 million a year have set up [lives] for themselves in which they are also at zero at the end of the year with credit cards and mortgage bills that are inescapable." All this and more was detailed in an absurd article in the establishment's newspaper of record, headlined, "You Try to Live on 500K in This Town."[318] Venture capitalist Tom Perkins, with a net worth of some $8 billion, actually compared the Occupy Wall Street movement and other criticism of the One Percent to Nazi Germany's campaign against the Jews, calling it a "Progressive Kristallnacht."[319] Perkins is married to high-profile novelist Danielle Steel and lobbies for giving the rich more votes than everyone else "because they pay more taxes."[320]

None of the issues covered in this book are exclusive to America. An Essex University study found that in Great Britain, children of the wealthy were more likely to be ungrateful and saw less of their parents on average after moving away from home than grown off-spring of lower-class families. Their research revealed that young adults with a college degree were 20 percent less likely to phone their mothers regularly and 50 percent less likely to visit them.[321] One can safely guess that this trend is even more prevalent in American society. *Time* magazine cited studies that show wealthier people are more likely to behave unethically in simulated business and charity scenarios. The rich also donate less on average to charities than even the poorest Americans, who give more than twice as much: 3.2 percent of their earnings, as opposed to 1.3 percent from the very wealthy. Researchers find increased levels of both narcissism and entitlement among those of a higher social class who have more wealth. The rich, as might be predicted, feel they are more deserving than other people. Madeline Levine, a California psychologist who has treated teens from affluent families for years, declared, "Their sense of entitlement is overpowering."[322]

There are eccentric billionaires who will waste their money on the most outlandish things. For instance, shipping fortune heir Alki David offered $1 million to anyone who streaked in front of President Obama. When twenty-four-year old Juan James Rodriguez took him up on the offer, David predictably rewarded him with an undisclosed, significantly smaller sum.[323] Amazon founder Jeff Bezos frittered away $42 million on a special clock designed to run for ten thousand years. Broadcom founder Henry T. Nicholas was accused of building a secret sex cave under his mansion.[324] Nicholas and other Broadcom executives had been charged with stock fraud, and he himself was indicted on drug charges, but predictably a judge threw out all the charges against him and blasted the prosecution for its "shameful" conduct.[325] Oracle founder Larry Ellison had a spare $400 million to spend in an egomaniacal quest to win the America's Cup. Ellison installed a basketball court on each of his two gargantuan yachts and employed a power boat to follow behind "to retrieve balls that go overboard." After buying out PeopleSoft, Ellison proceeded to lay off five thousand employees, nearly half of the company's workforce.[326] Where are the eccentric rich people who decide to divest themselves of large sums by giving it to those who desperately need it?

Actor Craig T. Nelson, who has a net worth of $45 million, during a 2009 appearance on right-wing, neoconservative Glenn Beck's talk show made this remarkable statement: "What happened to society? I go into business. I don't make it. I go bankrupt. I've been on food stamps and welfare; did anybody help me out? No." Many studies have confirmed the fact that with wealth comes a real attitude. Luxury cars, for instance, are far less likely to wait their turns at four-way intersections, and more apt to cut off pedestrians and other vehicles. A 2008 study led by a University of Amsterdam professor found that people in elevated social positions were less likely to feel compassion or distress over the suffering of someone else. This conclusion was supported by a 2011 University of California, Berkeley, study, which discovered that the less education and income someone had, the more likely they were to care about others. In fact, the level of generosity and compassion on the part of the participants in the study increased the lower their social status was.[327] The results of a study by New York University psychologists published in *Psychological Science* in 2016 showed that wealthy people literally don't acknowledge others or pay the slightest attention to them. Not surprisingly, a host of studies have bolstered the notion that while the poor tend to blame a larger set of circumstances for their situation, the rich simplistically attribute success to individual effort and failure to individual faults.[328]

Warren Buffett's frugality has been well publicized; for instance, refusing to help his daughter remodel her kitchen or his granddaughter pay her college tuition. Fellow billionaire J. Paul Getty set standards even he couldn't match. In 1973, Getty's sixteen-year-old grandson J. Paul Getty III was kidnapped in Rome. His parents were willing to pay the $17 million ransom but didn't have the cash. Getty Sr. refused to help, famously commenting "I have fourteen other grandchildren, and if I pay one penny now I'll have fourteen kidnapped grandchildren." Shortly thereafter, a newspaper in Rome received a gruesome package in the mail, containing the teenager's severed ear and a lock of his red hair. Getty Sr., still remarkably unmoved, loaned his son $2.5 million for a much-lower ransom amount on condition he pay it back with

4 percent interest. Despite losing an ear in the ordeal, Getty III tried to phone his grandfather to thank him after being released, but the old man wouldn't take the call. Like so many scions of great wealth, Getty's son and grandson were troubled souls; both of them had reportedly fought heroin addiction. Getty III overdosed on drugs and alcohol in 1981 and was incapacitated for the rest of his life. A California judge had to order Getty Jr. to help pay for his son's nursing care. Getty III's tragic life ended in 2011 at the premature age of fifty-four.[329] There are also online reports that Getty was so cheap he had pay phones installed in the guest bedrooms at his mansion.

Billionaire Howard Hughes exemplified how wealthy people whose behavior is out of the ordinary are considered eccentric rather than crazy. Mental illness is apparently another malady the wealthy are exempt from; back in the 1990s, the World Health Organization found that psychiatric conditions occur at higher rates in the poorest areas, while a 1963 Midtown Manhattan study concluded that poverty can be both a determinant and a consequence of poor mental health. A 2007 survey by the National Alliance to End Homelessness reported that some 744,000 Americans were homeless; around 250,000 of these were individuals with manic-depressive illness or schizophrenia. Mental institutions began deinstitutionalizing many patients during the Reagan years, a practice that the *New York Times* termed "a cruel embarrassment, a reform gone terribly wrong." In its 2016 report, the National Alliance to End Homelessness found that the rate of persons living with family or friends, "the most common prior living situation before becoming homeless," had risen 52 percent between 2007–2014.

Where we really see the dark side of human nature is in the effect winning the lottery has on many people. To my knowledge, not once has a single lottery winner smiled broadly, thanked God, or declared that he or she will help as many people as possible with the money. There is a better chance of someone getting struck by lightning twice in the same day than there is of winning millions in the lottery. Those who have profited from this incredibly unlikely good fortune should, one would guess, feel grateful and blessed. Instead, they frequently react as if someone is trying to take it away from them, as if they expect to be pestered by friends and family clamoring for money, and yes, they even behave as if they've earned it.

If winning the lottery once is an incredibly unlikely twist of fate, imagine the odds of winning it more than once. Amazingly, there are numerous examples of multiple lottery winners, suggesting that the entire system mimics the way our culture at large rewards the same people repeatedly. The most incredible example in this category is Seguro Ndabene, a Canadian who had won the lottery *five* times since 2004 for an aggregate $19.1 million. Ndabene's fifth win was held up in the courts over a dispute from another party claiming he was entitled to share in what was a group purchase, until Ndabene alone was eventually awarded the $17 million prize. Instead of celebrating, Ndabene threatened to sue the Lottery company, complaining, "This was amounting to torture, to torture me because I won several times. . . . I won the money and they refused to pay me right away." As one anonymous poster on a forum commented, "The five-time Lotto winner wants to talk about torture because the Lotto Corp. thought something might have been up after he won for a *fifth* time?"

Once they've been magically transformed into millionaires by a set of randomly selected numbers, people tend overwhelmingly to instantly catch the entitled attitude of the rich, the belief that they are special, while everyone else, who aren't winners, are trying to rob them of what isn't theirs. Many prove reluctant to share their good fortune even with their closest family members. Perhaps the old expression "fortune favors the bold" should logically be replaced with "fortune favors the cheap." Why aren't previous winners of large amounts in the lottery exempted from further winnings? While that makes eminent sense to me, I suppose it contradicts every aspect of our winner-take-all society.

As mentioned earlier, more rich celebrities are using Kickstarter to get their much less wealthy fans to finance their projects for them. However, the practice has been criticized to such a surprising extent that celebrities have felt the need to respond. Director Spike Lee defended his glorified begging for money with the well-thought-out response, "Fuck the haters!" As Emmy-award-winning writer Ken Levine explained, "The idea—and it's a great one—is that Kickstarter allows filmmakers who otherwise would have NO access to Hollywood and NO access to serious investors to scrounge up enough money to make their movies. Zach Braff has contacts. Zach Braff has a name. . . . He can get in a room with money people. He is represented by a major talent agency. But the poor schmoe in Mobile, Alabama, or Walla Walla, Washington, has none of those advantages."

Kickstarter is really no different from the illogical premise behind the 1985 Live Aid concert, conceived by the Boomtown Rats' front man Bob Geldof (now one of those pretentious British "Sirs"), and all its offshoots: Farm Aid, Comic Relief, USA for Africa, etc. In all those seemingly worthwhile efforts, rich celebrities were recruited to perform their music or tell their jokes while urging viewers (the vast majority of them far from wealthy) to contribute money, most often to end hunger and famine in Africa. The logical question, never asked by the always-adoring press, was why the wealthy entertainers didn't simply donate millions themselves instead of imploring those with substantially less means to do so. The purpose of the concert was, to quote Geldof, to get viewers to "Give us your fucking money!" Wouldn't it have been more effective to deliver food personally to the starving Africans so that it could be ascertained that the money actually was spent properly and that the food got to those who needed it? What exactly were the celebrities contributing, anyway, other than assuaging their consciences, and making themselves feel good? In reality, these celebrities were unneeded middlemen, collecting other people's money for their heartfelt "cause."

Geldof, not surprisingly, is now associated with his fellow Irish rock star Bono's notoriously unproductive foundation ONE as an advisor. As conservative critic Michelle Malkin put it in her September 23, 2010, blog entry regarding Bono's foundation's unbelievably high operating expenses and the corresponding pittance that is spent on the actual causes, "So ONE (percent) paid out around $8 million to employees to monitor the disbursement of about $185,000?" In 2008, "Sir" Bob gave a speech about Third-World poverty to the nonprofit group Diversity@Work, for which it was later revealed he was paid $100,000 and given luxury accommodations and first-class airfare.[330] By 2012, it was reported that Geldof, now running a large private equity firm, was speaking to wealthy investors about tapping into his beloved African continent for profits. Sir Bob was reported as having exploded with rage when a journalist dared to question his tax status. It was further revealed that "he has exploited off-shore companies based in the British Virgin Islands to ensure his two homes here—the mansion flat in Battersea, South London . . . and his rambling country home in Faversham, Kent—are both exempt from stamp duty and inheritance tax." Geldof summoned up every ounce of entitlement he possessed; as described in a UK newspaper, "Jabbing his finger, swearing and yelling, he exclaimed: . . . 'My time? Is that not a tax? I employ 500 people. . . . I have given my ideas. I have given half my life to this. How dare you lecture me about morals.'"[331] Only a thoroughly self-absorbed One Percenter could possibly believe that his time was a tax.

The focus of Live Aid's and USA for Africa's efforts, the starving people in Ethiopia, were evidently not helped much by the estimated $245 million raised by Geldof and company. In 1990, the media reflected upon the five-year anniversary of USA for Africa's huge hit record, *We Are The World,* by reporting, "Nevertheless, famine in Africa has not subsided. In fact, famine in Ethiopia, complicated by an ongoing civil war, is feared to be reaching the kind of crisis stage that existed in 1984–85."[332] By 2010, it was being reported by the BBC that some of the funds sent in by well-meaning people had gone to purchase guns for Ethiopian warlords. Geldof responded to these reports by calling them "total bullshit."[333]

Oprah Winfrey is very good at being a glorified middleman as well, having generated tons of goodwill from the fawning press and her adoring legions of fans for bestowing numerous gifts on her studio audience, most often automobiles. Winfrey, worth just under $3 billion, doesn't pay for the cars and other gifts; they are donated by the companies. And to top it all off, apparently the recipients have to pay taxes on these gifts. CNN studied the 276 new Pontiacs Oprah gave to a 2004 studio audience and found that—depending on individual tax brackets—a recipient would have to pay as much as $7,000 in taxes for it.[334] Oprah, being the rich elitist she is, had her accountants categorize them as prizes instead of gifts so that the winners would have to pay the taxes instead of her. So it cost this billionaire nothing—not even the pocket-change-type of taxes she would have been obligated to cover—yet she was given full credit for being a generous philanthropist.

The controversial author Kitty Kelly, in her biography of Oprah Winfrey, reported that many audience members, unable to come up with that much cash to pay for the taxes, turned to Oprah for help. As Kelly wrote, "her publicist said they had three options— they could keep the car and pay the tax, sell the car and pay the tax with the profit, or forfeit the car. There was no other option from Oprah." Louis Laze, in a *Chicago Sun-Times* piece, asked, "Was this really a do-good event Winfrey pulled off, or a cold-blooded pub- licity stunt designed to make the talk-show diva really look good at the expense of Pontiac, which gladly provided cars in exchange for some of Winfrey's promotional plugging?" Oprah was incensed over these accusations. As Kelly quoted her, she said, "For all the people who say, 'Oh, you didn't personally pay for the cars yourself,' which I heard, I say 'Well, I could have, and what difference does it make, if they get the cars? And why should I have paid for them if Pontiac was willing to do so?'" This billionaire spends $500 on mink eyelashes but wouldn't cover the taxes for those in her audience who simply weren't able to afford her gift. Kelly's book is full of gems that reveal the lifestyles of these rich and famous, celebrated hoarders of wealth. The ridiculous, over-the-top presents they give each other; such as the $100,000 convertible John Travolta (her "favorite white man") gifted Oprah; or the twin Bentleys that Tyler Perry, whom Oprah lovingly refers to as "my rich Negro man," gave to Oprah and her longtime friend Gayle King. Oprah revels in her wealth, proclaiming, "I have a closet full of shoes, and it's a good thing." When a fellow rich friend asked her, on the way back from a trip to Africa, if she felt guilty over having so much, Oprah replied, "No, I don't. I do not know how my being destitute is going to help them. . . . I'm going to sleep on my Pratesi sheets right now and I'll feel good about it."[335]

The luxuries never end for the wealthy, whether they are celebrated figures or anonymous corporate plutocrats. Special black platinum American Express cards to easily differentiate them from ambitious upper-middle-class wannabes. Private flights that bypass the onerous security checks—including the increasingly invasive, unconstitutional searches by TSA agents. Cinema services that will have the latest movies delivered to their mansion for viewing in their private theater on the same day it's released to the public. Heated driveways, personal shoppers, night nannies—the list goes on and on.[336]

Whether it's inherited wealth, a star who made it largely due to some wonderfully attractive genetics, or a fluky lottery winner, few who have great wealth appear to be thankful for it. They may relish it, or they may deny having it, but they simply don't appear capable of acting grateful about it. And they certainly don't like sharing it.

17 THE FUTURE OF WEALTH DISTRIBUTION

"I never got a job from a poor person."

—Sean Hannity

WHEN THE REMAKE OF FRANK Capra's timeless 1936 film *Mr. Deeds Goes to Town* was released in 2002, my interest was piqued, despite the fact it starred Adam Sandler, one of my least favorite entertainers. The original film explored the distribution of wealth in America during the time of the Great Depression. Longfellow Deeds, played by Gary Cooper, inherits a fortune and ultimately decides to give it away to the poor. He is summarily classified as insane and has to undergo a hearing to determine if he is mentally fit to handle his own finances. In the remake, with the shortened title of *Mr. Deeds,* there is no mention at all, not even cursorily, of Sandler's character giving away any money to those who need it. In other words, Hollywood remade a classic movie without even including the central theme of the original. This truly exemplified how much this country has changed and how untenable even a fictional account of a wealthy person divesting himself of his riches is now to the entertainment industry.

Long ago, socialist politician Eugene Debs (whose father came from a prosperous French family) said, "I am opposing a social order in which it is possible for one man who does absolutely nothing that is useful to amass a fortune of hundreds of millions of dollars, while millions of men and women who work all the days of their lives secure barely enough for a wretched existence." Debs was jailed and sentenced to ten years and disenfranchised for life for his opposition to World War I. When Debs was released from the Atlanta penitentiary, fifty thousand supporters were on hand to greet him back home in Terre Haute, Indiana.[337] Debs, like Huey Long, would be deeply disappointed at the massive inequity of wealth we have today in America and around the world. If a prominent socialist were released from prison today, can we picture fifty thousand people congregating anywhere to support him?

Those who benefit so lavishly from the inequitable system we currently have will not relinquish anything without kicking and screaming. In July 2014, former KISS band member Gene Simmons, who epitomizes someone whose "talent" doesn't match his fame or fortune, proudly defended the very wealthy in an interview with *U-T San Diego*. "I have been part of the 1 percent for the past 30 years," Simmons declared. "It's fantastic! The 1 percent pays 80 percent of all taxes. Fifty percent of the population of the US pays no taxes. The 1 percent provides all the jobs for everybody else. If the 1 percent didn't exist, there would be chaos and the American economy would drop dead. Try being nice to rich people. I don't remember the last poor person who gave me a job."[338] For the record, it doesn't appear that Simmons has ever been given a job by anyone, rich or poor. He's always been a rock star, which is not work in any traditional sense. And he, like most wealthy people, certainly isn't creating jobs. Simmons represents everything distasteful about modern capitalism; he revels in selling the KISS name any way possible; thus the band's name can be found on everything from M&Ms to condoms. Simmons told CNN that the KISS brand was worth as much as $5 billion.

We're bound to keep hearing the fluffy advice from experts regarding how those who can't pay their bills can learn to save money; for instance, the ridiculous "Feed the Pig" campaign, which advises people to put change into a literal piggy bank, or impossible admonitions to "pay yourself first," which of course no working-class or poor person can possibly do. How can you pay yourself if you're struggling to pay your bills? The European Central Bank has already started paying bank customers *negative interest rates* on their deposits—in other words, charging them for saving their own money. Economist Martin Armstrong warned that US banks are bound to follow suit, inventing a new array of additional, unnecessary account fees that will serve in effect as a negative interest rate. "The talk behind the curtain," Armstrong said, "is to impose negative interest rates on the consumer."[339] The bible of our marketplace, the *Wall Street Journal,* advertised the coming new normal in this area with a June 14, 2016, story headlined, "Everything You Need to Know About Negative Rates."

The gap between rich and poor is even growing in the area of life expectancy. That's right, in addition to all their other advantages, the rich live longer, too. A recent study by the Brookings Institution found that a rich man born in 1940 can expect to live nearly fifteen years longer than a poor counterpart of the same age. Incredibly, this longevity gap has grown by four years in just a single generation. If a wealthy male reaches the age of fifty-five, his average life expectancy is just under ninety (89.9). The poorest males at fifty-five, in contrast, have a life expectancy of 77.6. The wealthiest women, meanwhile, can expect to live to 90.3 years if they reach fifty-five, while the poorest females have an average life span of 82.9 once they hit fifty-five. The saddest statistic of all is the one that examines the change in life span for females born between 1920 and 1940. Incredibly, impoverished women have seen their overall life expectancy actually *drop* by 2.1 percent, while the females in the lowest 40 percent income level also saw their life expectancies dip slightly. The wealthiest 10 percent of women, meanwhile, saw their life expectancy increase by 5.9 percent during the same time frame.[340] *Smithsonian* magazine referred to this phenomenon as a clear "life expectancy gap" between the rich and poor. In 2013, new data revealed that average life spans in the United States had dropped to a full year lower than the international average, and the United States was now ranked twenty-sixth in the world, right behind Slovenia.[341] In 2015, for the first time in more than twenty years, life expectancy in the United States dropped slightly.[342]

Despite being the richest country in the world, Internet service in the United States is overpriced and slow, according to a State of the Internet report by delivery network Akamai. The study also found that America's Internet service is getting even slower, compared to other tech-savvy nations. Presently, the United States has only the ninth-fastest Internet connection speed in the world, ranking behind nations like Latvia and the Czech Republic. Why shouldn't the richest country have the best Internet service? While providers like Comcast charge consumers $320 a month for higher speeds like 305 Mbps, and Verizon beats that deal with the fastest available speed, 500 Mbps, for $310 per month, web surfers in Hong Kong can get that same 500 Mbps for only $25 monthly, or in Seoul, Korea, for $30. Predictably, several cable company CEOs have responded to the understandable criticism with editorials in the mainstream media, extolling American broadband prices and performance.[343] This is another aspect of the new norm in America: a rush to vanity where one should feel shame. I have a friend who comes from the Dominican Republic, and he has sworn for years that the Internet in that country is much faster and much cheaper as well. How have the wealthy CEOs who run Verizon, Comcast, and other Internet providers earned their great wealth, when they can't provide the same speed, or the same value, that is being provided in smaller, less wealthy nations? On August 7, 2013, *Forbes* trumpeted the good news that Comcast's CEO Brian L. Roberts was now a billionaire again, "for the first time since 2001." Not only is Roberts presiding over a company that charges more for Internet service and can't deliver the speeds Latvians enjoy, he can't claim credit for success, as he is the son of Comcast's cofounder. Ivan G. Seidenberg, Verizon's CEO, made over $18 million in 2016. Verizon's executive salaries were so high the *Huffington Post* headlined a May 1, 2016, story, "Are the Salaries of Verizon's Executives Being Charged to Low Income Families?" Does the kind of service his company provides, which is apparently not up to the level seen in the Dominican Republic, indicate that he is worth this kind of compensation?

Like so many science fiction novels, movies, and television shows predicted, robotics has developed to a point where it is yet another threat to working-class jobs. The *Washington Post* headlined a December 23, 2013, article, "Eight Ways Robots Stole Our Jobs in 2013." The jobs in question were all lower-class, blue-collar positions; Amazon, for instance, now uses robots to pick up online orders in warehouses, which means it "may not even have to hire the tens of thousands of temp workers it brings for the busy holiday season." In a partial response to 2014's unsuccessful fast-food worker strikes, "at least one company is working diligently" to replace line workers with mechanical cooks. Another company is working on technology to supplant "hundreds of thousands of menial laboratory jobs that pay decent money but could more efficiently be done by robots." As we discussed earlier, these advances will be at the expense of the poor and working class, as they invariably are. No one in the top 20 percent will be affected by them. You are not ever going to see a robot vice president or a robot consultant, and certainly never a robot CEO. The bestseller *The Second Machine Age,* by Erik Brynjolfsson and Andrew McAfee, addresses this issue, but in a peripheral, mainstream establishment way. In December 2016, reflecting the self-serve trend that has increasingly appeared in stores all over America, Amazon announced the introduction of the first grocery store without cashiers. Earlier in 2016, it was widely reported that self-driving trucks could cost the loss of some five million jobs.[344]

The whole robotics industry focuses attention on just how shortsighted, how narcissistic, our corrupt and incompetent leaders have become. How can they not have the foresight to understand that this shiny new employment pool can never pay taxes and can never purchase the products it will be making? Henry Ford, despite his antiunion stance, for instance, famously doubled his workers' wages in 1914 and defended the strategy by declaring that his employees had to be paid enough to afford to buy his product. It was not only a good public relations gesture, it was a brilliant business tactic that resulted in a lot more cars being sold. Henry J. Heinz, who founded the food empire, provided his employees with free medical care; allowed them to use on-site facilities like gyms, swimming pools, and libraries; and offered them free concerts and lectures. Milton Hershey the chocolate magnate provided similar leisure activities for his employees. While *Forbes* can headline an article "Happy Employees = Hefty Profits," and *USA Today* can proclaim "Do Happy Workers Mean Higher Company Profits?," and *Huffington Post* can report "Treat Workers Well to Boost Profits," few companies today seem to be heeding their advice or emulating old capitalists like Heinz and Hershey. On the contrary, the business world now operates with the draconian premise that employees must never feel secure about their positions and that the best worker is a lean and hungry, desperate worker.

Businesses can be incredibly generous. Google, for instance, which judging by the Glassdoor website, pays most of its employees more than $100,000 annually and offers an astonishing array of perks. Free breakfast, lunch, and dinner, all of it prepared organically by an on-site chef, free health and dental insurance, free haircuts, free dry cleaning, and subsidies for purchasing a hybrid car are benefits that Google employees receive. Gyms, swimming pools, video games, foosball, ping-pong, bonuses and stock options, on-site physicians, and even nap pods, where the exhausted workers can rest on the job, are also included in this lucrative package. These kinds of dream perks, however, are only extended to those who are already making a salary that puts them at least in the top 20 percent. Google's CEO, Sundar Pichai, has profited handsomely; by 2016, he had accumulated $489 million in stock options alone since 2013.[345] Apple, on the other hand, exemplifies the way the new normal works in the corporate world; while its top-paid employees are treated royally, about thirty thousand of its forty-five thousand workers work in Apple stores and earn $25,000 or so per year. As University of North Carolina Professor Arne L. Kalleberg described it, "In the service sector, companies provide a little bit of training and hope their employees leave after a few years."[346]

Once again, we see this constant theme of the marketplace channeling benefits and free stuff to those who make the most money already and are best equipped to deal with the costs of haircuts, dry cleaning, gym memberships, etc. Meanwhile, the poor suckers living from paycheck to paycheck are advised to live within their means and forego the trappings of modern technology. The costs of living are the same for everyone, but the freebies and perks go to those who least need them. If those who are unemployed or underemployed receive the smallest supplement from some inefficient government program, however, then the mob grabs their pitchforks indignantly over this outrageous handout. This same mob remains indifferent toward the far more significant corporate welfare that permeates the corrupt system, and is both privately and publicly funded.

Because of society's collective lust for winning at all costs, coaches at any level who succeed are considered worth any amount of money and are even preposterously labeled as geniuses. Bobby Knight, for instance, is still a respected talking head on television, despite a checkered career that featured temper tantrums and violent behavior unacceptable in any other field or industry. Knight once famously threw a chair onto the basketball court in anger, and more notably choked a player during a 1997 practice. After a cursory investigation, Knight was suspended for three games and fined $30,000. He was actually fired by Indiana University in 2000 after violating their zero-tolerance policy for the umpteenth time by physically assaulting a student. Over the years, Knight was involved in enough incidents to invite comparisons with the worst thug imaginable: head-butting players, kicking his own son (who was then playing for him), choking a man at a restaurant, throwing an assistant coach out of his chair (after which the *assistant coach* was subsequently fired), challenging another coach to a fight, to name just the highlights. Despite showing the impulse control of a pre-schooler, Knight is a revered figure, a legend in his field, with a $15 million fortune. Longtime UNLV basketball coach Jerry Tarkanian was awash in gambling, drug, and recruiting scandals involving his student athletes throughout his entire lengthy coaching career. Tarkanian, who certainly looked and sounded the part of a two-bit mobster, eventually sued the NCAA for harassment and, not surprisingly, he won again as they settled out of court with him for $2.5 million. Because of our culture's affinity for winners, it really wouldn't matter if the Bobby Knights of the world were caught cheating in the most blatant manner possible. Rules are for suckers.

Sport is a metaphor for life, as has been said numerous times. Talented athletes are granted incredible leeway by the law, and hot-headed, immature coaches are handled with kid gloves, in the same manner that successful corporate executives can flout convention and the mores of our society in pursuit of wealth. Winning, in any field, is rewarded, time and time again. Winners, because of their genes that gave them good looks or unusual size, or because of the circumstances of their birth, which gave them a solid foundation on which to pursue their goals, are always considered to have earned it. The fact of their success, in whatever field, is enough to prove their worth. It doesn't matter how you play the game as long as you win—to fracture the old Grantland Rice quote. Or as coach Vince Lombardi famously put it, "Winning isn't everything; it's the only thing." And it doesn't matter why you lost, you're still a loser, and no excuses are legitimate. There are no partial losers or partial winners.

The trends delineated in this book are illustrated clearly in the recent, widely reported statistics regarding middle-class wealth in America versus the rest of the world. Middle-class Canadians, for example, were lagging well behind their American counterparts as recently as 2000. As of 2014, they became wealthier. The poor in Europe now earn more than poor Americans. As the *New York Times* wrote, in an April 22, 2014, story, "Although economic growth in the United States continues to be as strong as in many other countries, or stronger, a small percentage of American households is fully benefiting from it." A low-income family in America now earns substantially less than similar families in Canada, Sweden, Finland, Norway, or the Netherlands. Thirty-five years ago, the exact reverse was true. "The idea that the median American has so much more income than the middle class in all other parts of the world is not true these days," the *Times* quoted Harvard economist Lawrence Katz as saying. "In 1960, we were massively richer than anyone else. In 1980, we were richer. In the 1990s, we were still richer." That is no longer the case, Professor Katz added. The article further noted that employee pay in Canada and several European countries had risen faster than it has in the United States, since at least 2010. Stating the obvious, the *Times* went on to write, "companies in the United States economy distribute a smaller share of their bounty to the middle class and poor than similar companies elsewhere. Top executives make substantially more money in the United States than in other wealthy countries." But the wealthiest Americans are doing just fine; those at the ninety-fifth percentile of income make 20 percent more than their counterparts in Canada, 26 percent more than those in Great Britain, and 50 percent more than those in the Netherlands.

The simple fact, which none of our political or business leaders seem willing to address, is that people have to be able to afford the costs of shelter and food at the bare minimum. If our society is willing to cast a good percentage of them to the winds of fate because of technology, outsourcing, or any other reason, they are ensuring that the system they are profiting so handsomely from will come crashing down. There is no way to be optimistic about anything in our society at this point. The average American citizen is less secure financially than ever. On July 26, 2014, the *New York Times* reported the startling reality that America had in effect gone through a "lost decade," as evident by its headline, "The Typical Household, Now Worth a Third Less." The article revealed that the inflation-adjusted net worth of a typical American household had declined 36 percent since 2003, citing figures from a study by the Russell Sage Foundation. During the same time period, the net worth of the wealthiest 5 percent of households increased by 14 percent. A myriad of other research has demonstrated that the increases for the top One Percent have been far greater than that. As the story in the *Times* concludes, "When only a few people are winning and more than half the population is losing, surely something is amiss."

In spite of the undeniable reality that the vast majority of workers aren't being paid enough to meet the ever-increasing costs of living, all the experts can offer are long-winded dissertations on the Gross National Product, stimulus plans, or incomprehensible discussions about economic growth. In the words of Dartmouth professor Charles Wheelan, "Politicians respond almost exclusively to the desires of special interests and the wealthiest citizens . . . average citizens have little or no independent influence."[347] As Martin Gilens pointed out in his book *Affluence and Influence: Economic Inequality and Political Power in America,* America's policymakers are only attuned to the concerns of the rich and powerful. "American citizens are vastly unequal in their influence over policymaking, and that inequality is growing." Gilens wrote. "In most circumstances, affluent Americans exert substantial influence over the policies adopted by the federal government, and less well-off Americans exert virtually none. Even when Democrats control Congress and the White House, the less well-off are no more influential."[348]

In December 2014, the US House of Representatives passed a huge funding bill that included another bailout provision for the big banks. Thanks to this $1.1 trillion monstrosity, the taxpayers, through the Federal Deposit Corporation, will be responsible for financial derivatives losses suffered by Citibank and its ilk. A confidential source told *Infowars* that J. P. Morgan CEO Jamie Dimon felt so strongly about the provision that he telephoned individual lawmakers himself, urging them to vote for the bill. As *Zero Hedge* put it in a December 12, 2014, piece, "At least we now know with certainty that to a clear majority in Congress—one consisting of republicans and democrats—the future viability of Wall Street is far more important than the well-being of their constituents." The message coming from our alleged representatives is that if you're a member of the poor or working class, get educated, learn a skill, scale back those luxuries, and basically do more with less. But if you're a large corporation, you're too big to fail, and those struggling taxpayers must lend you the assistance that society refuses them.

Those in the top 20 percent, who have been entrusted with managing this unjust monstrosity, are collectively whistling past the graveyard. The wealth in our society is plentiful, but it's been absconded by a relative handful of exceptionally greedy individuals. Even most Ayn Rand disciples would understand that it wouldn't be right for one child in a preschool to hoard all the toys while the others sat around and cried. But they fiercely defend a system that permits a fraction of humanity to have far more than they could ever need or hope to spend, while condemning most of the world's population to what Thomas Wolfe termed "lives of quiet desperation." What Huey Long deplored in an April 1935 speech rings astonishingly true today: "We find not only the people going further into debt, but that the United States is going further into debt . . . on which we must pay interest for the balance of our lifetimes, and probably during the lifetime of our children. And with it all, there stalks a slimy specter of want, hunger, destitution, and pestilence, all because of the fact that in the land of too much and of too much to wear." They killed Huey Long, and the glaring disparity in wealth is still there. What's truly tragic is that there is no modern-day Huey Long.

Recent Social Security statistics revealed yet another shocking fact; 51 percent of American workers made less than $28,851 in 2014, and 40 percent made less than $20,000. Twenty thousand dollars is what a full-time worker being paid $10 an hour would earn. Just as damningly, 62 percent of Americans made less than $40,000 in 2014, and 71 percent made less than $50,000. Consider that these numbers are skewered significantly by the wealth of the One Percent, obviously raising the averages. A common, but in my view unrealistic, estimate is that it takes $50,000 of income for an American family of four to support the idealized middle-class lifestyle. So even using that very conservative figure, this means that in 2014, *71 percent* of Americans failed to reach the level of middle class. It goes without saying, of course, that the lowest-paid workers are also the ones without pensions or many other benefits at all. Free meals, gym usage, and video games are for the six-figure boys and girls at Google.

The 2016 Oxfam report revealed that the richest sixty-two individuals in the world possess as much wealth as the bottom half of humanity. This elite group was noticeable for its absence of any Henry Fords or Thomas Edisons. The usual suspects were there; Bill Gates at number one, Warren Buffett, the Walton heirs, the Mars heirs, George Soros, the Koch brothers, and a multitude of others whose primary occupation was "investor." As Bernie Sanders noted, "Talk about wealth inequality. Between 2013 and 2015, the fourteen wealthiest people in this country saw their net worth increase by $157 billion dollars." Perhaps even more shockingly, the 2016 Oxfam study confirmed their prediction from a year before—that the richest *one* percent of people in the world now have more wealth than the remaining *99* percent of human beings on the planet.[349]

A November 11, 2014, headline in *The Huffington Post* informed us that "Americans Got to Enjoy Only Half as Many Vacation Days as Europeans in 2014." Residents of Denmark, France, Germany, and Spain enjoy thirty vacation days a year, while the median number for all of Europe was twenty-eight. Americans, on the other hand, had only an average of fourteen vacation days. Again, even these statistics are unquestionably skewered by the fact so many in that top 20 percent have lucrative benefits, elevating the overall numbers considerably. In reality, how many poor people can afford a vacation anywhere?

I was impressed by an essay published in the November 22, 2013, *Huffington Post,* titled "This is Why Poor People's Bad Decisions

Make Perfect Sense." Author Linda Tirado describes the hectic life of the working poor; she works two jobs and goes to school. "Rest is a luxury for the rich," she writes. She makes numerous other enlightening points. "Convenience food is just that. And we are not allowed many conveniences" and "We're aware that we're not 'having kids,' we're 'breeding'" and "We will never feel hopeful. We will never get a vacation. Ever. We know that the very act of being poor guarantees that we will never not be poor. . . . We don't apply for jobs because we know we can't afford to look nice enough to hold them. . . . 'Free' only exists for rich people . . . I make a lot of poor financial decisions. None of them matter, in the long term. . . . It's not like the sacrifice will result in improved circumstances. . . . I have proven that I am a poor person and that is all that I am or ever will be." This is the perspective of an individual who has to deal with financial hardships thumbing her nose at the ridiculous experts who urge her to stop wasting money on fast food and other frivolous pleasures, as if that will lift her out of poverty. Tirado went on to write and publish the bestseller *Hand to Mouth: Living in Bootstrap America.* Judging by the sales rankings, it may well be that she is finally not poor.

A 2013 study by the *Associated Press* revealed some truly alarming statistics, which were all but ignored by our political leaders. According to their research, "Four out of five U.S. adults struggle with joblessness, near-poverty or reliance on welfare for at least parts of their lives." This flew in the face of Barack Obama's empty rhetoric that his highest priority is to rebuild ladders of opportunity while reversing income inequality. A 2016 study found that nearly one in four Americans of "prime working" age—twenty-five to fifty-four years old—were unemployed. Demonstrating the global nature of this problem; in 2017, an estimated two hundred million persons will be unemployed around the world, the highest figure on record.[350]

The statistics are the same everywhere; Occupy Democrats, Bloomberg, and the Economic Policy Institute provided some US Labor Department data that distill what is happening into very understandable numbers. Since 1978, the cost of college tuition has risen by 1,120 percent, the cost of medical care has increased by 601 percent, the cost of food has increased by 244 percent, and the cost of shelter has gone up by 380 percent. During the same time period, the pay of a typical American worker rose just 10 percent, while minimum wage employees' pay actually fell by 5.5 percent. But the compensation of an average CEO rose an astronomical 937 percent. These tragic statistics summarize the situation we're in as well as anything I've written in this book. A 2016 Stanford University study found that 74 percent of Americans polled believed that CEOs are vastly overpaid, compared to the average worker.

Things aren't getting better. The US homeownership rate dropped to 62.9 percent in 2016, which was the lowest since 1965.[351] The Insured Retirement Institute recently concluded that nearly half of baby boomers have no retirement savings at all. The mainstream media, however, continues to deny reality, as indicated by an October 3, 2016, article in *U.S. News and World Report*, headlined "Why There is No Retirement Crisis." The "new normal" in corporate thinking is "retirement is not a right." A Pew Study released in 2016 delineated the situation very succinctly, finding that median expenditures had risen 14 percent since 2004, while median income had fallen by nearly the same amount.[352] The collective student loan debt is now an astounding $1.3 trillion, and the average 2016 college graduate owes $37,172.[353]

Jack London, over a century ago, lived among the poorest people in the western world at the time, in the East End of London, so he could research them and write about them in the book *People of the Abyss*. "Affluence means influence," he once said. London, like Huey Long, Eugene Debs, or anyone else who attempted to advocate for the poor, would be stunned at the consolidation of wealth now in America and around the rest of the world.

In response to this growing disparity, the 2016 presidential campaign featured two outsiders, one in each of the two major political parties. Donald Trump's upset victory was largely driven by the issues of immigration and trade. Trump simply said what a silent majority had been saying for over thirty years. He criticized not only illegal immigration, but also the foreign visa workers program, specifically citing the IT workers recently laid off by Disney. He blasted NAFTA, the TransPacific Trade Partnership, and other "bad deals" for America. Predictably, the mainstream media and establishment politicians in both parties branded him as a racist and invoked the inevitable comparisons to Adolph Hitler. Bernie Sanders, on the other hand, built his campaign around the growing disparity of wealth. While the Republicans failed to thwart Trump's grassroots campaign, the Democrats used the undemocratic superdelegates to deny Sanders even when he won primary after primary. When the media wasn't calling Trump racist, it was beating the drums for Hillary Clinton's nomination, which never lost momentum even when Sanders won seven straight primaries at one point.

Both Trump and Sanders stirred different elements of populist sentiment in a citizenry struggling amidst the worst economy since the Great Depression. Trump noted, in underpublicized comments, that "with the trillions and trillions of dollars we've spent on all these wars, we could have rebuilt America from top to bottom." Sanders declared that "one in four corporations doesn't pay any taxes." Both Trump and Sanders advocated the rebuilding of America's crumbling infrastructure. Trump's rhetoric targeted the "rigged process" and the corrupt insiders who run it. Sanders focused more on the manner in which wealth is funneled to the One Percent, instead of the millions and millions in need. "Let us wage a moral and political war against the billionaires and corporate leaders," Bernie Sanders proclaimed.

Sanders lost a good deal of credibility with his almost instantaneous endorsement of Clinton, right after one of her most controversial wins in the Californian primary. No one outside of WikiLeaks and the alternative media seemed remotely interested in this outright electoral theft—certainly not Green Party candidate Jill Stein, or even Sanders himself. As had been the case throughout both the Democratic and Republican primaries, there were countless allegations of voter fraud. In every instance, the fraud aided Clinton, or the opponents of Trump. Mainstream media coverage after the conventions became little more than a glorified coronation ceremony for Hillary Clinton.

Trump's unforeseen victory in the 2016 presidential election promised either breathtaking reform or greater public disillusionment. Even before he took office, Trump brokered a deal where one thousand jobs scheduled to be shipped offshore by Carrier in Indiana were saved in return for a reported $7 million in tax breaks. The deal was predictably criticized by the establishment media, as well as the head of Carrier's typically impotent union. On November 26, 2016, Senator Bernie Sanders issued a lengthy statement on the deal. Among his remarks were, "Let's be clear: it is not good enough to save some of these jobs. We cannot rest until United Technologies signs a firm contract to keep all of these good-paying jobs in Indiana without slashing the salaries or benefits workers have earned. United Technologies is not going broke. Last year, it made a profit of $7.6 billion and received over $6 billion in defense contracts." Chuck Jones, head of Carrier's union, lashed out at Trump for not saving even more jobs. The president of the AFL-CIO, Richard Trumka, backed Jones as well.

Donald Trump's most accurate piece of campaign rhetoric was "It's a rigged system, and you don't trust those who rigged it to fix it." The game *is* rigged, and in politics, or business, or any other aspect of life, the rich always win. The cards of the wealthy have been figuratively marked, and the great mass of humanity faces the impossible prospect of competing against a stacked deck.

At all levels of our society, those who have risen to the top are so decidedly unqualified, so distinctively incompetent, and so prone to corruption that it's impossible to envision an innocent reason for their success. Our elected representatives are seemingly incapable of doing the right thing, or often even of behaving properly. I firmly believe you could find a random group of 535 preschoolers and install them as our new Congress, and they would do a far better job. When discussing the One Percent, families like the

Rothschilds, on an international level, and the Rockefellers, here at home, are often forgotten. With the death of David Rockefeller, the Rockefeller name lives on publicly through philanthropic organizations. The Rothschilds are very private, but their power is undeniable. And the collective wealth of either family is rumored to dwarf that of Bill Gates, Warren Buffet, and the others at the top of any list of the richest people in the world.

If George Washington, Samuel Adams, John Hancock, Patrick Henry, Thomas Jefferson, James Madison, and the other leading statesman of the revolutionary era could see the condition of their republic now, there would be a collective weeping that would shake the heavens. Their lives, their fortunes, and their sacred honor were sacrificed for *this?* Those who have led us into this quagmire, this slippery ledge from which there appears to be no escape, must accept responsibility for the fiasco, the horrific nightmare they created.

Nearly two centuries ago, our shortest tenured president, William Henry Harrison, left this profound statement on the record: "All the measures of the government are directed to the purpose of making the rich richer and the poor poorer." Needless to say, every measure of business seems to work that way, as reflected in Calvin Coolidge's statement that "what's good for business is good for America."

In nature, it may be the fittest that survive, but in America, and the rest of the world, it is the rich that set the rules, control every contest, and invariably prevail. For the poor, it's "ours is not to question why." The world loves a winner, and nothing says winning like great wealth. The rich control everything, and every law, every tradition, and every aspect of our civilization proves it.

Most of the first-class passengers on the *Titanic* survived its sinking, while most of the poor in steerage perished. Few rich men die on any of our perpetual battlefields, or are behind bars in our burgeoning prison population. If anything, the odds for the rich are better than they've ever been. With every imaginable human advantage, it has become all but impossible for the rich, their children, and their children's children, not to thrive and prosper.

NOTES

1 *The Guardian,* January 20, 2014, https://www.theguardian.com/business/2014/jan/20/oxfam-85-richest-people-half-of-the-world.

2 *Think Progress,* July 17, 2012, https://thinkprogress.org/walmart-heirs-have-as-much-wealth-as-bottom-40-percent-of-americans-combined-7fe778936a32#.7n9xx28xr.

3 *CNN Money,* June 24, 2013, http://money.cnn.com/2013/06/24/pf/emergency-savings/.

4 *USA Today,* October 9, 2016, http://www.usatoday.com/story/money/personalfinance/2016/10/09/savings-study/91083712/?showmenu=true.

5 *CNN Money,* June 16, 2010, http://money.cnn.com/2010/06/16/news/economy/unemployed_need_not_apply/.

6 *Bloomberg,* May 3, 2014, https://www.bloomberg.com/news/articles/2014–05–02/miami-s-poor-live-on-11-a-day-as-boom-widens-wealth-gap.

7 *Realty Today,* February 21, 2014, http://www.realtytoday.com/articles/5204/20140221/top-10-american-cities-with-income-inequality.htm.

8 *US News & World Report,* September 23, 2014, http://www.usnews.com/news/blogs/data-mine/2014/09/23/there-are-more-homeless-students-now-than-ever-before.

9 *Los Angeles Times,* August 17, 2016, http://www.latimes.com/business/la-na-trump-economist-navarro-20160818-snap-story.html.

10 *CNN Money,* August 18, 2016, http://money.cnn.com/2016/08/18/pf/wealth-inequality/.

11 *The Guardian,* May 5, 2014, https://www.theguardian.com/commentisfree/2014/may/05/cecily-mcmillan-occupy-guilty-police-violence.

12 *Levy Economics Institute of Bard College,* March 2010 study.

13 Julie Bort, "Bill Gates: People Don't Realize How Many Jobs Will Soon Be Replaced by Software Bots," *Business Insider,* March 13, 2014.

14 *The Atlantic*, July 17, 2014, http://www.theatlantic.com/business/archive/2014/07/slaughter-at-microsoft-tech-giant-to-fire-14-percent-of-its-staff/374597/.

15 *Daily Caller*, March 17, 2014, http://dailycaller.com/2014/03/17/gates-tax-consumption-to-fix-unemployment-caused-by-technology-video/.

16 *New York Times*, May 2, 2014, https://www.nytimes.com/2014/05/03/business/steve-jobs-a-genius-at-pushing-boundaries-too.html?_r=0.

17 CNN, January 21, 2014.

18 Tom King, "Action Star Keanu Reeves Wants to Play the Field," *Wall Street Journal*, September 7, 2001.

19 *Huffington Post*, December 8, 2013.

20 *New York Times*, March 3, 1995, http://www.nytimes.com/1995/03/03/obituaries/f-lundberg-92-author-who-wrote-of-the-rich.html.

21 *Wall Street Journal*, July 31, 2009, http://www.wsj.com/articles/SB124896891815094085.

22 *Moyers and Company*, September 17, 2013.

23 *New York Times*, April 30, 2014, https://www.nytimes.com/2014/05/04/magazine/only-one-top-banker-jail-financial-crisis.html.

24 *USA Today*, March 28, 2013, http://www.usatoday.com/story/money/business/2013/03/28/departing-conocophillips-ceo-got-over-260-million-in-2012/2028085/.

25 *Newsmax*, April 15, 2015, http://www.newsmax.com/Finance/StreetTalk/Fortune-tax-corporate-GE/2015/04/14/id/638367/.

26 *MotherJones*, January 18, 2012, http://www.motherjones.com/mojo/2012/01/executive-pay-100-million-ceo-severance-packages.

27 *Bangor Daily News*, April 13, 2004.

28 *Huffington Post*, August 27, 2015, http://www.huffingtonpost.com/entry/ceo-worker-pay-gap_us_55ddc3c7e4b0a40aa3acd1c9.

29 *Huffington Post*, March 11, 2013, http://www.huffingtonpost.com/2013/03/11/general-electric-taxes_n_2852094.html.

30 *The Guardian*, February 29, 2012.

31 *New York Times*, October 15, 2010.

32 *The Guardian*, December 3, 2013, https://www.theguardian.com/money/us-money-blog/2013/dec/03/tax-breaks-for-ceos-pay-for-million-dollar-salaries.

33 *Huffington Post*, October 22, 2013, http://www.huffingtonpost.com/2013/10/22/ceo-pay-worker-pay_n_4143859.html.

34 *Daily Kos*, January 23, 2014, http://m.dailykos.com/story/2014/01/23/1271896/-Republicans-believe-rich-people-just-work-harder-So-how-do-they-explain-these-statistics.

35 *Politico*, December 25, 2013, http://www.politico.com/story/2013/12/pope-francis-catholic-church-republicans-gop-economics-101522.

36 *The Washington Post,* January 6, 2013, http://www.politico.com/story/2013/12/pope-francis-catholic-church-republicans-gop-economics-101522.

37 *Huffington Post,* January 15, 2013, http://www.huffingtonpost.com/2013/01/15/nike-indonesia_n_2481236.html.

38 *Small Business Trends,* December 17, 2012, https://smallbiztrends.com/2012/12/start-up-failure-rates-the-definitive-numbers.html.

39 *Washington Post,* May 19, 2016, https://smallbiztrends.com/2012/12/start-up-failure-rates-the-definitive-numbers.html.

40 *Orlando Sentinel,* December 9, 2013, http://articles.orlandosentinel.com/2013–12–09/business/os-disney-offshore-profits-taxes-20131206_1_walt-disney-world-u-s-senate-profits.

41 CNBC, May 21, 2013.

42 *US News & World Report,* February 7, 2011, http://money.usnews.com/money/retirement/articles/2011/02/07/7-reasons-you-dont-have-a-pension.

43 *Think Progress,* April 19, 2011, http://money.usnews.com/money/retirement/articles/2011/02/07/7-reasons-you-dont-have-a-pension.

44 *Washington Times,* July 24, 2014, http://www.washingtontimes.com/news/2014/jul/24/michael-moore-movie-making-critic-capitalism-has-n/.

45 *Hot Air,* November 14, 2006, http://hotair.com/archives/2006/11/14/video-report-pelosi-hired-illegal-immigrants-for-napa-valley-vineyard/.

46 *Boston Herald,* April 26, 2014, http://www.bostonherald.com/news/columnists/adriana_cohen/2014/04/cohen_one_percenter_liz_warren_milks_system_then_slams_it_in.

47 *Washington Post,* July 24, 2007, http://www.washingtonpost.com/wp-dyn/content/article/2007/07/23/AR2007072302011.html.

48 *Bloomberg,* May 30, 2013, https://www.bloomberg.com/news/articles/2013–05–30/board-director-pay-hits-record-251–000-for-250-hours.

49 *Minyanville,* October 1, 2010, http://www.minyanville.com/mvpremium/deepak-chopra-mens-wearhouse-boardmember/.

50 *Bloomberg,* June 15, 2016, https://www.bloomberg.com/news/articles/2016–06–15/nabors-directors-stay-on-board-after-being-voted-off-four-times.

51 *Reuters,* December 16, 2009, http://www.reuters.com/article/us-boardpay-idUSTRE5BF4TT20091216.

52 *The Fiscal Times,* November 1, 2016, http://www.thefiscaltimes.com/2016/11/01/20-Highest-Paid-Boards-Directors-SP-500.

53 *Bloomberg News,* May 30, 2013.

54 *Mother Jones,* May/June 2006, http://www.motherjones.com/politics/2006/05/how-rich-get-richer-sources.

55 *Breitbart,* May 18, 2015, http://www.teaparty.org/report-jebs-education-company-paid-hillary-225k-speech-99522/.

56 ABC News, January 17, 2016, http://abcnews.go.com/Politics/bernie-sanders-hillary-clintons-speaking-fees/story?id=36351691.

57 *The Washington Post,* July 11, 2013, https://www.washingtonpost.com/news/post-politics/wp/2013/07/11/hillary-clinton-isnt-alone-former-politicians-rake-it-in-on-speaker-circuit/?utm_term=.d82cc0426fd5.

58 *Forbes,* December 10, 2007, http://www.forbes.com/2007/12/10/celebrity-hollywood-entertainment-biz-media-cx_kb_1210celebparties.html.

59 *Huffington Post,* January 29, 2012, http://www.huffingtonpost.com/2012/01/29/kim-kardashian-snoop-dogg_n_1240339.html.

60 *Business Insider,* June 6, 2012, http://www.businessinsider.com/celebrities-who-received-honorary-doctorates-2012–5.

61 *Wall Street Journal,* December 15, 2011 http://www.wsj.com/articles/SB10001424052970204026804577098774037075832.

62 *Sports Business Daily,* January 31, 2011, http://www.sportsbusinessdaily.com/Daily/Issues/2011/01/Jan-31/People-and-Pop-Culture/Bornstein.aspx.

63 *USA Today,* February 15, 2013, http://www.usatoday.com/story/gameon/2013/02/15/roger-goodell-nfl-commissioner-30-million/1923857/.

64 *US News & World Report,* January 30, 2014, http://www.usnews.com/news/articles/2014/01/30/senators-seek-to-punt-nfls-tax-exempt-status.

65 *Sports Business Journal,* September 3, 2013, http://www.sbnation.com/nhl/2013/9/3/4689464/gary-bettman-salary-nhl-commissioner.

66 "NFL Star Donte Stallworth Pleads Guilty to DUI Manslaughter," *Fox News,* June 16, 2009.

67 *Miami Herald,* June 17, 2009, http://articles.sun-sentinel.com/2009–06–17/news/0906160285_1_donte-stallworth-mario-reyes-reyes-family.

68 *Prison Legal News,* February 1, 2014, https://www.prisonlegalnews.org/news/issue/25/2/.

69 *Los Angeles Times,* May 12, 2006, http://articles.latimes.com/2006/may/12/local/me-jails12.

70 *Prison Legal News,* July 15, 2010, https://www.prisonlegalnews.org/news/issue/21/7/.

71 *New York Post,* September 2, 2002, http://nypost.com/2002/09/02/brodericks-guilt-actor-to-meet-with-irish-kin-of-fatal-87-car-wreck/.

72 *People,* August 8, 2001, http://people.com/celebrity/ex-90210-star-wrongful-death-suit/.

73 *Chicago Tribune,* July 12, 1936.

74 *New York Times,* August 29, 1987, http://www.nytimes.com/learning/general/onthisday/bday/0805.html.

75 *Before I Get Old: The Story of the Who,* by Dave Marsh, p. 355.

76 *Denver Post,* July 1, 2009, http://www.denverpost.com/2009/07/01/
    victims-mom-forgives-nuggets-j-r-smith/.

77 *Mother Jones,* May 6, 2013.

78 *Slate,* October 8, 2010, http://www.slate.com/articles/news_and_poli-
    tics/jurisprudence/2010/10/toxic_persons.html.

79 *The Washington Post,* June 3, 2011.

80 *Bloomberg Businessweek,* December 13, 2012, https://www.washingtonpost
    .com/opinions/why-are-diplomats-free-to-abuse-in-america/2011/05/
    24/AG6RgPIH_story.html?utm_term=.c67b77b12bf8.

81 *Mother Jones,* September 5, 2013, http://www.motherjones.com/politics/
    2013/09/university-president-financial-perks-petraeus.

82 *Forbes,* May 2, 2012.

83 *Fox 8 News,* December 6, 2016.

84 *Forbes,* December 5, 2016, http://www.forbes.com/sites/karstenstrauss/
    2016/12/05/the-highest-paid-private-college-presidents/#633846724443

85 *New York Times,* September 17, 2006, http://www.nytimes.com/2006/09/
    17/books/review/Wolff2.t.html.

86 *Forbes,* May 31, 2012, http://www.forbes.com/sites/jamesmarshallcrotty/
    2012/05/31/sean-diddy-combs-is-reportedly-worth-550-million-should-
    his-son-have-received-a-54000-scholarship-to-attend-cash-strapped-
    ucla/#f1a5ef9d172a.

87 *Chicago Now,* June 5, 2012, http://www.chicagonow.com/good-bad-
    parents/2012/06/kids-scholarships-and-their-1-parents/.

88 *Forbes,* August 7, 2013, http://www.forbes.com/sites/specialfeatures/2013/
    08/07/how-the-college-debt-is-crippling-students-parents-and-the-
    economy/#645c687e1a41.

89 *Wall Street Journal,* February 3, 2015, http://www.wsj.com/articles/big-gap-
    in-college-graduation-rates-for-rich-and-poor-study-finds-1422997677.

90 *Forbes,* May 2, 2012, http://www.forbes.com/sites/danielfisher/2012/05/
    02/poor-students-are-the-real-victims-of-college-discrimination/
    #66bde2972007.

91 *New Jersey On-Line,* December 19, 2013, http://www.nj.com/rutgers-
    football/index.ssf/2013/12/pinstripe_bowl_gift_packages_provide_val-
    uable_reward_for_players.html.

92 *Gothamist,* June 17, 2010, http://gothamist.com/2010/06/17/carvel_black_
    card_is_real_lohans_ab.php.

93 *Time,* March 21, 2013, http://business.time.com/2013/03/21/stealth-
    celebrity-endorsement-no-money-changing-hands-just-free-burritos/.

94 *Nando's Black Card,* March 29, 2012, http://www.nandosblackcard.com/
    which-celebrities-have-a-nandos-black-card/.

95 *Time,* January 31, 2012, http://business.time.com/2012/01/31/celeb-
    schwag-famous-people-get-100k-worth-of-free-stuff-annually/.

96 *Vulture,* January 28, 2012, http://www.vulture.com/2012/01/how-celebrities-get-almost-everything-for-free.html.

97 *The New York Times,* February 15, 2006, http://www.nytimes.com/2006/02/15/movies/redcarpet/celebrity-freebies-a-force-irresistible.html.

98 *LaughSpin,* April 29, 2013, http://www.comedyofchicago.com/2013/04/laughspin-kickstarter-abuse-why-are-you.html.

99 *The Atlantic,* October 2013.

100 *Think Progress,* September 16, 2013, https://thinkprogress.org/meet-three-billionaires-asking-taxpayers-to-buy-them-new-stadiums-a082d804771b#.knbi7x7xl.

101 *Washington Post,* May 11, 2015, https://www.washingtonpost.com/news/early-lead/wp/2015/05/08/national-guard-paid-millions-to-nfl-teams-for-in-game-soldier-salutes/?utm_term=.28f1363c483c.

102 *Villanova Center for the Study of Sports Law,* March 6, 2013, http://lawweb2009.law.villanova.edu/sportslaw/?p=1853.

103 *Washington Post,* October 3, 2016, https://www.washingtonpost.com/news/wonk/wp/2016/10/03/why-thousands-of-millionaires.

104 *Forbes,* May 6, 2013, http://www.forbes.com/sites/christopherhelman/2013/05/06/as-irani-exits-oxy-a-question-lingers-is-he-a-billionaire/#4032c2115c71dont-pay-federal-income-taxes/?utm_term=.440017234a33.

105 *Kiplinger,* March 30, 2011, http://www.kiplinger.com/article/investing/T052-C008-S001-8-outrageous-executive-perks.html.

106 *Forbes,* March 27, 2013, http://www.forbes.com/sites/kurtbadenhausen/2013/03/27/baseballs-highest-paid-players-on-and-off-the-field-2/#7c7649e310c1.

107 *Huffington Post,* April 25, 2014, http://www.huffingtonpost.com/2014/04/25/celebrity-endorsements_n_5213495.html.

108 CNBC, May 10, 2012, http://www.cnbc.com/id/47324363.

109 *Gawker,* March 18, 2013, http://gawker.com/5990571/bill-oreillys-divorce-is-so-ugly-god-got-involved.

110 *Huffington Post,* May 16, 2012, http://www.huffingtonpost.com/2012/05/16/poverty-salvation-army-report_n_1521577.html.

111 *Christian Science Monitor,* February 22, 1984.

112 *Dutch* by Edmund Morris, pp. 645–646.

113 *Huffington Post,* January 10, 2014, http://www.huffingtonpost.com/2014/01/10/jack-kingston-free-lunch_n_4572915.html.

114 *Huffington Post,* December 18, 2013, http://www.huffingtonpost.com/2013/12/18/jack-kingston-school-lunch_n_4467711.html.

115 *Politico,* October 21, 2010, http://www.politico.com/story/2010/10/fincher-under-fire-for-campaign-loan-043969.

116 *If You Only News,* March 11, 2015, http://www.ifyouonlynews.com/human-interest/christian-pastor-john-hagee-welfare-recipients-dont-deserve-to-live/.

117 *Daily Kos,* May 7, 2015, http://www.dailykos.com/story/2015/5/7/1383156/-Wisconsin-Republicans-push-bill-to-bar-poor-people-from-buying-shellfish-Oh-or-Wisconsin-cheese.

118 Rachel Bade, "Israel Hawks to Pope Francis: Stay Out of Politics," *Politico,* May 13, 2015, http://www.politico.com/story/2015/05/israel-hawks-to-pop-francis-stay-out-of-politics-117929.

119 *Portland Press Herald,* July 24, 2014.

120 *The Atlantic,* January 13, 2014, http://www.theatlantic.com/business/archive/2014/01/it-is-expensive-to-be-poor/282979/.

121 *True Activist,* August 27, 2013, http://www.trueactivist.com/it-is-illegal-to-feed-the-homeless-in-cities-all-over-the-united-states/.

122 *Huffington Post,* November 3, 2014, http://www.huffingtonpost.com/2014/11/03/fort-lauderdale-feeding-homeless_n_6094234.html.

123 *Newsweek,* October 28, 2014, http://www.newsweek.com/two-years-later-no-charges-after-police-kill-homeless-man-barrage-46-shots-280609.

124 CNN, June 22, 2014, http://www.cnn.com/2014/06/20/us/albuquerque-police-investigation/.

125 *Huffington Post,* September 30, 2014, http://www.huffingtonpost.com/2014/09/30/james-boyd-lunatic-penis_n_5907696.html.

126 *World Socialist website,* June 24, 2015.

127 *Think Progress,* August 30, 2012, https://thinkprogress.org/worlds-richest-woman-says-people-are-poor-because-they-re-lazy-drunks-d7dfeeade06c#.2mfwtbkie.

128 *CNN Money,* May 19, 2015, http://money.cnn.com/2015/05/19/news/economy/issa-poor/.

129 *Yahoo Finance,* December 9, 2016, http://finance.yahoo.com/news/give-poor-money-directly-and-they-dont-spend-it-on-alcohol-and-cigarettes-135858208.html.

130 *Information Clearing House,* May 12, 2010, http://www.informationclearinghouse.info/article25430.htm.

131 *Talking Philosophy,* October 9, 2011, http://blog.talkingphilosophy.com/?p=3291.

132 *Seattle Times,* February 22, 2010, http://www.seattletimes.com/nation-world/in-hard-times-americans-blame-the-poor/.

133 *Wall Street Journal,* July 21, 2011, http://blogs.wsj.com/washwire/2011/07/21/bachmann-everybody-should-pay-taxes/.

134 *The Atlantic,* June 6, 2012, http://www.theatlantic.com/business/archive/2012/06/35-000-rich-people-arent-paying-any-income-tax-how-is-that-possible/258183/.

135 Ibid.

136 CBS News, July 1, 2013.

137 *Hot Air*, March 12, 2014, http://hotair.com/archives/2014/03/12/obama-health-insurance-isnt-expensive-just-cancel-cable-and-phones/.

138 *Huffington Post*, November 27, 2011, http://www.huffingtonpost.com/2011/11/27/black-friday-target_n_1115372.html.

139 *The Milwaukee Journal*, September 5, 1965.

140 *Kingfish: The Reign of Huey P. Long* by Richard White, p. 209.

141 Ibid.

142 *Monroe-News Star*, November 14, 1934, https://www.newspapers.com/newspage/87443768/.

143 *Maverick Marine: General Smedley D. Butler and the Contradictions of American Military History*, by Hans Schmidt, p. 231.

144 *The FDR Years: On Roosevelt and His Legacy* by William Edward Leuchtenburg, p. 87.

145 *The Times-Picayune*, September 5, 2010, http://www.nola.com/politics/index.ssf/2010/09/the_enduring_mystery_of_who_ki.html.

146 *Associated Press*, September 10, 2010.

147 *New York Times*, April 27, 2008, http://www.nytimes.com/2008/04/27/arts/music/27hime.html.

148 *New York Times*, January 13, 2009, http://www.nytimes.com/2009/01/14/us/politics/14geithner.html?pagewanted=all&_r=0.

149 *New York Times*, February 8, 2001, http://www.nytimes.com/2001/02/08/us/onetime-illegal-immigrant-sheltered-by-chavez-recalls-painful-past.html.

150 *Huffington Post*, January 24, 2012, http://www.huffingtonpost.com/2012/01/24/mitt-romney-maids-salary-tax-returns-election-2012_n_1228843.html.

151 *Al Jazeera America*, September 26, 2013, http://america.aljazeera.com/articles/2013/9/26/california-governorsignsbillgrantingdomesticwork-ersovertimepay.html.

152 *Los Angeles Daily News*, January 4, 2014, http://www.dailynews.com/business/20140104/middle-class-hollywood-workers-lose-jobs-in-come-when-filming-flees-los-angeles.

153 *Business Insider*, December 12, 2011, http://www.businessinsider.com/rich-people-do-not-create-jobs-2011–12.

154 *Human Events*, April 7, 2006, http://humanevents.com/2006/04/07/emexclusive-emthe-truth-about-la-raza/.

155 *Arizona Sentinel*, October 22, 2009, https://thearizonasentinel.wordpress.com/2009/10/22/la-raza-acorn-our-dollars-are-funding-our-demise/.

156 *Investor's Business Daily*, August 27, 2014, http://www.investors.com/politics/editorials/holders-bank-of-america-settlement-includes-pay-offs-to-democrat-groups/.

157 *Washington Times,* June 3, 2015, http://www.washingtontimes.com/news/2015/jun/3/irs-illegals-can-get-back-taxes-obama-amnesty/.

158 Fox News, February 18, 2015, http://www.foxnews.com/politics/2015/02/18/memo-telling-border-patrol-agents-dont-have-to-detain-intoxicated-drivers-draws.html.

159 *Federation for American Immigration Reform,* "Lower Wages for American Workers," http://www.fairus.org/issue/lower-wages-for-american-workers.

160 ABC News, May 21, 2010, http://abcnews.go.com/Business/illegal-immigrants-cost-us-100-billion-year-group/story?id=10699317.

161 *Washington Times,* May 6, 2013, http://www.washingtontimes.com/news/2013/may/6/report-legalizing-illegal-immigrants-cost-6-3-t/.

162 *New Republic,* April 29, 2013, https://newrepublic.com/article/113065/immigration-reform-low-wage-workers-will-benefit-too.

163 *New York Times,* June 3, 2015, http://www.nytimes.com/2015/06/04/us/last-task-after-layoff-at-disney-train-foreign-replacements.html.

164 *New York Times,* June 11, 2016, http://www.nytimes.com/2016/06/12/us/laid-off-americans-required-to-zip-lips-on-way-out-grow-bolder.html.

165 *Center for Immigration Studies,* January 2010, http://cis.org/h-2b-guestworkers.

166 *Economic Policy Institute,* December 5, 2011, http://www.epi.org/blog/j-1-h-2b-guest-worker-programs-youth-unemployment/.

167 *Daily Caller,* May 6, 2014, http://dailycaller.com/2014/05/06/obama-outsources-100000-more-jobs-to-guest-workers/.

168 *US News & World Report,* May 9, 2016, http://www.usnews.com/education/best-colleges/paying-for-college/slideshows/10-student-loan-facts-college-grads-need-to-know.

169 *The New York Times,* July 27, 2012, http://www.nytimes.com/2012/07/28/business/striking-palermos-pizza-workers-say-immigrants-were-fired-to-stop-a-union.html.

170 *The Boston Globe,* January 8, 2010, http://archive.boston.com/news/local/massachusetts/articles/2010/01/08/detained_immigrants_were_set_to_clear_gillette_snow/.

171 *The Los Angeles Times,* June 22, 2009, http://articles.latimes.com/2009/jun/22/local/me-harris22.

172 *Arizona Daily Sun,* November 13, 2007, http://azdailysun.com/news/national/lebanese-woman-faked-marriage-for-u-s-citizenship-hired-by/article_4ee199b6–6c5a-5aa2-a154–164dd4b447b4.html.

173 *Newsmax,* August 22, 2014, http://www.newsmax.com/Newsfront/TSA-immigration-travel-ID/2014/08/22/id/590367/.

174 *The American Spectator,* June 18, 2013, https://spectator.org/55379_irs-immigration-fraud-scandal/.

175 Robert W. Wood, "IRS Admits It Encourages Illegals to Steal Social Security Numbers," *Forbes,* April 13, 2016.

176 *Forbes,* January 14, 2014, http://www.forbes.com/sites/clareoconnor/2014/01/14/outgoing-lululemon-ceo-christine-day-to-take-helm-at-healthy-fast-food-firm-luvo/#7e3ca5b86f84.

177 Lindsey Rupp, "Abercrombie CEO Leaves Chain After Overseeing Rise and Fall," *Bloomberg,* December 9, 2014.

178 *CNBC,* May 3, 2014, http://www.cnbc.com/2014/05/03/buffett-didnt-want-to-go-to-war-with-coca-cola.html.

179 *Business Wire,* March 21, 2014, http://www.businesswire.com/news/home/20140321005785/en/Wintergreen-Advisers-LLC-Expresses-Disappointment-Coca-Cola%E2%80%99s-Proposed.

180 *New York Times,* September 30, 2011, http://www.nytimes.com/2011/10/01/business/lets-stop-rewarding-failed-ceos-common-sense.html.

181 *CPS News,* July 2, 2008, http://www.cps-news.com/2008/07/02/another-ceo-is-rewarded-for-poor-performance/.

182 *ABC News,* September 2, 2013, http://abcnews.go.com/Business/highest-paid-worst-performing-chief-executives/story?id=20111337.

183 *Bloomberg,* August 17, 2016, https://www.bloomberg.com/graphics/2016-golden-parachutes/.

184 *CNN,* January 2, 2014, http://money.cnn.com/2014/01/02/technology/enterprise/blackberry-alicia-keys/.

185 *Forbes,* January 19, 2012, http://www.forbes.com/sites/nathanielparish-flannery/2012/01/19/billion-dollar-blowout-top-10-largest-ceo-severance-packages-of-the-past-decade/#68a4e1232565.

186 *Think Progress,* June 4, 2012, https://thinkprogress.org/verizon-to-lay-off-1-700-workers-after-paying-ceo-22-million-last-year-314f8f8a4734#.kv7joo1jp.

187 *Huffington Post,* February 7, 2014, http://www.huffingtonpost.com/2014/02/07/time-inc-bonus-layoffs-magazine-million-norman-pearlstine_n_4747913.html.

188 *USA Today,* December 17, 2013, http://www.usatoday.com/story/money/cars/2013/12/16/general-motors-gm-bailout-repayment/4043607/.

189 *USA Today,* April 24, 2015, http://www.usatoday.com/story/money/cars/2015/04/24/mary-barra-pay-gm/26308957/.

190 NBC News, September 1, 2010, http://www.nbcnews.com/id/38935053/ns/business-us_business/t/ceos-lay-thousands-rake-millions/.

191 *Fortune,* April 5, 2013, https://www.bloomberg.com/news/articles/2013-04-04/hp-s-lane-giving-up-chairmanship-whitworth-interim-chair.

192 *Business Insider,* June 3, 2015, http://www.businessinsider.com/meg-whitman-hints-at-more-layoffs-again-2015-6.

193 *National Journal,* March 5, 2014, http://csbaonline.org/about/news/how-the-government-pays-defense-contractors-tens-of-billions-for-nothing.

194 *Forbes,* December 19, 2011, http://www.forbes.com/sites/lorenthompson/2011/12/19/how-to-waste-100-billion-weapons-that-didnt-work-out/#351a25326150.

195 *Huffington Post,* August 24, 2010 http://www.huffingtonpost.com/richard-skip-bronson/post_733_b_692546.html.

196 *The Guardian,* February 23, 2014, https://www.theguardian.com/society/2014/feb/23/europe-11m-empty-properties-enough-house-homeless-continent-twice.

197 *The Washington Post,* July 2, 2006, http://www.washingtonpost.com/wp-dyn/content/article/2006/07/01/AR2006070100962.html.

198 *Bloomberg,* September 9, 2013, https://www.bloomberg.com/news/articles/2013-09-09/farmers-boost-revenue-sowing-subsidies-for-crop-insurance.

199 *New York Times,* February 4, 2014, https://www.nytimes.com/2014/02/05/us/politics/senate-passes-long-stalled-farm-bill.html.

200 *Daily Kos,* November 7, 2013, http://www.dailykos.com/story/2013/11/7/1253828/-50-billionaires-received-11-3-million-in-farm-welfare-could-get-more-in-new-farm-bill.

201 *Daily Caller,* November 14, 2011, http://dailycaller.com/2011/11/14/coburn-report-bon-jovi-springsteen-quincy-jones-ted-turner-received-federal-funds/.

202 *New York Post,* December 23, 2013, http://nypost.com/2013/12/23/experts-fears-health-risks-with-micro-apartments/.

203 *San Francisco Chronicle,* November 11, 2013, http://www.sfgate.com/business/article/Micro-apartment-developments-on-rise-in-S-F-4951775.php.

204 *Austin Chronicle,* June 20, 2014, http://www.austinchronicle.com/news/2014-06-20/prof-dumpster-fighting-for-the-one-percent/.

205 *The Guardian,* April 22, 2007, https://www.theguardian.com/environment/2007/apr/23/musicnews.music.

206 *The Examiner,* April 29, 2009.

207 *NewsBusters,* July 23, 2011, http://www.newsbusters.org/blogs/nb/noel-sheppard/2011/07/23/reasons-nick-gillespie-exposes-maher-hypocrisy-would-you-give-show.

208 *E Online,* October 25, 2009, http://www.eonline.com/news/150413/does-jennifer-aniston-only-take-three-minute-showers.

209 *USA Today,* April 16, 2014, http://www.usatoday.com/story/money/business/2014/04/16/cpi-shows-food-prices-rising/7742669/.

210 *USA Today,* April 17, 2012.

211 *Washington Times,* August 17, 2011, http://www.washingtontimes.com/news/2011/aug/17/prepping-debt-plan-obama-calls-shared-sacrifice/.

212 *The Guardian,* May 5, 2012.

213 *Christian Science Monitor,* November 2, 2008, http://www.csmonitor.com/USA/Politics/2008/1102/sacrifice-theme-returns-to-us-politics.

214 *Washington Times,* December 15, 2016, http://www.washingtontimes.com/news/2016/dec/15/obama-heads-to-hawaii-for-the-holidays/.

215 *The Washington Times,* November 25, 2014, http://www.washingtontimes.com/news/2014/nov/25/obama-amnesty-obamacare-clash-businesses-have-3000/.

216 *News Busters,* November 13, 2014, http://www.newsbusters.org0/blogs/curtis-houck/2014/11/13/abc-nbc-continue-blackout-gruber-video-cbs-ignores-clip-pelosi.

217 *USA Today,* September 23, 2013, http://www.usatoday.com/story/opinion/2013/09/23/not-affordable-care-act-avik-roy-editorials-debates/2858175/.

218 *Daily Kos,* June 27, 2012, http://www.dailykos.com/story/2012/6/27/1103667/--Sometimes-poor-people-will-die-just-because-they-are-poor.

219 CBS News, October 11, 2015, http://www.cbsnews.com/news/for-third-time-in-40-years-no-social-security-increase-coming/.

220 *Common Dreams,* November 24, 2013, http://www.commondreams.org/views/2013/11/24/one-entitlement-really-does-need-trimming.

221 *Forbes,* June 26, 2013, http://www.forbes.com/sites/susanadams/2013/06/26/the-worlds-most-outrageous-pension-deal/#742da1585505.

222 *Bloomberg,* October 28, 2015.

223 *Congressional Research Service,* July 31, 2015, https://fas.org/sgp/crs/misc/RL30631.pdf.

224 *Bloomberg,* January 19, 2012, http://www.govexec.com/pay-benefits/2012/01/many-federal-retirees-receiving-six-figure-pensions/40874/.

225 *US News & World Report,* January 16, 2009, http://money.usnews.com/money/blogs/planning-to-retire/2009/01/16/president-bush-will-get-a-196700-pension.

226 *Los Angeles Times,* July 11, 2012, http://articles.latimes.com/2012/jul/11/local/la-me-chief-compensation-20120711.

227 *Wirepoints Illinois News,* September 24, 2014, http://www.wirepoints.com/upside-down-demographics-of-chicago-public-safety-pensions-wp-original/.

228 *Time,* March 14, 2016, http://time.com/money/4258451/retirement-savings-survey/.

229 *Chicago Sport and Society,* May 9, 2013, http://www.chicagosport andsociety.com/2013/05/09/rich-mans-game-rising-ticket-prices-in-taxpayer-funded-facilities/.

230 *Business Insider,* October 9, 2012, http://www.businessinsider.com/attractive-people-are-more-successful-2012–9.

231 *Wall Street Journal,* June 9, 2014.

232 *Forbes,* March 20, 2013, http://www.forbes.com/sites/tykiisel/2013/03/20/you-are-judged-by-your-appearance/#15c89b0e30f0.

233 *Chapters in the History of Social Legislation in the United States to 1860,* by Henry Walcott Farnam, p. 257.

234 *New York Times,* January 26, 2007, http://www.nytimes.com/2007/01/26/business/26walmart.html.

235 *Huffington Post,* May 2, 2012, http://www.huffingtonpost.com/2012/05/02/walmart-overtime-labor-department-settlement_n_1470543.html.

236 *New York Times,* March 8, 2013, http://www.nytimes.com/2013/03/09/business/man-who-helped-image-of-wal-mart-steps-down.html.

237 *NBC News,* May 9, 2014, http://www.nbcnews.com/business/consumer/obama-wal-mart-touts-efficiency-angers-labor-n101181.

238 *Yahoo News,* March 13, 2014, https://www.yahoo.com/news/fast-food-workers-sue-mcdonalds-for-wage-theft-171757955.html?ref=gs.

239 *CNN Money,* September 27, 2016 http://money.cnn.com/2016/09/27/news/economy/donald-trump-nafta-hillary-clinton-debate/.

240 *NBC Bay Area,* August 31, 2012, http://www.nbcbayarea.com/investigations/series/children-in-the-field/Children-in-the-Field-Picking-Our-Food-164796976.html.

241 *The Oregonian,* September 29, 2012, http://www.oregonlive.com/pacific-northwest-news/index.ssf/2012/09/child_farm_labor_in_oregon_and.html.

242 *Fortune,* December 9, 2016, http://fortune.com/2016/12/09/ohio-state-legislature-cities-local-minimum-wages/.

243 *Bloomberg,* April 24, 2016, https://www.bloomberg.com/news/features/2016–04–24/inside-one-of-the-world-s-most-secretive-iphone-factories.

244 *CNN Money,* August 11, 2016, http://money.cnn.com/2016/08/11/news/modern-slavery-china-india/.

245 *Wall Street Journal,* March 18, 2012, http://www.wsj.com/articles/SB10001424052702304459804577288572845949222.

246 *New York Times,* February 14, 2014, https://www.nytimes.com/2014/02/16/fashion/millennials-internships.html.

247 *Think Progress,* August 11, 2015, https://thinkprogress.org/the-olsen-twins-empire-is-worth-1-billion-but-they-don-t-pay-their-interns-now-their-interns-are-86916129ab5e.

248 *Huffington Post* and others, July 9, 2012, https://americankabuki.blogspot.com/2012/07/mexican-drug-cartel-laundered-money.html?m=1.

249 *Washington Post,* February 12, 2016, https://www.washingtonpost.com/business/economy/2016/02/12/1359a004-d1e5–11e5–88cd-753e80c-d29ad_story.html?utm_term=.0ee43770ecf6.

250 *New York Times,* June 29, 2010, http://dealbook.nytimes.com/2010/06/29/money-laundering-the-drug-problem-at-banks/?_r=0.

251 *CNN Money,* October 13, 2016, http://money.cnn.com/2016/10/13/investing/wells-fargo-ceo-resigns-compensation/.

252 *CNN Money,* September 9, 2016, http://money.cnn.com/2016/09/08/investing/wells-fargo-created-phony-accounts-bank-fees/.

253 *Huffington Post,* March 19, 2014, http://www.huffingtonpost.com/2014/03/19/bitcoins-drugs-dopecoin-potcoin_n_4980749.html.

254 *CNN Money,* September 1, 2015, http://money.cnn.com/2015/09/01/news/unpaid-tolls-debt/.

255 *Think Progress,* March 21, 2014, https://thinkprogress.org/alabama-town-allegedly-imprisons-poor-people-and-tells-them-to-scrub-floors-to-pay-off-traffic-fines-d7861cc4b00a#.mnk5yxjzv.

256 *Daily Finance,* August 6, 2009, http://www.aol.com/article/2009/08/06/why-is-magic-johnson-shilling-for-rent-a-center/19112131/.

257 *Time,* January 31, 2012, http://business.time.com/2012/01/31/study-poor-people-pay-more-for-auto-insurance/.

258 *Huffington Post,* April 30, 2013, http://www.huffingtonpost.com/2013/04/30/ceo-to-worker-pay-ratio_n_3184623.html.

259 *Washingtonian,* November 11, 2010, https://www.washingtonian.com/2010/11/11/who-makes-how-much-media-professionals/.

260 *Cleveland Scene,* January 27, 2011, http://www.clevescene.com/scene-and-heard/archives/2011/01/27/don-king-on-killing-a-man-those-are-the-things-that-happen.

261 *New York Magazine,* August 28, 1978, "And in This Corner…Robert Arum," https://books.google.com/books?id=_OACAAAAMBAJ&pg=PA51&lpg=PA51&dq=august+28,+1978,+new+york+magazine,+bob+arum&source=bl&ots=r6QVdFldUQ&sig=_v8z-ttsO-CyXMZh8vVLxdrurrx8&hl=en&sa=X&ved=0ahUKEwidq7jrr-rPRAhVMpY8KHd2BBnwQ6AEIHzAB#v=onepage&q=august%2028%2C%201978%2C%20new%20york%20magazine%2C%20bob%20arum&f=false.

262 *National Review,* February 7, 2012, http://www.nationalreview.com/corner/290190/why-do-companies-pay-consultants-so-much-tell-them-what-they-already-know-jim-manzi.

263 *New York Observer,* August 13, 2013, http://observer.com/2013/08/the-godfather-of-ceo-megapay-mckinsey-consultant-arch-patton-didnt-invent-wealth-inequality/.

264 *Business Insider,* March 20, 2013, http://www.businessinsider.com/ sam-palmisano-ibm-office-2013–3.

265 *Wall Street Journal,* November 19, 2012 http://www.wsj.com/articles/ SB10001424127887324073504578115163336933032.

266 *Bloomberg,* September 12, 2016, https://www.bloomberg.com/news/ articles/2016–09–12/retiring-swift-ceo-to-get-paid-more-as-consult-ant-than-as-boss.

267 *CNN Money,* August 31, 2015.

268 Center for American Progress, February 10, 2014.

269 "Today in Energy," December 16, 2014, http://www.eia.gov/todayine-nergy/detail.php?id=19211.

270 *Think Progress,* July 24, 2012, https://thinkprogress.org/what-five-oil-companies-did-with-their-375-million-in-daily-profits-920ad33d1641#.hn5g94lna.

271 *Columbus Dispatch,* July 8, 2007.

272 *UK Daily Mail,* July 26, 2011, http://www.dailymail.co.uk/news/arti-cle-2018807/Walnuts-DRUGS-FDA-makes-bizarre-claim-seller-says-reduce-risk-heart-disease-cancer.html.

273 *San Francisco Chronicle,* June 7, 2011, http://blog.sfgate.com/politics/ 2011/06/07/food-safety-chief-defends-raw-milk-raids/.

274 *Washington Post,* May 3, 2016, http://blog.sfgate.com/politics/2011/ 06/07/food-safety-chief-defends-raw-milk-raids/.

275 *Huffington Post,* May 14, 2012, http://www.huffingtonpost.co.uk/dr-raj-persaud/when-doctors-go-on-strike_b_1513689.html.

276 *Wall Street Journal,* September 21, 2012, http://www.wsj.com/articles/ SB10000872396390444620104578008263334441352.

277 *Economic Policy Institute,* June 11, 2013, http://www.epi.org/press/ unemployed-workers-outnumber-job-openings/.

278 *Huffington Post,* November 20, 2014, http://www.huffingtonpost.com/ allen-frances/why-are-medical-mistakes-_b_5888408.html.

279 *New York Daily News,* December 17, 2013, http://www.nydailynews. com/news/national/woes-not-texas-affluenza-boy-article-1.1550043.

280 *Forbes,* July 16, 2013, http://www.forbes.com/sites/dorothypomer-antz/2013/07/16/robert-downey-jr-tops-forbes-list-of-hollywoods-highest-paid-actors/#56fe006a2c24.

281 *US News and World Report,* October 1, 2007, http://www.usnews.com/news/ national/articles/2007/10/01/crack-vs-powder-cocaine-a-gulf-in-penalties.

282 *Daily Mail UK,* March 31, 2013, http://www.dailymail.co.uk/news/article-2301867/Bill-Wyman-Police-interested-Rolling-Stones-affair-13-year-old-Mandy-Smith-claims-slept-14.html.

283 *Daily Mail UK,* September 28, 2012, http://www.dailymail.co.uk/news/article-2209821/The-Whos-Pete-Townshend-breaks-year-silence-child-pornography-scandal.html.

284 *People,* March 19, 2004, http://people.com/celebrity/pee-wee-actor-settles-kiddie-porn-case/.

285 *Spin,* December 16, 2013, http://www.spin.com/2013/12/r-kelly-sex-crimes-jim-derogatis/.

286 Kurt Loder, "More Charges May Be Pending in Henley Arrest," *Anchorage Daily News,* December 10, 1980, p. 86.

287 *New York Post,* April 25, 2014, http://nypost.com/2014/04/25/peter-yarrow-the-guest-of-dis-honor/.

288 *Forbes,* March 31, 2014, http://www.forbes.com/sites/rickungar/2014/03/31/american-justice-for-the-wealthy-no-prison-for-du-pont-heir-convicted-of-sexually-molesting-his-child-because-he-would-not-fare-well-in-jail/#3e79e41d1db0.

289 *Daily Caller,* March 2, 2011, http://dailycaller.com/2011/03/02/congressional-bosses-from-hell-sheila-jackson-lee/.

290 *CBS News,* April 1, 2010, http://www.cbsnews.com/news/hank-johnson-worries-guam-could-capsize-after-marine-buildup/.

291 *New York Times,* January 29, 2014, https://www.nytimes.com/2014/01/29/nyregion/rep-michael-grimm-physically-threatens-a-ny1-reporter.html?_r=0.

292 *New York Daily News,* December 23, 2014, http://www.nydailynews.com/news/politics/grimm-plead-guilty-felony-count-tax-evasion-article-1.2053630.

293 *Washington Times,* April 12, 2000.

294 *Huffington Post,* May 1, 2008.

295 *Huffington Post,* March 2, 2012, http://www.huffingtonpost.com/2012/03/02/ken-mehlman-i-am-sorry-fo_n_1316199.html.

296 *Politico,* May 19, 2010, http://www.politico.com/story/2010/05/souder-i-am-so-shamed-037400.

297 *Seattle Times,* March 1, 1992, http://community.seattletimes.nwsource.com/archive/?date=19920301&slug=1478550.

298 *USA Today,* June 5, 2013, http://www.usatoday.com/story/news/politics/2013/06/05/gutierrez-chicago-lobbyist-scofield-staff-congress-democrat/2391499/.

299 *Fox News,* April 17, 2014.

300 *Huffington Post,* November 15, 2012.

301 *Portland Independent Media Center,* December 13, 2003 http://portland.indymedia.org/en/2003/12/276578.shtml.

302 *UK Daily Mail,* July 2, 2010, http://www.dailymail.co.uk/femail/article-1291661/A-inconvenient-masseuse-How-saint-Al-Gore-sanctimonious-eco-crusader-lost-halo-wife.html.

303 *Business Insider,* July 21, 2010, http://www.businessinsider.com/two-more-women-accuse-al-gore-of-assault-2010–7.

304 *New York Times,* July 11, 2008, http://cityroom.blogs.nytimes.com/2008/07/11/rangel-defends-use-of-rent-stabilized-apartments/.

305 *New York Times,* May 1, 2008, http://www.nytimes.com/2008/05/01/nyregion/01cars.html.

306 *New York Times,* March 27, 2013, http://www.nytimes.com/2013/03/28/us/politics/senate-barbers-get-trimmed-in-latest-budget-cuts.html?mtrref=www.google.com&gwh=8F0B5F21CAF2946681AE0CB-117C4BA0E&gwt=pay.

307 *My First Class Life,* February 3, 2015, http://myfirstclasslife.com/hidden-financial-perks-united-states-president/?singlepage=1.

308 *Daily Caller,* January 15, 2013.

309 *News Busters,* June 24, 2014, http://www.newsbusters.org/blogs/nb/jeffrey-meyer/2014/06/24/nbcs-chuck-todd-rushes-defend-hillary-clinton-its-not-bubble-she.

310 *UK Daily Mail,* June 24, 2014, http://www.dailymail.co.uk/news/article-2667949/Taxpayers-spend-944–000-support-multimillionaire-Bill-Clintons-post-presidential-lifestyle-2014.html.

311 *Breitbart,* August 14, 2013, http://www.breitbart.com/big-government/2013/08/14/ny-times-clinton-foundation-rife-with-cronyism/.

312 *Naked Capitalism,* May 22, 2012, http://www.nakedcapitalism.com/2012/05/its-not-about-reelection-bill-clintons-80-million-payday.html.

313 *CNN,* February 6, 2016.

314 *ABC News,* April 23, 2010, http://abcnews.go.com/Politics/Supreme_Court/life-supreme-court-cushy-job-justice/story?id=10449434.

315 *Think Progress,* September 19, 2011, https://thinkprogress.org/multi-millionaire-rep-says-he-cant-afford-a-tax-hike-because-he-only-has-400k-a-year-after-feeding-68990814b15f#.hz0zqwlec.

316 *Politico,* October 5, 2011.

317 *New York Daily News,* June 23, 2014, http://www.nydailynews.com/news/politics/chelsea-clinton-care-money-article-1.1840138.

318 Allen Salkin, "You Try to Live on $500K in This Town," *New York Times,* February 6, 2009.

319 *Wall Street Journal,* January 24, 2014, http://www.wsj.com/articles/SB10001424052702304549504579316913982034286.

320 *Time,* February 14, 2014, http://time.com/8466/tom-perkins-taxes/.

321 *UK Daily Mail,* March 19, 2014, Can-t find anywhere- maybe can just remove note?.

322 *Time,* August 20, 2013, http://healthland.time.com/2013/08/20/wealthy-selfies-how-being-rich-increases-narcissism/.

323 *ABC News,* October 14, 2010.

324	*Los Angeles Times,* July 18, 2007, http://www.latimes.com/business/la-fi-nicholas18jul18-story.html.

325	*Los Angeles Times,* December 16, 2009, http://articles.latimes.com/2009/dec/16/business/la-fi-broadcom16–2009dec16.

326	*Moyers & Company,* October 10, 2014, http://billmoyers.com/2014/10/10/americas-ridiculously-rich-2014-edition/.

327	*The Economist,* July 29, 2010, http://www.economist.com/node/16690659.

328	*Forbes,* November 1, 2016, http://www.forbes.com/sites/janetwburns/2016/11/01/research-shows-rich-people-dont-really-notice-the-rest-of-us/#1e4abd4b5d43.

329	*Forbes,* February 8, 2011, http://www.forbes.com/sites/christopherhelman/2011/02/08/troubled-grandson-of-j-paul-getty-dies/#15ab642c11cd.

330	*Daily Telegraph,* November 14, 2008, http://www.dailytelegraph.com.au/sir-bob-geldof-wants-100000-for-anti-povery-speech/news-story/3a30bc21002a9d9c068be06fa573f77a.

331	*UK Daily Mail,* May 25, 2012, http://www.dailymail.co.uk/news/article-2150195/How-Saint-Bob-words-private-equity-whore-launching-125m-investment-fund.html.

332	*Sun Sentinel,* April 15, 1990, http://articles.sun-sentinel.com/1990–04–15/features/9001030011_1_africa-hunger-usa.

333	*UK Daily Mail,* March 18, 2010, http://www.dailymail.co.uk/news/article-1259061/Sorry-Bob-Geldof-Band-Aid-millions-DID-pay-guns.html.

334	*New York Post,* November 26, 2010, http://nypost.com/2010/11/26/no-thanks-oprah-you-can-keep-the-new-car/.

335	*Oprah: A Biography* by Kitty Kelly, pp. 401–402.

336	*Business Insider,* June 25, 2013, http://www.businessinsider.com/14-secret-services-for-the-wealthy-2013–6.

337	*New York Times,* October 21, 1926.

338	*Breitbart,* July 6, 2014, http://www.breitbart.com/california/2014/07/06/gene-simmons-defends-1-percent/.

339	*Infowars,* June 6, 2014, http://www.infowars.com/economist-u-s-banks-preparing-to-charge-customers-for-deposits/.

340	*The Atlantic,* April 18, 2014, http://www.theatlantic.com/business/archive/2014/04/more-money-more-life-the-depressing-reality-of-inequality-in-america/360895/.

341	*The Washington Post,* November 21, 2013, http://www.theatlantic.com/business/archive/2014/04/more-money-more-life-the-depressing-reality-of-inequality-in-america/360895/.

342	*Huffington Post,* December 8, 2016, http://www.huffingtonpost.com/entry/us-life-expectancy-2015_us_58498eaee4b04002fa802713.

343 *Huffington Post,* July 24, 2013, http://www.huffingtonpost.com/2013/07/24/us-internet-speed_n_3645927.html.

344 *Los Angeles Times,* September 22, 2016, http://www.latimes.com/opinion/op-ed/la-oe-greenhouse-driverless-job-loss-20160922-snap-story.html.

345 *CNN Money,* March 31, 2016, http://money.cnn.com/2016/03/31/technology/google-ceo-pay-sundar-pichai/.

346 *Forbes,* June 25, 2012, http://www.forbes.com/sites/stevedenning/2012/06/25/apples-employees-have-a-hell-of-a-ride/#9bc764d7926e.

347 *US News & World Report,* April 22, 2014, http://www.usnews.com/opinion/blogs/charles-wheelan/2014/04/22/study-shows-wealthy-americans-and-businesses-control-politics-and-policy.

348 *Boston Review,* July 1, 2012 http://bostonreview.net/forum/lead-essay-under-influence-martin-gilens.

349 *International Business Times,* January 19, 2015, http://www.ibtimes.com/richest-1-will-have-more-wealth-remaining-99–2016-oxfam-study-1787200.

350 *The Guardian,* January 19, 2016, https://www.theguardian.com/business/2016/jan/19/global-unemployment-3-million-rise-next-two-years-international-labour-organization-report.

351 *Zero Hedge,* July 28, 2016, http://www.zerohedge.com/news/2016–07–28/us-homeownership-rate-crashes-lowest-1965.

352 *Pew Charitable Trusts website,* March 30, 2016, http://www.pewtrusts.org/en/research-and-analysis/issue-briefs/2016/03/household-expenditures-and-income.

353 *US News & World Report,* May 9, 2016, http://www.usnews.com/education/best-colleges/paying-for-college/slideshows/10-student-loan-facts-college-grads-need-to-know.

BIBLIOGRAPHY

Abdelnour, Ziad K. *Economic Warfare*. New Jersey: Wiley, 2011.

Barry, John M. *Rising Tide: The Great Mississippi Flood of 1927 and How It Changed America*. New York: Simon & Schuster, 1998.

Benedict, Jeff. *Public Heroes, Private Felons: Athletes and Crimes Against Women*. Boston: Northeastern, 1999.

Brynjolfsson, Erik and Andrew McAfee. *The Second Machine Age*. New York: W. W. Norton, 2016.

Buchanan, Patrick J. *Day of Reckoning*. New York: St. Martin's Griffin, 2009.

Buchanan, Patrick J. *The Death of the West*. New York: St. Martin's Griffin, 2002.

Carroll, Robert Todd. *The Skeptic's Dictionary*. New York: Wiley, 2003.

Corley, Tom. *Rich Habits: The Daily Success Habits of Wealthy Individuals*. Minnesota: Langdon Street, 2010.

Davis, Forrest. *Huey Long: A Candid Biography*. Montana: Kessinger, 2010.

Deal, Terrance E. and Allan A. Kennedy, *The New Corporate Cultures: Revitalizing the Workplace After Downsizing*. New York: Perseus Books, 2010.

Domhoff, G. William. *Who Rules America?*. New York: Prentice-Hall, 1967.

Domhoff, G. William. *Who Rules America Now?*. Illinois, Waveland, 1997.

Ehrenreich, Barbara. *Nickel and Dimed: On (Not) Getting by in America*. New York: Henry Holt, 2001.

Farley, James. *Behind the Ballots*. New York: Harcourt-Brace, 1938.

Farnam, Henry Walcott. *Chapters in the History of Social Legislation in the United States to 1860*. New Jersey: Lawbook Exchange, 1938.

Flynn, John T. *Meet Your Congress*. New York: Doubleday, Doran, 1944.

Flynn, John T. *The Roosevelt Myth*. Connecticut: Devin-Adair, 1948.

Freeland, Chrystia. *Plutocrats: The Rise of the New Global Super Rich and the Fall of Everyone Else*. New York: Penguin, 2012.

Gilens, Martin. *Affluence and Influence: Economic Inequality and Political Power in America*. New Jersey: Princeton University Press, 2012.

Golden, Daniel. *The Price of Admission: How America Buys Its Way into Elite Colleges—and Who Gets Left Outside the Gates*. New York: Three Rivers, 2006.

Hamermesh, Daniel. *Beauty Pays: Why Attractive People Are More Successful*. New Jersey: Princeton University Press, 2011.

Kelly, Kitty. *Oprah: A Biography*. New York: Three Rivers, 2010.

Lamm, Richard D. *The Immigration Time Bomb*. New York: Truman-Talley Books, 1985.

Leuchtenburg, William Edward. *The FDR Years: On Roosevelt and His Legacy*. New York: Columbia University Press, 1995.

London, Jack. *The People of the Abyss*. New York: Macmillian Company, 1904.

Long, Huey P. *My First Days in the White House*. Pennsylvania: The Telegraph Press, 1935.

Lundberg, Ferdinand. *The Rich and the Super-Rich*. New York: Bantam Books, 1973.

Malik, Kenan. *The Quest for a Moral Compass: A Global History of Ethics*. Brooklyn: Melville House, 2014.

Marsh, Dave. *Before I Get Old: The Story of the Who*. New York: St. Martin's Press, 1983.

McGowan, David. *Weird Scenes Inside the Canyon: Laurel Canyon, Covert Ops & The Dark Heart of the Hippie Dream*. London: Headpress, 2014.

Morris, Edmund. *Dutch*. New York: Modern Library, 1999.

Newfield, Jack. *The Life and Crimes of Don King: The Shame of Boxing in America*. New York: William Morrow, 1995.

Olen, Helaine. *Pound Foolish: Exposing the Dark Side of the Personal Finance Industry*. New York: Penguin Group, 2012.

Patton, Arch. *Men, Money and Motivation: Executive Compensation as an Instrument of Leadership*. New York: McGraw-Hill, 1961.

Patton, Arch. *What is an Executive Worth?*. New York: McGraw-Hill, 1961.

Patzer, Dr. Gordon. *Looks: Why They Matter More Than You Ever Imagined*. New York: Amacom, 2008.

Pizzigati, Sam. *The Rich Don't Always Win: The Forgotten Triumph Over Plutocracy That Created the American Middle Class, 1900–1970*. New York: Seven Stories, 2012.

Rand, Ayn. *Atlas Shrugged*. New York: Random House, 1957.

Randel, Jim. *Skinny on Success*. Connecticut: Rand Publishing, 2010.

Reed, Ed. *Requiem for a Kingfish: The Strange and Unexplained Death of Huey Long*. Louisiana: Award Publications, 1986.

Reich, Wilhelm. *The Mass Psychology of Fascism*. New York: Orgone Institute Press, 1946.

Ringer, *Robert. Looking Out for #1: How to Get from Where You Are Now to Where You Want to be in Life.* New York: Random House, 1983.

Rivlin, Gary. *Broke, USA: From Pawnshops to Poverty, Inc.* New York: Harper, 2010.

Schmidt, Hans. *Maverick Marine: General Smedley D. Butler and the Contradictions of American Military History.* Kentucky: University Press of Kentucky, 1987.

Schweizer, Peter. *Do as I Say, Not as I Do.* New York: Broadway Books, 2005.

Stone, Duel. *The Huey P. Long Assassination: Conspiracy Unveiled.* Louisiana: Lloyds of Louisiana, 1997.

Szasz, Thomas. *The Manufacture of Madness.* New York: Harper & Row, 1977.

Szasz, Thomas. *The Myth of Mental Illness.* United States: Paladin Press, 1972.

Tirado, Linda. *Hand to Mouth: Living in Bootstrap America.* New York: G. P. Putnam's Sons, 2014.

Trunk, Penelope. *Brazen Careerist: The New Rules for Success.* New York: Business Plus, 2014.

Veblen, Thorstein. *The Theory of the Leisure Class.* New York: Macmillan, 1899.

Vonnegut, Kurt. *Slaughterhouse Five.* New York: Delacorte, 1969.

Wallach, Dr. Joel. *Dead Doctors Don't Lie.* California, Wellness Publications, 2004.

White, Richard. *Kingfish: The Reign of Huey P. Long.* New York: Random House, 2006.

Williams, T. Harry. *Huey Long.* Louisiana, Easton Press, 1969.

Zinman, David. *The Day Huey Long Was Shot.* Louisiana, University of Louisiana at Lafayette Press, 1993.

ACKNOWLEDGMENTS

I would like to thank Skyhorse Publishing for agreeing to publish this controversial book, and especially my editor Joseph Craig, for his invaluable assistance. Joseph Bockman, Juan Morrobel, Mark Ottey, "Young" Dave Johnson, and Mike Sanders helped with research. Talk-show hosts Ed Opperman, Tim Kelly, Meria Heller, and Richard Syrett were so interested in this subject that they asked me to appear on their programs to discuss it before this book was even published. One of our greatest living writers, Alexander Theroux, offered me support and encouragement. Renowned attorney Douglas Caddy consistently promoted my work. I can never repay all the advice and assistance that David Wayne has given me. Roger Stone took time out from his incredibly busy schedule to give me advice and encouragement. I was thrilled and honored to make the acquaintance of Huey Long's great-granddaughter Audra Snider during the course of writing this book, and she was not only an important resource, but a real kindred soul. Most of all, I want to thank my wife Jeanne, son John Jeffries, daughter Julianna Jeffries, brother Richard E. Jeffries, Jr., sisters Joyce Foroobar and Janet Marcellino, and the rest of my huge extended family for their love and inspiration.

Index